RAF WINTH.
The Story of an Airfield 1939-1959

Colin Savill BA (Hons)

November 2014

Registered Charity No. 256434. Accredited Museum No. AN551
Front cover photograph – Howard Heeley

Acknowledgements

This book has been made possible thanks to the excellent help and support of all at Newark Air Museum particularly Mike Smith the curator who over the years has garnered much material, recollections and records of RAF Winthorpe, fellow trustees Museum secretary Howard Heeley and archivist Mrs. Kathy Smith and member Bill Taylor.

The many former personnel or their relatives and other, civilian, individuals, who have either recorded and left their stories with the Museum previously or have contacted us since this project began, they have all provided a valuable contribution to the story; James Sands in particular, ex Radar Officer at Winthorpe, for allowing me to use extracts from his recollections and the use of his photographs. Wilhelm Ratuszynski for the use of material and pictures on the Polish Squadrons and David Gardner of the RAAF Museum for his help on No. 455 Squadron.

Thanks must also go to Karen Shanahan, a fellow graduate of Bishop Grosseteste University College, Lincoln, for her research help at the National Archives Kew, Ian Lane of Mill Design and Advertising for transferring my original Word documents into the book format, Carol Morgan, Archivist at the Institution of Civil Engineers for pointing me in the right direction re airfield construction and a special mention for Dr. Hazel Kent at Bishop Grosseteste University, Lincoln who first 'planted the seed' saying that I could (and would) write a book.

I apologise in advance if I have missed anyone.

The Author

Colin Savill was born in Newark and educated at the Magnus Grammar School. Following RAF service he worked in engineering for many years before becoming a mature student at, then, Bishop Grosseteste University College, Lincoln graduating in 2010 with a BA (Hons). He joined Newark Air Museum in 2009 as a volunteer and became a trustee of the Museum in 2012. He is widowed with two daughters and several grandchildren.

Foreword

RAF Winthorpe may not be a station that is known well by the Royal Air Force, but located close to my home town of Newark-on-Trent in Nottinghamshire, it is one that holds close family connections for me.

During the early part of World War II RAF Winthorpe was home to two Polish Air Force squadrons, later becoming home to a major No 5 Group Heavy Conversion Unit training bomber crews from around the Commonwealth. My grandparents witnessed the activities at the base and often recounted their memories to me as a youngster during my upbringing in Newark.

Post-World War II the RAF Central Servicing Development Establishment was housed at Winthorpe and provided a valuable service with the compilation of documentation and servicing manuals.

Later, parts of the former RAF station were returned to agriculture, while other facilities became home to the Newark & Nottinghamshire Agricultural Society. The aviation connection has been maintained by the Newark (Nottinghamshire & Lincolnshire) Air Museum, who have researched and published this book that details the history of Royal Air Force Winthorpe.

This history allows us to remember and commemorate the past while paying tribute to those who went before us as we play our own part in the present. As a history of brave and courageous people I commend it to you.

Air Chief Marshal Sir Andrew Pulford KCB CBE ADC RAF
CHIEF OF THE AIR STAFF

Contents

CHAPTER ONE

Creating an Airfield

Cartoon – NAM archives/ Mr. John Dove

During the period of the Second World War airfield development was the largest civil engineering project ever undertaken in the UK. In the East Midlands prior to September 1939 there were 14 airfields, an increase from 9 in 1935, and only one - Hucknall - in Nottinghamshire, all with grass runways, by 1945 this had risen to 106, the majority having concrete runways, Nottinghamshire having a total of 14 airfields and landing grounds.

RAF Expansion Scheme airfields, built to house the expanding RAF to counter the looming German threat in the early 1930s, were built to a standard design and well constructed with permanent buildings. In spite of the urgency the Royal Fine Arts Commission was consulted as to the aesthetics of the proposed building designs and layout and the Society for the Protection of Rural England was also involved in the process. A standard airfield and domestic site layout, including neo-classical red-brick residential blocks and standard mess layouts, office space and hangars, is still evident at many airfields today. A typical airfield at the time only required grass runways as aircraft weights had not yet reached the heavy bomber proportions of WW2.

The onset of war called for a further massive expansion in the construction programme to meet the needs of the expanding RAF and Royal Navy. These war time airfields were austere in comparison to the 1930s Expansion Scheme and had less permanent structures. Accommodation was generally in Nissen Huts, with semi-permanent hangars and brick built operations block, control tower and perhaps Station HQ. The layout of some may have included Expansion Phase buildings but more than likely they did not.

Approval for the acquisition of land for an airfield at Winthorpe came in August 1939. The land was requisitioned under the Emergency Powers (Defence) Act of 1939; Landowners and Farmers had no immediate recompense or grounds for appeal and many did not get their land back until long after the war was over, if at all.

Built in 1940 as a satellite airfield for RAF Swinderby, construction of Winthorpe airfield took place mainly on what had been Carr Farm, Winthorpe, the property of Capt. Walter Need, which also involved the closing of one road - Drove Lane - and some farm tracks and footpaths. Under the Defence (General) Regulations 1939 anything from a footpath or farm track to a trunk road could be closed without appeal, around 4,000 such 'highways' were closed in this way in the UK during the wartime period.

The name Carr is derived from the Old Norse kjarr, originally meaning a swamp; here it means land that is submerged by fresh water along a river or lake margin. The old Carrs or marshes had been drained and woods planted and the better land, enclosed in 1778, formed excellent farm fields extending from Drove Lane to the Private Drive to Coddington Hall. The approach to the farmhouse and farm buildings which stood two fields away from the A46 followed the original footpath across the old pastures and Carrs to Coddington.

The farm and its outbuildings was demolished, the stream was piped in, the trees in Oak Wood and Carr Plantation cut down and the ground levelled, and the airfield with its grass runways opened in September 1940, Two Mile House, which stood at the junction

Windrome Cottage – Joyce Golland

of Drove Lane and the A46, near to the present day roundabout, was also demolished as it was a hazard to aircraft taking off being adjacent to the main runway, and later the Bleach Houses at the other end of the runway were also ordered to be demolished for the same reason.

Joyce Golland (nee Godson), as a young girl, lived in a cottage "Windrome" - pictured in about 1910 on Drove Lane with her parents, Harry (the smallest boy in the photo) and Lydia and Grandparents.

The cottage being right next to the airfield was provided with a Morrison shelter which replaced the kitchen table – the family lived in the cottage throughout the war; Joyce was regularly warned to keep clear of the well at the back of the cottage. A man with a

Steamroller towing his caravan arrived to work on the airfield and one of Joyce's aunts later married him. Joyce's other grandparents Henry and Edith Charity had lived in Two Mile House before the war, they had to move to Winthorpe when the house was demolished and Joyce recalls having to travel 'the long way round' to Winthorpe via Coddington and Newark to visit them with Drove Lane being closed.

Winthorpe was one of the few airfields in the area to be attacked; a parachute mine was dropped on the 14th November 1940; some personnel thinking it was a parachutist began firing at it but upon realising that it was a parachute mine they ran. It landed on the south side of the airfield near to the Bleach Houses leaving a crater 38ft. (11.5m) across and 20ft. (6m) deep and destroying a guard hut but caused no loss of life or damage to aircraft.

The Bleach Houses, actually three cottages, were the former homes of linen bleachers and stood on the Winthorpe side of the A46, somewhere close to where the A17/A46 roundabout is today. Two faced the A46 and the third, behind them, faced a field. Before the construction of the airfield the bridge under the road was made of handmade bricks and a flight of steps enabled residents to get water from the stream, and a pump in front of one house served all three homes.

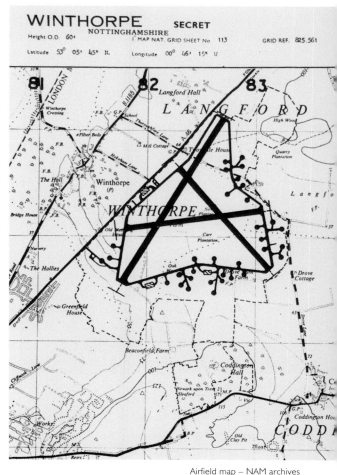

Apart from broken windows, the Bleach Houses suffered no damage when the land mine was dropped; scores of windows were shattered though in Winthorpe and on the outskirts of Newark. Five year old David Hallam who lived on Middleton Road in Newark suffered shock and lost most of his hair and recalls having to go to school wearing a balaclava. Following this incident the Bleach Houses were demolished.

Further land was requisitioned in 1942 when part of Hall Farm, Coddington was taken over. In some cases only parts of fields were used as Mr Alan Geeson whose Father was the farm tenant explains:

We had four fields along Drove Lane, the second field, First Footits Close was 9.13 acres and 3 acres were

Airfield map – NAM archives

requisitioned, all of Middle Footits Close 8.56 acres and Bottom Footits Close 9.13 acres were taken (dispersal hard standings were built on these fields). *The final field was known as Long Meadow of 8.61 acres, this was back from Drove Lane behind the untouched Fairfields Close and First Footits, but only 3 acres were taken* (which was covered by the end of runway 33 and taxiways).

All the fields had been used for growing crops such as potatoes, grain and sugar beet. What was once Middle Footits and Bottom Footits Closes' today houses Newark Air Museum.

Winthorpe is located 2 miles (3km) northeast of Newark-on-Trent to the west of and adjacent to the A46 Newark to Lincoln road or the Roman Fosse Way, whilst Coddington is 3 miles (5km) east of Newark-on-Trent and until a new bypass was built, which incidentally runs across the old airfield, was on the A17.

Aerial photograph – detail from c1970 aerial image at NAM by Author

Why call it RAF Winthorpe? The accommodation and technical sites were all in Coddington Parish as was the main gate, so logic would say it should have been RAF Coddington. There are two theories.

The first was that it was done to confuse an enemy – by calling it after an adjoining Parish making it harder to locate; there are local examples of this in other RAF station names, RAF Swinderby is in Morton Parish, RAF Syerston in Flintham Parish and RAF Gamston sits next to Elkesley village. The second theory is that it avoided confusion within the RAF itself, there were already two stations with a similar spelling - RAF Cardington and RAF Cheddington, and similarly RAF Brize Norton in Oxfordshire is actually at Carterton, all phonetically sounding somewhat the same.

Winthorpe was one of six airfields built near to Newark-on-Trent; the others were Balderton, Syerston and Ossington in Nottinghamshire and Swinderby and Fulbeck in Lincolnshire, all less than ten miles from the town with Newton to the South-west near to Bingham and Gamston near to Retford to the North a little further distance away.

The main runway was the usual (post 1941) 2,000 yards (1,829m) long and the two other, shorter, runways 1,400 yards (1,280m) and were aligned 09/27 and 15/33. Runways are usually numbered in compass degrees at 180° to each other, so for example with 09/27 aligned east/west the runway orientation is between 085° and 094° heading east on one side and 265° and 274° heading west on the other. The compass dial demonstrates this.

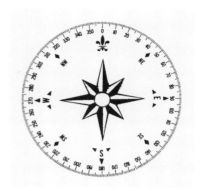

Local legend has it that Winthorpe airfield was built in error and never used operationally because the main runway 04/22 was aligned so that a fully laden bomber taking off on runway 04 for a mission would pass over the town and more importantly the Ransome and Marles (today the multi-national NSK company) ball bearing factory (see aerial photo taken in c1970) which supplied bearings vital to the war effort.

This would lead to the fairly high risk, that if an aircraft did crash on takeoff, of destroying the factory, stopping bearing production and causing the deaths of the factories skilled workforce - doing something that Göering and the Luftwaffe failed to do, although a raid did take place in March 1941 killing 41 and injuring 165 men and women.

Winthorpe's history supports this and after 1940 the airfield was not used again for operational flying.

All the accommodation and technical sites including two of the three hangars were to the south of the airfield with the third hangar to the north-west by the side of the, then single carriageway, A46 road the Indoor Bowls Centre today is exactly where this Hangar was sited, the bomb dump was to the north east near to High Wood.

Coddington Hall – NAM archives

Practically all of the accommodation was in Coddington parish, sited around Coddington Hall (left) which was used as the Officers Mess and Beaconfield Farm. This was not the first time Coddington Hall had been used by the military; in the First World War it had housed No.11 Company Royal Engineers Training Depot, it failed to sell in a 1918 auction, but was bought later and split into two units. By 1936 Anglo-Iranian Oil used it for offices.

There was one B1 type hangar (next page left) with a clear span of 120ft. (36.5m), 227ft. (69m) long with a centre door clearance height of 27ft (8.2m). There was 135 tons (137 tonnes) of steel in the building with another 28 tons (28.45 tonnes) for the doors

B1 and T2 Hangars – NAM archives

and their guides. B1 hangars were from a series of prefabricated buildings intended to supplement existing hangars on airfields.

The other two hangars were the T2 type (the photograph right shows one of these hangars and the control tower with a Lancaster on the dispersal point). A development of the 1937 designed Bellman Hangar they were introduced in 1940. Constructed of welded and bolted steel typically clad in galvanized corrugated iron sheets (22 gauge for the roof and 24 gauge for the walls) the T2 became the standard temporary (the T standing for transportable) hangar for the RAF in WW2. These came in differing lengths, with a variable amount of internal bays, 113ft 6in (34.6m) wide with a 90-97ft. (27-29.5m) doors open span and a maximum door height of 25ft (7.62m).

Accommodation and working/technical buildings were typical of a 1940s airfield, gone were the Art Deco and neo-Georgian permanent buildings of the pre-war expansion airfields to be replaced by the utilitarian using a variety of materials from wooden and Nissen huts to brick.

SSQ – NAM archives / Bill Taylor

The Nissen hut had many uses on an RAF station including accommodation, messes, churches, offices, armouries, workshops and stores (above is the Station Sick Quarters at Winthorpe). They come in three internal spans, 16ft (4.9m), 24ft (7.3m) or 30ft (9.2m); length was in sections in multiples of 6ft (1.83m), usually with wooden or brick ends each containing two windows and a door frame. They could be erected quickly and windows and extra doors could be added to the sides by adding either a dormer window form or door frame by taking out a piece of corrugated sheet and replacing it. Thousands of all the sizes were mass produced.

Nissen huts are pre-fabricated structures made from a half-cylindrical skin of corrugated steel sheets designed and first used during World War I, its arched shape made it very strong. A Canadian, Major Peter Norman Nissen, a mining engineer and inventor, of the 29th Company Royal Engineers began to experiment with hut designs and constructed three prototype semi-cylindrical huts. Following completion of the third prototype the design was formalised and the Nissen hut was put into production in August 1916, at least 100,000 were produced in World War I. The Quonset in the United States was the American built version.

Similar-shaped huts were also developed notably the Romney used mainly for stores and workshops but were also used for messes and cinemas, A span of 25 feet (7.62m) with a corrugated metal skin, they could be built in 8ft (2.45m) lengths to suit requirements.

Pre-war wooden huts were assembled using timber framed sections. Each section bolted together to form huts of any length; originally they had 3/4in (19mm) rebated weather boarding with the inside walls lined with plasterboard and with standard metal windows. Roofs were timber trussed and panelled and covered externally either with corrugated asbestos or timber and felted. The floors were of timber.

At the start of the War the standard hut was a timber framed, weather boarded, excellent quality and long life span building known as the 'B' Type; by 1940 timber shortages had seen the development of 'X' 'Y' and 'Z' designs using less timber and which were quicker to produce. By 1941 other types of hut had also been developed, mainly the Laing, Thorne and Maycrete.

The Laing hut was of standard prefabricated lightweight timber wall sections bolted together; end sections had one central door 2ft 8in (80cm) wide. Side were usually made up of 10 sections each 6ft (1.83m) wide and incorporating a steel half window frame which when combined with a left or right hand section would form a standard sized window. The walls were lined both inside and out with plasterboard and additionally the outside covered with felt. Lightweight composite roof trusses were spaced every 4 feet (1.2m) and supported corrugated asbestos sheeting outside and plasterboard inside. They were heated by a single stove placed in the middle of the hut.

Seco or Uni-Seco Structures (the Selection Engineering Company) mass produced timber huts in WW2. They were a timber frame clad with asbestos sheets and a timber roof of shallow pitch with a plasterboard ceiling beneath. The prefabricated panels were a sandwich with a wood-wool filling between sheets of corrugated asbestos-cement. Seco huts at Winthorpe were used for amongst others the Radar Workshops and Signals apparatus section.

Accommodation huts would normally be either Nissen or Laing. Winthorpe like most airfields had both, they lacked any sort of luxury, cold and damp with sparse heating in winter the Nissen huts could be hot in summer, with probably a mile or so walk or cycle to and from their workplace for the airmen and women.

Accommodation Nissen huts were used for all ranks but space in each hut depended on the rank, officers had a room each with a room for a batman for senior officers, 8 sergeants shared a single room while junior ranks were 12 to a room.

Laing huts when used for accommodation housed six senior officers plus a batmen's room with a central corridor whilst airmen and women were housed 24 to a single room hut, airwomen had the 'luxury' of an internal chemical toilet but men used communal ablutions blocks, heating was from a single pot bellied stove in the centre of a room, officers had a small stove for each room.

The WAAFs at Winthorpe also had some BCF huts for accommodation, manufactured by the British Concrete Federation; these light huts were made from prefabricated sections of reinforced concrete. Prefabricated 'cruck' uprights on brick plinths held concrete blocks fixed horizontally to form walls, and steel trusses supported corrugated Asbestos roof panels. The huts were usually 65ft (19.8m) x 18ft 6ins (5.6m) in size.

Temporary/Half Brick buildings were designed to have a life span of 10 years and built of single brick, without a cavity wall, with piers at 10 feet (3m) intervals. The walls supported a light steel frame carrying asbestos sheeting or board and felt roofing. Outside the brickwork was rendered with cement whilst inside the walls were painted. The buildings had concrete floors. Buildings at Winthorpe of this type included the control tower, guard room, parachute and dinghy stores and the latrines.

Winthorpe's control tower shortly before it was demolished and how it may have looked when in use - this is RAF Elvington.

Winthorpe Control Tower – NAM archives   Elvington Tower – Author

CHAPTER TWO

Polish Squadrons

The history of RAF Winthorpe would not be complete without an account of Nos.300 and 301 Polish Squadrons, although not based at Winthorpe they did make use of the airfield when they were based at Swinderby especially in the winter of 1941.

> '*Somewhere in England... the first detachment of the Polish Air Force is already training with enthusiasm to form itself into the first of several Squadrons that will soon become part and parcel of the Royal Air Force...*'
>
> Extract from an Air Ministry announcement dated 13th December 1939.

RAF Squadron numbers in the 300 series were allocated to flying units manned by Allied personnel who had escaped from occupied Europe; there were 14 Polish Squadrons (300-309 and 315-318), four operated as bombers. All the Squadrons bore names for regions or cities of Poland.

Forming the Squadrons

Order WAR/B.C.127 dated 14th March 1940 had confirmed the establishment of a Polish training unit as part of No.18 Operational Training Unit at Bramcote, near Nuneaton in No.6 Bomber Group. Its task was to give conversion training to crews for the Polish bomber Squadrons that were being formed.

The first Polish Squadron, No.300 (Masovia) formed at RAF Bramcote, near Nuneaton, Warks. on 1st July 1940 as a light bomber unit, equipped with Fairey Battles and it was on this date that the Polish Air Force flag was first hoisted in Great Britain. No.301 (Pomerania) Squadron followed and was officially formed at Bramcote on 24th July 1940. The history of these two units runs parallel for a long time; both were formed at the same airfield, stationed together on others, were manned by a similar number of personnel and flew the same types of aircraft.

The Squadron badge for No.300 combines the arms of both Poland and England - it has the Polish White Eagle 'Orzeł Biały' (an eagle argent armed, crowned) and the English

No.300 Sqn. Badge – www.polish squadronsremembered.com

Lion (a lion passant guardant, crowned) and has the letters CCC - 300 in Roman numerals.

The personnel of both Squadrons consisted of Polish airmen who had arrived in England, mainly from France, in early 1940. Training commenced with the pilots at Redhill (some 40 miles south of London), with the navigators and gunners firstly at Eastchurch in Kent then at Hucknall near Nottingham.

The first Squadron, No.300, initially had 10 flying crews with 180 maintenance and other personnel. They were equipped with Fairy Battle light bombers which had a crew of three; the Squadron code letters BH were designated to the unit. Its first joint commanders were W/Cdr K. P. Lewis, RAF and W/Cdr W. Makowski, C.O. of the Polish Training Centre at Hucknall (Makowski had been the general manager of LOT the Polish state airline before the war). F/Lt S. Cwynar commanded A Flight and F/Lt M. Pronaszko B Flight. The Squadron's technical officer was F/Lt S. Budzinski with RAF technical and advisory staff temporarily attached to the Squadron until the Poles became fully conversant with RAF systems and procedures.

No.301 Sqn. Badge – www.polish squadronsremembered.com

Similarly No.301 Squadron consisted of 10 aircrews and 172 other personnel freshly arrived in England. Its first CO was W/Cdr Rudkowski, advised by British officer S/Ldr C.G. Skinner also with a number of RAF personnel on temporary attachments. Like its twin Squadron No.301 was equipped with 16 Fairey Battles. The code letters GR were assigned to the 'Pomeranian'. It used a badge with a Pomeranian red griffin rampant shield design.

The Fairey Battle was a light bomber powered by a single Rolls-Royce Merlin engine, designed as a two-seat day bomber to replace the ageing Hawker Hart and Hind biplanes. The prototype first flew on 10th March 1936. An all-metal, low-wing cantilever monoplane, equipped with retractable landing gear its clean design with its long, slim fuselage and cockpit for three (pilot, navigator and gunner) seated in tandem with a continuous glazed canopy, was more like a large fighter rather than a bomber.

Fairey Battles – Wilhelm Ratuszynski

The armament and crew were similar to the twin engined Bristol Blenheim. The Battle's standard payload of four 250lb (110kg) bombs was carried in cells inside the wings and two additional bombs could be carried on underwing racks. As the engine took up the nose area the bomb aimer's position was under the wing centre section sighting through a sliding panel in the floor of the fuselage. The first RAF Squadron, No.63, was equipped with Battles in June 1937.

Despite being a great improvement on the aircraft that preceded it by the time it saw action it was virtually obsolete. It was slow, weighed down with a three-man crew and bomb load with a limited range and highly vulnerable to both anti-aircraft fire and fighters with only a single defensive .303 machine gun. It also lacked an armoured cockpit and self-sealing fuel tank.

The Battle recorded the first RAF aerial victory of the Second World War but by May 1940 was suffering heavy losses. In six weeks in 1940 almost 200 Battles had been lost yet on the return from France, for a short period, the RAF continued to rely on the light bomber. Reforming No.1 Group it continued to be deployed in operations against shipping massed in the Channel ports for Operation Sealion. The last combat sortie by the type was mounted on the night of 15/16th October 1940 by No.301 (Polish) Squadron in a raid on Boulogne while Nos.12 and 142 Squadrons bombed Calais.

On the 20th August, just as Poland's President in Exile General Sikorski (in the centre) had conferred a Polish decoration on RAF Bramcote's Station Commander, G/Capt. A. P. Davidson, H.M. King George VI (on the left) unexpectedly visited the Squadrons. The King signed the Squadron's logbooks and wished everybody well.

H.M. King George VI and Gen. Sikorski – Wilhelm Ratuszynski

A few days later the Squadrons were transferred to RAF Swinderby as part of No.1 Bomber Group, where No.300 Squadron landed their aircraft on August 22nd. The following phone call is said to have taken place:

"We're at Swinderby, at the new aerodrome. You've no idea what we haven't got here!"

"Well, what?" inquires the Bramcote end.

"Well, there's no water; there's no officers' mess; no beds and no chairs in the rooms. We haven't got - in short - anything."

"Good God! There must be something there. We're coming there next week."

"Well, there's an airfield and nothing else."

Swinderby was still being constructed but with hard work by all concerned the airfield became a bomber Squadron base.

On the 9th of September Group informed Swinderby that 'S C I' practice would not be allowed at Winthorpe as recorded in the operations room log book.

David Hallam then a young boy remembers two Polish airmen being briefly billeted with his family (his Mother and his four other siblings) where they lived on Middleton Road in Newark, his Mother complained they would grind their teeth as they slept.

Operations from Swinderby and Winthorpe

On 12th September the Squadrons were ordered to designate three crews for a mission to bomb barge concentrations in the German occupied French ports, the sortie was cancelled just before take-off. Two days later, however, orders for an attack on Boulogne were received. Three crews from No.300 Squadron and three from No.301 took off at dusk. It was the first Polish bomber raid from Britain.

From then on weather permitting, the Squadrons flew missions over the continent alternately every night. Each time, the targets were the German invasion barge concentrations at Boulogne, Dunkirk, Ostend and Calais. On the 25th September a Battle of No.301 Squadron was shot up by a night fighter during a raid on Boulogne and the crew in attempting an emergency landing at Honington, Devon crashed, P/Os. Waronski and Kulinski and Sgt. Paliwoda were all lost.

On the night of 13/14th October No.300 Squadron suffered their first loss when the airfield was subjected to attacks by German bombers, 10 bombs were dropped on the runway at Swinderby one aircraft was destroyed and two were damaged. A German plane cruised near the airfield and kept it blacked-out so that the homing bombers had to wait in the air until they were almost out of fuel. Finally having to make forced landings in darkness and mist one bomber crashed in Watchwood Plantation, Calverton, the aircraft burst into flames and F/O Gebicki and Sgts. Egierski and Morawa, all perished, they are buried in the Wilford Hill Cemetery, Nottingham. Another aircraft also crashed but the crew survived

Winthorpe had at least three aircraft from each Squadron based there and buses, official and private cars all maintained communication between the two aerodromes, the bombers were housed near the Newark to Lincoln road (the A46). The Swinderby ORB notes that in October '...*the detachment appears to be well cared for and contented'*. A former Farndon and Newark resident, Mr. Maurice Price, recalls seeing Battles and later three Wellingtons parked on the grass there next to the hangar.

On the 29th October a Fairey Battle of No.300 Squadron crashed near Sutton-upon-Trent, Nottinghamshire when the Port wing fell off during a training flight, reports stated that the aircraft went into a steep dive causing the port wing to fail, F/O Firley-

Bielanski and Sgts. Szmajdowicz and Goebel all died and were buried in the Polish Cemetery at Newark.

In late October 1940 the units began to receive the Wellington Mk I and flying personnel almost doubled to 144 airmen (24 full crews), while each Squadron's personnel increased to about 400.

The longest serving of the trio of medium bombers (the others were the Hampden and Whitley) which equipped Bomber Command at the outset of World War II. The Wellington had its origins in 1932 when, in answer to Air Ministry Specification B9/32, Vickers proposed a twin engined 'heavy' bomber with an empty weight of 6,500lbs. Utilising geodetic construction, a method of 'weaving' the individual struts of the fuselage structure it provided an incredibly resilient airframe able to absorb tremendous damage combined with a low weight penalty.

The first aircraft flew in June 1936 and was, for a short time, known as the Vickers Crecy before the name Wellington was adopted. The first true Wellington made its maiden flight just before Christmas 1937, less than two years after a revised Air Ministry Specification B29/35 had been drawn up around the Vickers design, and the first order for 180 aircraft placed; the aircraft featured nose and tail turrets.

The first Squadron to receive the Wellington was No.99 at RAF Mildenhall, Suffolk, in October 1938 and by September 1939 a further seven Squadrons had traded their Heyfords and Hendons for Wellingtons with a payload some three times greater than the Heyford. Over 11,000 Wellingtons of all marks were built.

After two months of intensive training, the Squadrons resumed missions over occupied Europe. After a successful attack on Mannheim, Germany they were finally detailed for operational service. Their first target was the complex of fuel tanks and the petroleum refinery at Antwerp, Belgium which they attacked on 22nd December 1940. The raid went off well and all the aircraft returned safely. A few days later, on the 28th six more aircraft bombed the same target. While returning from this mission one No.300 Squadron Wellington crashed after hitting trees on its landing approach about half a mile from the airfield killing F/Lt Krynski, Sgt. Wegrzyn died the following day from his injuries and both were buried in the Polish Cemetery at Newark, F/O Golko, P/O Szymanski and Sgts. Graczyk and Suczynski were wounded.

In 1940, No.300 Squadron had flown 55 missions flying 212 hours and No.301 had made 42 operational sorties in 156 flying hours, both bombing targets in France and Belgium.

The beginning of 1941 was marked by a raid by No.301 Squadron aircraft on Bremen, Germany on the night of January 1st/2nd. Bremen was considered one the most difficult target to attack and the Poles welcomed the chance to have a crack at it. It was to be their first sortie of nearly seven hours and it was planned that the Poles would be some of the first aircraft over the target so their Wellingtons carried incendiaries.

The crews reached the target and dropped their loads. On the way back to England they encountered a snow blizzard with limited visibility. Three of the Squadron's aircraft crashed, killing 11 airmen, including the OC A Flight, S/Ldr Floryanowicz.

One Wellington crashed when the undercarriage collapsed on a heavy landing at Swinderby but without casualties. One crashed during a landing approach at Digby. All the crew, S/Ldr Floryanowicz, F/O Kulbacki, P/O Olszyna and Sgts. Guzowski, Gackowski and Hejnowski died and are buried in the Polish Cemetery at Newark. The second was shot down near to Digby by a German fighter; killed were F/O Sadowski, P/Os. Murawski and Dziubinski and Sgts. Kasianowski and K. Sawicz and they also were buried in the Polish Cemetery; tail-gunner Sgt Wancisiewicz surviving.

For the next three weeks, the bombers were grounded by heavy rains which made the airfield unserviceable. On the 27th January H.M. the King and Queen Elizabeth visited Swinderby; they spoke with several Polish officers and to the King's question what he found most difficult to master in training one Polish officer answered 'King's Regulations, Your Majesty'.

During January and most of February Swinderby which then did not have concrete runways was practically out of use following the heavy rainfall. Very few sorties were made and Winthorpe was used in order to maintain flying duties. Newton, Syerston, Waddington and Bircham Newton/Langham in Norfolk were among those airfields used to mount operational sorties, the aircraft flying to them empty then loading their bombs and fuel there.

The following extracts from the Operations Record Book of No.300 Squadron shows this.

> **15 February 1941.** *Low clouds and drizzle, clearing in the afternoon. Instrumental and photographic flights. Tests before operational flight. Total flying hours 06.35. At night operational flights of four crews over Boulogne from Waddington. Usual ground training and Link Trainer practice.*
>
> **16 February 1941.** *Few clouds and strong wind. Ferrying of aircraft from Waddington to Winthorpe. Total flying hours 03.00. One slightly damaged aircraft left at Waddington. Link trainer practice.*

Not until nearly the end of February did anything like normal flying resume; on the 25th February 2 crews were on operations over Dusseldorf and on the 26th 3 crews on operations over Cologne.

Slowly, the frequency of flights increased and targets included Bremen, Hamburg and Brest to attack German battleships. Also marshalling yards at Mannheim, Düsseldorf and Frankfurt were bombed. A No.301 Wellington overshot the runway at Bramcote during a training flight on 21st March killing three crew members F/O Korycinski and Sgts. Lenczowski and Chrzanowski.

On 23rd March, it was announced that the Poles were to bomb Berlin. Seven No.300 Squadron aircraft were detailed for the raid flying first to Bircham Newton/Langham. Two Wellingtons swung on takeoff in strong cross winds and hit the boundary fence and a third was damaged, fortunately without injury to the crews. The remaining four crews dropped their bombs over Berlin. All returned safely and photographs showed that their bombing was accurate.

The four No.300 Squadron crews which bombed Berlin taken soon after the mission:

Back row, from left: Julian Talkowski, Alfons Kowalski, Tadeusz Baczak, Jan Jabłonski, Kazimierz Szymanowski, Aleksander Suczynski, Jozef Kuflik, Nikodem Kozinski, Marian Sztul, Jan Artymiuk and Tadeusz Swidzinski.

Front, from left: Edmund Jura, Edmund Rygiel, Czeslaw Dziekonski, Roman Miarczynski, Piotr Nowakowski, Waclaw Makowski, Romuald Sulinski, Czeslaw Dej, Antoni Zychowski, Władysław Rogalski and Jan Biezunski.

No.300 Squadron crews – Wilhelm Ratuszynski

The Polish bombers went to Berlin again on the night of 17/18th April. Air defences had been strengthened and Allied bomber losses started to mount. The Polish Squadrons were not immune and one crew of F/Os. Dudek and Brzozowski, P/O Rewkowski and Sgts. Bojakowski, Lipecki and Golebiowski, was lost over the sea when the aircraft was probably shot down returning from an operation against Bremen on the 9th May.

The Swinderby ORB noted in May 1941 that '... a number of 301 Squadron's Officers, Sergeants and Airmen have been dispersed, some taking over the five huts at Winthorpe satellite aerodrome and the remainder going to Coddington Hall. These arrangements have proved very satisfactory; the Polish personnel of No.301 Squadron are living entirely as a separate unit and are comfortably installed and well fed and appear to prefer their new conditions to life at the parent Station. Work is proceeding satisfactorily with the buildings at Coddington Hall but still nothing has been done towards extending the aerodrome and building runways and dispersal points at Winthorpe.

The beginning of June was marked with increased activity; operational sorties led to Lorient, Osnabrück, Bielefeld, Nuremberg and other targets. On 11th June the Squadrons were visited by the AOC-in-C Bomber Command, Air Marshal Sir Richard E. C. Peirse followed by H.R.H. the Duke of Kent the day after. A No.301 aircraft was shot down over the sea coming back from Düsseldorf on the 12th June, F/Os. Sedzik and Sojka and

The crew of No.301 Squadron Wellington GR-O, Swinderby May 1941: S/Ldr Brejnak (left), F/O Lapa, Sgt. Hasinski, Sgt. Zaremba, P/O Bylenski and P/O J. Wojcik.

– Wilhelm Ratuszynski

Sgts. Kruk-Szuster, Weinberg and Maciej were all rescued and taken prisoner but Sgt Chowanski died. A similar fate befell a No.301 aircraft off Terschelling Island, Holland on 19th June during a raid on Bremen with all the crew, F/Os. Krassowski and Bernas and Sgts. Wagner, Bonkowski, Franaszczuk and Manasiak lost.

On the 23rd June a No.301 aircraft returning from a sortie on Bremen lost a propeller and crashed at Roewood Farm Kirkington. Lost were P/O Pietruszka and Sgt Tegowski who are buried in the Polish cemetery at Newark. F/O Sawlewicz and Sgts. Popiawski, Florczak and Grzyrnski were rescued by Farmers Mr. and Mrs. Broadberry who pulled them from the burning aircraft. Both Mr. and Mrs. Broadberry were awarded British Empire Medals.

A No.300 Squadron aircraft after attacking Bremen ditched in the North Sea 40 miles E of Grimsby, Lincolnshire on the 29th June, with all the crew, F/O Dej and Sgts. Nowakowski, Wielondek, Kudelko, Socha and Sosinski, safe and rescued. On the 30th June a No.301 aircraft was shot down by a night fighter near to Nienburg, between Bremen and Hanover, during a raid on Bremen. Sgt Korab-Brzozowski was killed and the rest of the crew bailed out and were taken prisoners.

Both Squadrons lost one aircraft each on the 4th July on another raid on Bremen. On its target approach a No.300 Squadron aircraft was shot down by a night fighter and crashed near Augustenfeld north of Hanover. F/O Kula and Sgts. Mieczkowski, Urbanowicz, Herman all died with F/Lt Krupowicz and W/O Przybylski both taken prisoner. Similarly the No.301 Squadron aircraft was also shot down by a fighter over Holland and crashed into the sea. Killed was the Swinderby Station Commander G/ Capt. Stachon who although disqualified from operational flying, took every chance to fill-in on missions for incomplete crews, the rest of the crew F/Lt Butkiewicz, F/O Palka, W/Os. Dydo and Idzikowski and Sgt Dziegiel were taken prisoner.

Shot down by a night fighter over Holland on a raid to Cologne on the 10th July all the No.300 Squadron crew were taken prisoner, F/Lt Janicki, P/Os Kuflik and Kozinski and Sgts. Sztul, Artymiuk and Suczynski.

On 16th July 1941 No.300 Squadron as the senior Polish Air Formation was entrusted with the Polish Air Force standard (right). The standard had been made in Wilno (Vilnius), Poland by women working in secret and carried to Britain; the BBC broadcast a message telling the women that it had arrived safely. The motto on the standard reads *'Miłosc zada ofiary - Love Demands Sacrifice'*.

A service took place celebrated by Mgr. Gawlina, Military Bishop for the Polish

The Polish Air Force Standard – Wilhelm Ratuszynski

Forces, also taking part were the President, the Commander-in-Chief and many other distinguished Polish and British visitors. It remained with No.300 Squadron for three months after which it was kept in turn for the same period by each of the Polish bomber and fighter Squadrons.

S/Ldr. Cwynar was appointed as Officer Commanding No.300 Squadron on the 17th July and an operation over Cologne was carried out by six crews from the Squadron who all returned to base.

David Hallam again recalls evenings spent with his brother at their bedroom window recording the Wellingtons' numbers as they took off from Winthorpe and crossing them off when they were not seen again, and Joyce Golland remembers watching Wellingtons taking off and waving at them with her Grandfather from a bedroom window of their cottage (although she cannot remember anyone waving back!)

On the 18th July 1941 No.300 Squadron left Swinderby (and Winthorpe) for RAF Hemswell, near Gainsborough followed by No.301 the following day.

Postscript - subsequent operations

Both Squadrons moved from Hemswell to Ingham in 1942 and back to Hemswell in January 1943; following No.301s disbanding No.300 moved to Ingham again in June 1943 and finally Faldingworth in March 1944, where the Squadron disbanded on 11th October 1946.

No.300 later converted to Wellington IIIs, IVs and Xs and finally in 1944 to Lancasters. Over 2½ years it flew 3,684 operational sorties and dropped nearly 10,000 tons of bombs on enemy targets and it also laid more than 1,400 mines in enemy waters. The last operational mission was on 25th April 1945 when 14 Lancasters bombed Berchtesgaden.

When offensive duties finished No.300 took part in Operation Manna - the dropping of food supplies to the Dutch, and its last mission before VE Day was on 7th May 1945 when it dropped relief supplies to the Dutch in Rotterdam. It took part in Operation Exodus the repatriation of British ex-POWs, Operation Dodge the transport of British troops from Italy to Great Britain and the carrying of Red Cross supplies for liberated Poles in German concentration camps. The Squadron won 107 decorations including 1 OBE, 63 DFCs, 1 CGM, 1 MM and 37 DFMs.

In March 1943 No.301 Bomber Squadron was disbanded and the majority of the crews and aircraft were merged with No.300 Squadron. Whilst in Bomber Command No.301 Squadron had flown 7,367 operational hours in 1,260 sorties against enemy targets and dropped 1,428 tons of bombs and laid 222 tons of mines.

The remaining crews were attached to No.138 Squadron at RAF Tempsford as the newly formed C Flight, temporarily renamed as 301 Squadron Special Duties Flight RAF, operating Handley-Page Halifax special duties aircraft; it was later to become No.1586 (Polish Special Duties) Flight RAF at Derna Libya.

The second incarnation of No.301 'Pomerania' Squadron was formed from No.1586 Flight at Brindisi, Italy on 7th November 1944, as part of the Mediterranean Allied Air Forces. This version of the Squadron operated a mix of Halifax's and Liberators in supply dropping missions over Poland, Yugoslavia and northern Italy. The Squadron returned to Britain during March 1945 and disbanded in 1946.

Two No.301 Squadron airmen who survived their aircraft being shot down over Germany, F/O Pawel Whilem Tobolski (left) service no. P.0375, shot down on the 25/26th June 1942 and F/O Wlodzimierz Kolanowski (right) service no. P.0243, shot down on the 8th November 1942, became escapees from Stalag Luft III near Sagan (now Zagan in Poland) 100 miles (160km) southeast of Berlin on the 24/25th March 1944 (the Great Escape). They were among the 50 of the 73 escapees who were recaptured and killed by the Germans.

www.pegasusarchive.org/pow/cSL_3_Fifty.htm

Their service numbers would indicate that they were some of the first Polish airmen within the RAF and were probably stationed at Swinderby and Winthorpe.

The following is a fitting tribute to all the Polish personnel:

> *'...we remember with affection and pride the Polish air and ground crew who fought so valiantly throughout the war of 1939-45. Their courage and gallantry became legendary. The Royal Air Force was honoured by their presence, inspired by their example and enlivened by their gaiety. We salute a brave band'.*

Air Chief Marshal Sir John Grandy GCB, KBE, DSO.

CHAPTER THREE

1942, relief landing ground and concrete runways

No.455 Squadron Badge – Royal Australian Air Force Museum

In November 1941 control of Winthorpe passed to RAF Ossington and used for a period as a Relief Landing Ground by No.14 (Pilots) Advanced Flying Unit ((P) AFU) who arrived at Ossington in January 1942 from Lyneham, Wiltshire. On February 7th 1942 control of the station passed to RAF Syerston as a second satellite ground and on the 15th October 1942 Winthorpe returned to being under Swinderby control.

No.455 Squadron, Royal Australian Air Force was formed at Williamtown, New South Wales, on 23rd May 1941, in accordance with Article XV of the Empire Air Training Scheme for service in Europe with the RAF. While the Williamtown party waited shipping overseas other personnel, predominantly members of the RAF, began assembling at Swinderby on 6th June 1941 equipped with Handley-Page Hampden medium bombers. The Australian contingent arrived on 1st September.

The squadron had use of Winthorpe as a dispersal and relief landing ground although there is no record in the squadron ORB of their using the airfield but the Swinderby ORB records Squadron personnel located at Winthorpe in October 1941 '… *a number of airmen of No.455 Squadron are accommodated at Winthorpe*' and '… *members of No.455 Squadron returned to Swinderby*' in November 1941. The squadron moved to RAF Wigsley in early February 1942 and transferred to Coastal Command.

In all around 10,000 Australians served with Bomber Command; squadrons which were predominantly Australian aircrew were designated as RAAF squadrons and 17 of these were formed, 12 in Britain and 5 in the Middle East.

The squadron achieved a couple of notable firsts; it was the first Australian squadron in the RAF when it joined No.5 Group, and in the bombing raid against Frankfurt on

Nissen huts (Site 2) – AIR 29/2408 National Archives

the night of 29th August the first Australian squadron to bomb Germany. Most of its operations until February 1942 was in the bombing campaign although it also took part in mine laying sorties in enemy waters. Although notionally Australian the squadron has been described during this period as a 'League of Nations' composed of Australian, British, Canadian, New Zealand and Rhodesian personnel.

It was during 1942 that Winthorpe's concrete runways were laid, wrongly, as local lore would have it, due to the Ransome and Marles ball bearing factory located in a direct line just over a mile away from the end of the main runway. This is though supported by official records – any aircraft based at Winthorpe that took part in operational raids was 'bombed up' at other airfields.

From 1943 to 1945 the airfield was expanded with much of the work carried out by Sir Robert McAlpine Ltd; this included construction of the watch (control) tower, hard standing aircraft dispersals, hangars, sick quarters, cinema and accommodation (Site two pictured).

The main Communal Site was developed around Coddington Hall with Site 5 to the NE. The Sick Quarters was on the far side of Beaconfield Farm, with the Sewage Disposal area on the edge of the site between Sick Bay and Site 5. Site No1 was the officers' quarters, built to the north of Newark Rd at the bend where Parkland's Close is today. A fence ran behind (what is today Newark Road housing) Site 4 past the hall driveway where the guardroom was and around the buildings either side of the drive (Site 2). The WAAF Site was at the far side of the field behind Site 4.

From the 1930s McAlpine's had employed large numbers of Irish (Republic of Ireland) nationals (commonly known as navvies). During the wartime period they built or upgraded more than 20 RAF airfields including Mildenhall, Fairford, Boscombe Down, Prestwick and Northolt in addition to Winthorpe and Ossington.

Sir Archibald Sinclair, the Secretary of State for Air, addressed the House of Commons during the Estimates Debate on 29th February 1944:

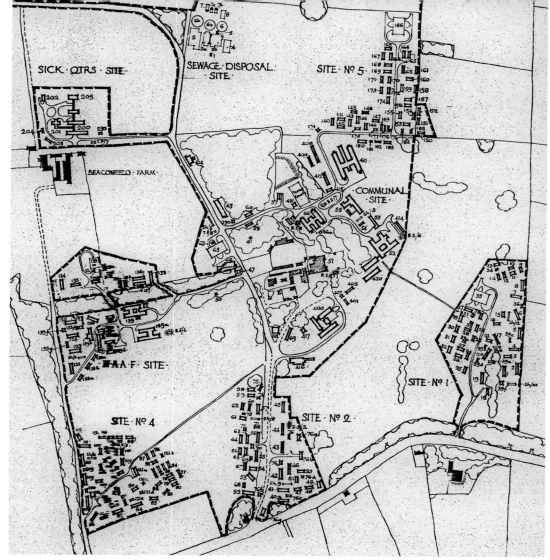

Domestic site map – NAM archives/Author

'Four and a half years ago, we started the most gigantic civil engineering and building programme ever undertaken in this country...' this had required the government to dispossess people of their land, houses and crops often with little notice and with no appeal. He went on to say, '... it has not been a pleasant thing for the people of this country to have had their land turned into an air base...' and he was '... glad to say that we have almost reached the end of our territorial demands'.

Sinclair had good reason to comment about the amount of land taken up by the Air Ministry. The typical Bomber Command airfield in 1939 varied very little from those used during World War I, they occupied an area of approximately 617 acres (250 hectares) and provided permanent facilities and accommodation for the personnel who maintained and operated a single squadron of aircraft. Each of these had a satellite station manned by further personnel which duplicated some of the essential services. The RAF Pocket Book 1937 (AP1081) gave guidance on the size and layout of an airfield.

In 1942 the average size of a Bomber Command airfield was an area of 790 acres or 320 hectares or about 1 mile x 1.5 miles (1.6 x 2.4km); there were 79 airfields, by 1944 the number had grown to 131. These give a total area for Bomber Command airfields of 62,410 acres (25,256 hectares) in 1942 increasing to more than 103,490 acres (41,881 hectares) by late 1944. Approximately 272,000 acres (110,000 hectares) in total were requisitioned for the RAF along with a wide variety of buildings. In terms of loss of potential crops this represented in excess of 3 million tons of potatoes or over 500,000 tons of wheat or 4 million tons of sugar beet by Bomber Command alone, a significant amount given wartime food rationing.

Of the 27 airfields in Bomber Command in 1939, only nine had any sort of paved landing strips. This did not cause a problem because the aircraft then in service could take off and land on grass airstrips; in 1939/40 the largest aircraft operated by Bomber Command was the Wellington weighing 28,500lbs (12,955kg) at its takeoff weight. By comparison, the four engined heavy bombers, the Stirling, introduced in 1941, Halifax and Lancaster eventually had loaded weights up to a maximum 72,000lbs (32,727kg).

Ernest Bevan, the Minister of Labour, had called on Southern Ireland to release men for a labour force for the construction of airfields on the mainland of Britain in 1940. Over 100,000 tons of concrete would be needed at each of over two hundred sites. During 1942 around 127,000 men were employed indirectly by the Air Ministry on airfield construction; 136 different contractors spread over 800 contracts were employed between 1939 and 1945.

The WW2 airfield was a pattern of three intersecting runways linked by a perimeter track and with its technical and maintenance areas close by but with its instructional, communal and domestic sites dispersed. From 1941 the main runway, usually aligned to the prevailing wind, was normally 2,000yds (1,829m) long with two subsidiary runways 1,400yds (1,280m) long. The perimeter track (or peritrack) encircled the interlocking A-shape of the three runways with a concrete surface of approximately 50ft (15.2m) wide with Dispersals/Hardstandings at intervals; on Class 'A' Bomber Command stations there were 34 'frying pan' dispersals each 125ft (38m) in diameter.

In constructing airfields sites had to be surveyed, land cleared and levelled, drainage pipes, conduits for communication systems, tarmac and concrete had to be laid and buildings constructed. This required a large workforce and the movement by road of enormous quantities of soil, hardcore, concrete and equipment to and from the sites. The construction of landing strips, taxiways and hard standings (excluding building construction) for Bomber Command alone required thousands of daily round trips by lorries.

Amongst the services required were facilities for maintenance, flying operations, personnel and utility supply. Maintenance facilities included hangars, workshops, offices, stores and the mechanical and electrical engineering installations needed to maintain

Technical site under construction in 1942 – NAM archives

the aircraft. For flying operations there were control towers, metrological offices, briefing rooms, gun butts, bomb dumps, armouries, POL (petrol, oils and lubricants) storage and rudimentary lighting systems at some airfields. For personnel there were water reservoirs and pumping systems, sewage systems, sleeping quarters, messes, medical centres, offices and rest and leisure facilities including churches and cinemas.

To operate all of the above facilities each airfield required electricity, gas, water and telecommunications. All of these had to be planned, designed, manufactured and constructed before a single aircraft could begin operations. The drinking water came from a mains supply as did the electricity, but standby electricity generating sets were placed in various important locations around the airfield. Sewage and waste water was taken from all sites to a sewage farm. As can be imagined, the grid work of drains, pipes and cables were that of a small town with around 34 miles of drains, 10 miles of cable ducts and 7 miles of water main. The RAF carried out 59 differing tasks on each station.

Along with hard standings and bases for hangars and technical buildings a total of around 130,000 tons of hardcore and concrete was required for each airfield with the number of airfields built during the period 1939-45 the equivalent to building a concrete highway 9,000 miles (14,500km) long and 30ft (9m) wide - enough from London to Beijing. Over 175 million square yards (146 million square metres) of concrete, asphalt and other hard surfacing is estimated to have been laid. With expected stress factors of 2,000 pounds per square inch runways were six to nine inches thick concrete laid on a hardcore base.

Much of the sand and aggregate used in the construction of Winthorpe was extracted locally along the River Trent; amongst these was a site at Farndon which helped to form what is now Farndon Marina. At one time during the war there were around 200 lorries operating from Farndon alone ferrying loads not only to airfields but to Newark Northgate railway station where there was a specially constructed ramp to load the goods wagons.

A former wartime Farndon schoolboy Maurice Price recalls:

"I had an uncle and he was a lorry driver working at the Farndon gravel pits. During the school holidays he would take me with him when delivering gravel to the airfields ... I kept a list of all the airfields which I visited ..."

These airfields included most of the Nottinghamshire and Lincolnshire airfields including Winthorpe and as far afield as Cottesmore and North Luffenham.

In 1944 the runways and perimeter tracks at Winthorpe were covered with a layer of tarmac applied because it was more flexible and less liable to dusting or cracking which was happening with the concrete due to the effects of the weather (water percolation and frost) and aircraft weights (the perimeter tracks were particularly susceptible).

The wartime airfield buildings were, generally all of the same types, a mixture of timber framed, brick or prefabricated steel used for both accommodation and technical sites. In total there would be about one hundred buildings built upon an airfield.

The cost of constructing an airfield in 1942 with its three runways and linked taxiways and hard standings was estimated as being in the region of £500,000 excluding any buildings; by 1944 the increased demands on infrastructure by the heavy bombers and the numbers of personnel required to be housed, fed and entertained meant that the price had increased to around £1 million; in 1944 the total cost of the building programme for both the RAF and USAAC was estimated at £615 million.

At the peak of construction in 1942 there were around 60,000 men employed directly on civil engineering work on airfields in the UK; during the period 1939-1945 444 RAF airfields were constructed in the UK.

CHAPTER FOUR

No.1661 Heavy Conversion Unit

The Royal Air Force introduced Heavy Conversion Units (HCU) in late 1941 to qualify crews trained on medium (twin engined) bombers to operate and to gain experience on the new heavy (four engined) bombers then beginning to enter Squadron service, before final posting to the operational Squadrons.

There were 20 HCUs and two HCFs (Heavy Conversion Flights) formed between 1941 and 1944 - one becoming a Lancaster Finishing School (LFS); Syerston became an operational training station as No.1668 HCU in November 1943 then becoming No.5 Group LFS in January 1944 until disbanding at the end of March 1945.

Some HCUs also supplied aircraft for bombing operations over Germany when required, usually crewed by the instructors (as did Winthorpe in January 1943). The HCUs initially had a combined total of over 700 aircraft with 1,720 Officers and 25,520 other ranks which included WAAFs, this rose to a peak of aircraft numbers in January 1944 of 1,860 including those used for fighter affiliation.

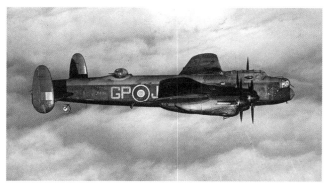

Lancaster B.I W4113 GP-J of No.1661HCU. The aircraft had flown on a number of raids with Nos. 49 and 156 Squadrons in 1942 and 1943. – NAM archives

The heavy bombers, the four engined Shorts Stirling, Avro Lancaster and Handley-Page Halifax, needed a crew of seven - pilot, flight engineer, navigator, wireless operator, bomb aimer, mid-upper gunner and rear gunner.

The RAF pilot wore full wings, or brevet, with the letters RAF in a wreath, surmounted by a crown, with a wing on each side as had been usual from the beginning of the RAF in 1918 and indeed by its predecessor the RFC. Other members of the crew wore half brevets which was a single wing emerging from a wreath which contained up to three letters. These letters indicate the crew member's function, N for Navigator, B for Bomb Aimer, AG for Air Gunner, WAG for Wireless Operator/Air Gunner, and E for the Flight Engineer; these badges were introduced in late 1942 with the exception of the Air Gunner introduced in 1939.

The air gunner had had a designated badge since 1923 when ground tradesmen who fulfilled the role had been granted a winged bullet badge; upon receipt of the badge the men gained 3d (just over 1p) extra per day with an extra 6d (2½p) also paid for each day actually engaged in flying (an Aircraftman 2nd class (AC2) earned 3s 6d (17½p) a day in 1937); from 1939 the Air Gunner became a recognised separate specialist flying trade.

Prior to 1942 the Navigator and Bomb Aimer had been a combined role known as an Observer with an O badge; the Flight Engineer was a new aircrew classification needed for the four engined 'heavy' bombers, he also operated as the reserve pilot and undertook some flying training in order to be able to carry out this role. A later addition saw the S for an Air Signaller introduced in 1944 when the Wireless Operator/Air Gunner became two separate roles.

Each member of the aircrew had been taught their trade at specialist schools, either in the UK or overseas as part of the British Commonwealth Air Training Plan. Having completed their basic training five of the trades, (pilot, navigator, wireless operator, bomb aimer and one (rear) air gunner) crewed up at an Operational Training Unit (OTU) and trained as a five man crew on twin engined medium bombers, mainly Wellingtons.

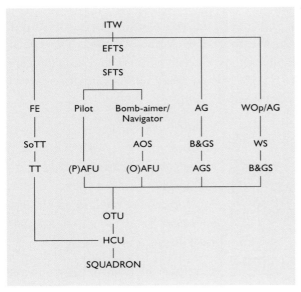

The training routes for each aircrew specialist are shown in the diagram (left). From the Initial Training Wing (ITW) the crew took differing routes.

A Flight Engineer would pass through a School of Trade Training and then specialist Technical Training for the aircraft type he would be flying before arriving at the HCU. Air Gunners and Wireless Operator/Air Gunners would take a different route through Bombing and Gunnery School or Wireless School onto either Advanced Gunnery School or Bombing and Gunnery School then to an OTU.

Pilots would first attend an Elementary Flying Training School and then a Service Flying Training School, onto a Pilots (Advanced Flying Unit) then to the OTU whilst a Navigator went to an Air Observers and Navigators School followed by an Observers (Advanced Flying Unit) and then to an OTU. Bomb Aimers were also the assistant navigator so a Bombing and Gunnery School provided training for bomb aiming and firing of the (nose turret) machine guns and from there onto an Air Observer and Navigators School and then to an OTU.

Each new intake at the OTU was paraded in a hangar and told to form themselves into a crew. Whilst many crews formed quite happily on this ad-hoc basis it was not unknown for a crew to fail to become a team and to voluntary split up or even be separated by the flight commander or commanding officer, if necessary. Some men tried several crews 'for size' until they were happy; a misfit quickly became apparent. At the OTUs they flew together and acquired their team skills, sometimes with a relatively easy operational task (mine laying or leaflet dropping) thrown in.

Once they were competent, the five man crew would transfer to a HCU, where they would be joined by a flight engineer, who came direct from training, and an additional air gunner (for the mid-upper turret position) to form the seven man crew needed for the heavy bombers.

The four to six week Heavy Conversion course consisted of ground instruction, along with approximately 40 hours of flying and included the following exercises, Familiarisation, Circuits and Landings, Bombing, Fighter Affiliation and Cross Country flying. Experienced instructors (pilots, navigators and flight engineers), normally crew who had completed at least one operational tour, would first fly with the crew and then the crew would repeat the exercise alone. The training syllabus was split into two parts with alternate days of flying and ground instruction with the course designed to last six weeks.

Once qualified the crew was then posted to an operational Squadron, although from late 1943 until early 1945, when the Lancaster was replaced by the Halifax and Stirling at the HCUs, crews destined for Lancaster equipped units did a very short course at a Lancaster Finishing School which were formed in November 1943 (No 5 LFS at Syerston for No.5 Group or No 1 LFS at Lindholme (moving to Hemswell in January 1944) for No.1 Group and No.3 LFS at Feltwell for No.3 Group), before an operational posting. Most OTUs and the HCUs supplied crews to a particular Group.

John Nettleton – Public domain RAF Bomber Command

No.1661 Heavy Conversion Unit was formed at RAF Waddington on the 7th October 1942 from Nos.9 (formed on the 8th August 1942) and 44 Squadron conversion flights (formed on the 1st January) along with 49 Squadron conversion flight at RAF Scampton (formed on the 16th May). These became A, B, and C flights respectively and remained at Waddington and Scampton as part of No.5 Group under the command of Squadron Leader (S/Ldr.) J. D. Nettleton VC a South African (above), with a mixed strength of Manchester and Lancaster aircraft.

John Nettleton had gained his VC on the 17th April 1942 as the leader of six Avro

Lancaster bombers of No.44 Squadron on a daylight attack on a diesel engine factory at Augsburg, Germany.

When they had just crossed the French coast at low level near Dieppe, German fighters attacked the aircraft a short way inland and four Lancasters were shot down. The two remaining continued towards the target and both aircraft attacked the factory, bombing it amidst heavy anti aircraft fire; Nettleton's damaged Lancaster was the only aircraft to return, landing at Squires Gate near Blackpool. His VC was gazetted on the 24th April 1942.

Nettleton, by now a Wing Commander, died on the 13th July 1943 when his No.44 Squadron Lancaster KM-Z (ED331) took off from Dunholme Lodge for a raid on Turin, Italy. His aircraft was believed to have been shot down by a night fighter off the Brest peninsular. His body and those of his crew were never recovered and they are commemorated on the Runnymede Memorial.

Some records show that the HCU was stationed at RAF Skellingthorpe from October 1942 but the ORB for the unit shows that the flights remained at Scampton and Waddington although some flying was carried out from RAF Woodhall Spa due to '... Scampton aerodrome being unserviceable'.

The Operational Record Book for No.1661 HCU on the 9th November 1942 stated that: *The Policy of this Conversion Unit is to train O. T. U. Crews and Second Pilots from 5 Group Squadrons to fly Manchester and Lancaster aircraft, finally passing them out fully trained for Operational duties.*

All of the flying instructors it continues '... *have all completed one or two operational tours.'* The Chief Ground Instructor was S/Ldr. McClure.

On the 12th November the King accompanied by the AOC was '... *graciously pleased to inspect the unit...'*

On the 1st January 1943 the HCU transferred to RAF Winthorpe, the aircraft, 8 Manchesters and 10 Lancasters, carried the unit code letters GP or KB under the command of Wing Commander Beauchamp DSO DFC; S/Ldr. Nettleton was promoted and posted back to No.44 Squadron on the 4th of January and F/Lt. Oakley DFM took command of A flight, S/Ldr. McClure was posted to No.83 Squadron and was replaced by S/Ldr. McFarlane posted in from RAF Wigsley.

Beauchamp had joined the RAF in the 1930s and in October 1937 was posted to No.49 Squadron flying Hampdens based at Scampton, completing 38 missions until November 1940. He later went to No.207 Squadron flying Manchesters and Lancasters and completed a tour between September 1941 and August 1942.

The original aircraft strength of Manchesters and Lancasters was changed with the withdrawal from service of the Manchesters in late 1943 replaced by the Handley-Page

Halifax which arrived in early September, the first recorded Halifax flight in the ORB is on the 3rd September and the last recorded Manchester flight is the 5th October.

Halifaxes in turn were replaced by Short Stirling IIIs; the last Halifax recorded in the ORB is the 11th December whilst the first flight for a Stirling is the 10th December. At the same time due to a shortage of operational Lancasters these too were withdrawn with their last record of a flight on the 7th January 1944, thus the HCU became a purely Stirling unit; the Lancasters did not return to the HCU until December 1944 when aircraft availability had improved and the HCU became solely Lancaster by March 1945 with 32 aircraft 'on charge'.

The expansion of Bomber Command in 1942/3 put a severe strain on the organisational administration of its units resulting in the introduction of an intermediate level of command between Group HQs and Stations (see diagram). War Establishment WAR/BC/313 came into effect in March 1943 which created the Base system consisting of a Base Station with one or two substations.

Each Base was commanded by an Air Commodore and was initially identified by the name of the Base Station and the role of the Base.

Air Commodore E. I. Bussell who had been the Officer Commanding, RAF Syerston arrived on the 15th March 1943 to become the AOC, Swinderby Training Base and G/Capt. E. S. Butler OBE arrived from Bomber Command Headquarters to command RAF Winthorpe and S/Ldr. W. I. Deas DFC became the Chief Flying Instructor.

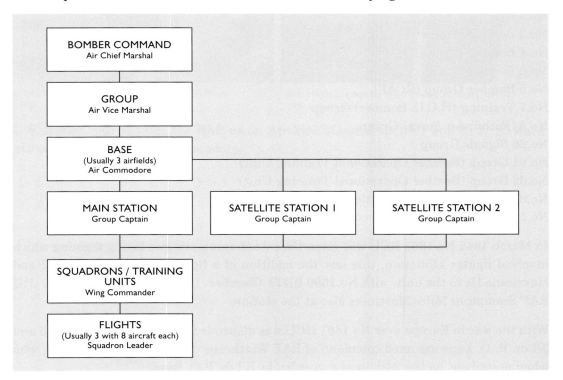

Wireless operator and flight engineers positions in a Lancaster – NAM archives

CHAPTER FIVE

The aircraft of No.1661 HCU - 1

From the beginning the Heavy Conversion Units usually operated aircraft that had seen long hours of operational flying and subsequently these aircraft could be difficult to maintain in a flying condition. This resulted in some claims that many training aircraft accidents were the result of the aircraft not being airworthy. One aircraft, Lancaster DV246, had served with the famous No.617 Dambusters Squadron and flown on at least 28 missions (these missions are recorded in a separate chapter) before its use by the HCU at Winthorpe.

This chapter deals with the three main types. Aircraft known to have been operated by No.1661 HCU are listed in appendices 1 to 3.

Avro Manchester

The Avro Manchester was originally designed to Air Ministry Specification P.13/36, for a twin engined medium bomber for worldwide use, capable of carrying out shallow (30°) dive bombing attacks and be able to carry heavy bomb loads of 8,000lbs (3,630kg) or two 18in (457mm) torpedoes. Provision for catapult assisted takeoff to permit the maximum load was also part of the

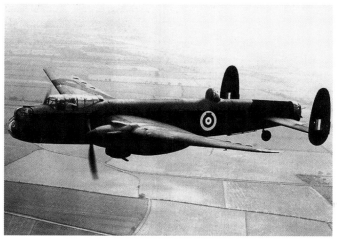

Avro Manchester – Public domain Canadian Forces Expired crown copyright

specification. Cruising speed was to be a minimum of 275mph at 15,000ft. The Air Ministry was expecting an aircraft of similar weight to the B.1/35 specification but smaller and faster, the Airspeed A.S.29 (not built), Armstrong Whitworth A.W.39 a Whitley development (not built), Handley Page H.P.55 (not built), a Hawker project and Vickers Warwick were offered to this specification.

Against Specification P.13/36, Avro had 2 Manchester prototypes ordered with Rolls-Royce Vulture engines, the Handley-Page H.P.56 twin engined bomber had one prototype ordered with Vulture engines but it was never built, soon after Handley-Page was told to redesign the HP.56 for four engines (Rolls-Royce Merlin X) rather than two, which became the HP.57 Halifax, as the Vulture was already suffering technical problems. One Vickers Warwick with Vulture engines was also ordered.

Avro had already started work on a design before the invitation to tender. In early 1937 both the Avro and Handley-Page designs were accepted, and prototypes ordered but in mid 1937 the Air Ministry exercised their right to order off the drawing board thus side stepping the usual procurement process, an action necessary due to the rapid expansion of the RAF in expectation of war. From 1939 it was expected that the P.13/36 specification would replace existing medium bombers in production.

The Rolls-Royce Vulture 24 cylinder X-block engine was basically two Rolls-Royce Peregrine V12 cylinder blocks mounted one on top of the other, the bottom one inverted to give the "X" shape. When developed in 1935, the engine had promise, it was rated at 1,760hp (1,310kW) but it proved unreliable and had to be derated to 1,480-1,500hp (1,100-1,120kW). Avro's prototype Manchester L7246 was assembled by their experimental department at Manchester's Ringway Airport and first flew from there on the 25th July 1939, with the second aircraft following on the 26th May 1940. The Rolls-Royce engine was chosen by Avro and not stipulated by the Air Ministry as is sometimes claimed.

Manchester L7477 with flak damage following an operation (this aircraft served with No.1661 HCU) – NAM archives

The Manchester was designed with twin fins but the first production aircraft, designated the Mk.I, had a central fin added and 20 aircraft with this configuration were completed. They were succeeded by the Mk.IA which reverted to the twin-fin system but used enlarged, taller fin and rudders mounted on a new tailplane with its span increased from 22ft (6.71m) to 33ft (10.06m). This configuration was carried over to the Lancaster, except for the first prototype which also used a central fin.

Avro built 177 and Metropolitan-Vickers 32 aircraft; plans for Armstrong-Whitworth and Fairey Aviation at Stockport/Ringway to build the Manchester were abandoned with the Fairey order for 150 Manchesters replaced by orders for Halifaxes.

The Manchester entered service with No.207 Squadron of Bomber Command in November 1940, flying its first operational mission on the 24/25th February 1941 in a raid on the French port of Brest. Equipping eight bomber Squadrons serving with two others and also being used by Coastal Command it operated with Nos.408 and 420 Squadrons Royal Canadian Air

Force and Nos. 49, 50, 57, 61, 83, 97, 106, 144 and 207 Squadrons in the RAF.

The 193 operational Manchesters flew 1,269 operations with Bomber Command, dropping 1,826 tons (1,657 tonnes) of bombs; its last operation was against Bremen on the 25th June 1942. Of the 78 aircraft lost, 45 were non-operational of which 30 involved engine failure.

VARIANTS:	
Prototype	L7246 originally with twin tail, due to a lack of directional stability it had a third fin added.
Mk.I	First production version with twin tail and additional central fin added; 20 built.
Mk.IA	Main production version with twin tail and enlarged tail plane, it also had taller fins and rudders.
Mk.II	Projected version powered by a pair of Napier Sabre or Bristol Centaurus engines, none built.
Mk.III	BT308 powered by four Merlin engines with increased wingspan; the three fins and rudders of the Manchester I were retained, the prototype Avro Lancaster.

SPECIFICATIONS (Mk.I):			
Crew:	7 (including 2 pilots)	Length:	70ft (21.34m)
Wingspan:	90ft 1in (27.46m)	Max takeoff weight:	50,000lb (22,680kg)
Engine:	2 x 1,760hp (1,310kW) Rolls-Royce Vulture 24 cylinder X-type		
Maximum speed:	265 mph (230 knots, 402kmh) at 17,000ft (5,180m)		
Range:	1,200 miles (1,930km) with maximum bomb load		
Service ceiling:	19,500ft (5,852m)		
Armament:	8 x 0.303in (7.7mm) Browning machine guns in nose, dorsal and tail in Nash & Thomson turrets		
Bomb load:	10,350lb (4,695kg)		

Avro Lancaster Mks.1 and 3

Manchester Mk.III, BT308, which first flew on the 9th January 1941, was essentially the first Lancaster, being powered by four Merlin engines and with increased wingspan, although initially retaining the three fins and twin outboard rudders (the central fin had no movable control surface) of the Manchester I. BT308 received the Lancaster name immediately after its first flight. The second prototype Lancaster DG595 featured the twin, enlarged fins and rudders of the Mk.IA. Manchester production continued until November 1941 but some aircraft in production were completed as Lancasters.

There were 7,377 Lancasters built in all its variants with the two main types the Mk.1 and Mk.3 the most numerous; both models were manufactured concurrently, the only significant difference being the Merlin's manufactured by either Rolls-Royce for the Mk.1 or the American Packhard company for the Mk.3; there were 300 Mk.2s built using Bristol Hercules engines.

The Lancaster entered service with No.44 Squadron at Waddington in December 1941 and the first operation by the Squadrons Lancasters was on the 3rd March 1942. Forty-two Squadrons, Heavy Conversion Units, Lancaster Finishing Schools and various other Development and Training Flights all used the Lancaster during the war.

Avro Lancaster – Public domain photograph TR 197 of the Imperial War Museum

Specially modified Lancasters known as Type 464 Provisioning (below left) were used in the Dambusters Raid in May 1943, the bomb bay doors were removed and struts to carry the bomb were fitted in their place. A hydraulic motor, driven by the pump previously used for the mid-upper turret was fitted to spin the bomb. Lamps, fitted in the bomb bay

Lancaster Type 464 Provisioning – NAM archives

and nose, were used for the simple height measurement system which enabled the accurate control of low-flying altitude at night. The mid-upper turret was removed to save weight, and the gunner moved to the front turret to relieve the bomb aimer from having to man the front guns so that he could assist with map reading.

Each Lancaster required over 50 personnel including the crew to maintain, provision and fly the aircraft, this number excluded all the ancillary staff (cooks, clerks etc.) that any RAF Station needed to operate efficiently.

SPECIFICATIONS (Mk.I):			
Crew:	7 (pilot, flight engineer, navigator, bomb aimer/nose gunner, wireless operator, mid-upper gunner and rear gunner)		
Length:	69ft 4in (21.11m)	Wingspan:	102ft (31.09m)
Max takeoff weight:	72,000lb (32,727kg) with 22,000lb (10,000kg) bomb		
Engine:	4 x 1,280hp (954kW) V12 Rolls-Royce Merlin XX liquid-cooled		
Maximum speed:	282mph (455.6kmh) at 63,000lb (28,576kg) at 13,000ft (3,962m)		
Range:	2,530 miles (4,073km)		
Service ceiling:	21,400ft at 63,000lb (32,659kg)		
Armament:	8 x 0.303in (7.7mm) Browning machine guns in nose, dorsal and tail turrets		
Bomb load:	Maximum normal bomb load of 14,000lb (6,300kg) or 1 x 22,000lb (10,000kg) Grand Slam with modifications to the bomb bay		

VARIANTS:

B.I	Rolls-Royce Merlin XX engines and SU carburettors, later production Lancasters had Merlin 22 and 24 engines.
B.I Special	32 Aircraft adapted to take the super heavy Tallboy and then Grand Slam bombs. Upgraded engines with paddle-bladed propellers and the mid-upper turret removed. For Tallboy the bomb bay doors were bulged, for Grand Slam they were removed completely and the area faired over and later the nose turret was removed.
PR.I	Modified photographic reconnaissance B.1 operated by Nos. 82 and 541 Squadrons in the war. All armament and turrets removed with a reconfigured nose and a camera carried in the bomb bay.
B.I (FE)	For operations against the Japanese (the Tiger Force) in the Far East (FE), a tropicalised variant based on late production aircraft with modified radio, radar, navaids, and a 400 gallon (1,818L) tank installed in the bomb bay. Most were painted with white upper surfaces and black undersides.
B.II	Bristol Hercules (VI or XVI) engine powered variant, 300 were produced by Armstrong-Whitworth.
B.III	Packard built Merlin engines produced at the same time as the B.I, the two being indistinguishable externally. Minor differences were related to the engine installation.
B.III (Special)	Known at the time of modification as the Type 464 Provisioning Lancaster, 23 built to carry the Upkeep mine (bouncing bomb) for the Dams' raids.
ASR.III	B.III modified for air-sea rescue, with three dipole ventral antennas fitted aft of the radome and carrying an airborne lifeboat in the re-configured bomb bay. Armament was often removed and the mid-upper turret faired-over.
GR.III/MR.III	ASR.III modified for maritime reconnaissance.
B.IV	The Lincoln B.1, an increased wingspan and lengthened fuselage and new Boulton Paul F turret (two x 0.5in Browning machine guns) with re-configured framed "bay window" nose glazing. The prototypes (PW925, PW929 and PW932) were powered by two stage Merlin 85s inboard and later Merlin 68s outboard.
B.V	Increased wingspan and lengthened fuselage, two-stage Merlin 85s, became the Lincoln B.2.
B.VI	Nine aircraft converted from B IIIs fitted with Merlin 85/87 engines with two-stage superchargers giving much improved high altitude performance. These aircraft were only used by Pathfinder units Nos.7, 83 and 635 Squadrons and No.405 Squadron RCAF as a Master Bomber. Two were retained by Rolls-Royce for installation and flight testing.
B.VII	The final production version with the Martin 250CE mid-upper turret with two 0.5in (12.7mm) Browning Mark II machine guns and the Nash & Thomson FN-82 tail turret with twin 0.5in Browning machine guns replacing those with 0.303in (7.7mm) Browning machine guns.
B.X	Canadian-built B.III with Canadian and US made instrumentation and electrics. Canada used the aircraft in post war maritime patrol, search and rescue, and photo-reconnaissance roles until 1964.
B.XV	As per Lancaster B.IV/Lincoln B.1 but built in Canada and renamed Avro Lincoln XV one example was built before the order was cancelled when the war ended.

Short Stirling

The Short S.29 Stirling was the RAFs first four-engined heavy bomber built by Short Brothers to an Air Ministry specification B.12/36 of 1936, and entered service in 1941. The Stirling had a relatively brief operational career as a bomber, being relegated to secondary duties from 1943 onwards when the Handley-Page Halifax and Avro Lancaster entered service.

Short Stirling Mk.1 - NAM archives

The specification had several requirements; the bomb load was to be a maximum of 14,000lb (6,350kg) carried to a range of 2,000 miles (3218km) or a lesser payload of 8,000lb (3,629kg) to 3,000 miles (4,800km), cruise at 230mph or more at 15,000ft (4,600m) and have three gun turrets (in the nose, amidships and rear) for defence. The aircraft should also be able to be used as a troop transport for 24 soldiers and be able to use catapult assistance for takeoff. The idea was that it would fly troops to far corners of the Empire and then support them with bombing.

Shorts were producing four-engined flying boat designs of the required size and created the S.29 by removing the lower deck and boat hull of the S.25 Sunderland. The new S.29 design was largely identical: the wings and controls were the same, construction was identical and it even retained the slight upward bend at the rear of the fuselage, originally intended to keep the Sunderland's tail clear of sea spray.

Short Stirling Mk.1 - NAM archives

The first S.29, now named the Stirling, first flew on the 14th May 1939 with four Bristol Hercules II radial engines; production started in August 1940 at Shorts' Rochester factory.

The massive bomb load put it in a class of its own; double that of any other bomber (it was larger than the Handley-Page Halifax and the Avro Lancaster which replaced it but both of these were originally designed to have twin engines). The Stirling was the only British bomber of the period to see service that had been designed from the start with four engines.

The first few Mk.Is had Hercules II engines but the majority had 1,500hp (1,100kW) Hercules XIs. The Mk.III, introduced in 1943, was similar with the exception of a new dorsal turret and the improved 1,635hp (1,200kW) Hercules VI or XVI engines, which improved maximum speed from 255 to 270mph (410 to 435kmh).

No.7 Squadron were the first to receive the Stirling in August 1940 and the night of the 10/11th February 1941 saw 3 Stirlings of the Squadron in action for the first time as part of a force of 43 aircraft, attacking oil storage tanks in Rotterdam. The aircraft equipped fifteen Squadrons in the bombing role and a further thirteen in transport and towing roles, with a short post war career in the civilian transport role. Total Stirling production was 2,383 aircraft of all variants, excluding 6 rebuilt aircraft (serials TS261- 6).

SPECIFICATIONS (Mk.I):

Crew:	7 (First and second pilot, navigator/bomb aimer, front gunner/WT operator, two air gunners, and flight engineer)		
Length:	87ft 3in (26.6m)	Wingspan:	99ft 1in (30.2m)
Max takeoff weight:	70,000lb (31,752kg)		
Engine:	4 x 1,375hp (1,025kW) Bristol Hercules II radials		
Maximum speed:	282mph (454kmh) at 12,500ft (3,800m)		
Range:	2,330 miles (3,750km)		
Service ceiling:	16,500ft (5,030m)		
Armament:	8 x 0.303in (7.7mm) Browning machine guns: in nose tail and dorsal turrets		
Bomb load:	Up to 14,000lb (6,350kg)		

VARIANTS:

Mk.1	Initial production version Series 1 totalling 267 with 1,375hp Hercules II engines. Series 2 (117 built) had 1,590hp Hercules XI engines with two-speed superchargers The Series 3 (307) had Hercules XIs in Bristol designed power plants.
Mk.2	Proposed Canadian production version but planned production of 140 cancelled.
Mk. III	Improved Mk.I Series 3 with 1,615hp Hercules VI and XVI engines with under-slung oil coolers, 1,037 built.
Mk. IV	Adaptation of the Mk.III as glider tug and/or paratroops transport with the nose and dorsal turrets removed and exit hatch in rear fuselage, delivery commenced in late 1943. Production totalled 460 with at least a further 130 Mk.IIIs converted.
Mk.V	Transport derivative of the Mk.III to carry 20 paratroops, 40 troops, two jeeps with trailers or 12 stretchers and 14 sitting wounded. Lengthened nose fairing, hinged to give access to cargo compartment and large loading door in starboard side, 160 built at Belfast ending in November 1945.

CHAPTER SIX

The aircraft of No.1661 HCU - 2

Apart from the three main types operated by the HCU other aircraft were also at some time on the unit's strength.

Handley-Page Halifax

The Halifax served only briefly on the unit from September to December 1943. The aircraft known to have flown with the HCU are listed in Appendix 4.

Handley-Page Halifax - NAM archives

Handley-Page produced the HP.56 design to meet Air Ministry Specification P.13/36 for a twin-engine medium bomber, soon after Handley-Page was told to redesign the HP.56 for four engines rather than two. This redesign, powered by four 1,280hp (950kW) Rolls-Royce Merlin X engines, increased the span from 88 feet (27m) to 99 feet (30m) and increased the weight by 13,000lbs (5,900kg) with a top speed of 265mph. These modifications resulted in the HP.57, which was named the Halifax; such was the promise of the new model that the RAF had placed their first order for 100 Mk.I Halifaxes 'off the drawing board' before the first prototype even flew.

The prototype first flew on the 25th October 1939 and the first production Halifax on the 11th October 1940, it was the second four engined bomber to enter service. The first Squadron, No.35, received its first Halifax, at RAF Leeming in November 1940.

The first operational flight came on the night of 11/12th March 1941 when No.35 Squadron attacked Le Havre and was the first RAF four engined bomber to drop bombs on Germany in an raid on Hamburg on the night of the 12/13th March 1941. Along with the Lancaster, the Halifax shared the major burden of the night offensive over Germany. At the peak of its strength in 1944 Bomber Command had 26 Halifax Squadrons in operation. With a total Halifax production of 6,178 the last aircraft was delivered in April 1945.

The Halifax Mk.I series I, II and III were closely followed by the Halifax MK.II series I and series I (Special) and series IA. Although the MK.I had no mid-upper turret, the Mk.II had a Boulton Paul two gun turret fitted, and the Merlin X engines were replaced by 1,390hp Merlin XX engines. The next variant the Mk.III was fitted with the Bristol Hercules engine as opposed to the Merlin.

Coastal Command, the Airborne Forces (the Hamilcar glider could only be towed by the Halifax) and the Special Duties (SOE) Squadrons (for the parachuting of agents, and the dropping of weapons to resistance fighters), as well as Bomber Command, all used the Halifax.

The MK.VI and MK.VII, produced at the end of the war, were the last of the bomber versions off the assembly lines. The first Halifax MK.VI first flew on October 10th 1944. The MK.VI had 1800hp Hercules 100 engines fitted along with extra fuel capacity for longer range with a pressurized fuel system and special carburettors fitted, ready for operations against the Japanese. Although similar to the MK.VI, the Halifax MK.VII had Hercules XVI engines fitted; these aircraft served mainly with the Canadian Squadrons and also with the 2 Fighting French Squadrons stationed at Elvington.

The Halifax operated in the Middle East, with No.462 Squadron; stationed in Palestine it was the only British four engined bomber in the Middle East to bomb the Africa Korps from Egypt.

SPECIFICATIONS (Mk.II):

Crew:	7 (pilot, flight engineer, navigator, bomb aimer/nose gunner, wireless operator, mid-upper gunner and rear gunner)		
Length:	71ft 7in (21.82m)	Wingspan:	104ft 2in (31.75m)
Max takeoff weight:	54,400lb (24,675kg)		
Engine:	4 x 1,615hp (1,205kW) Bristol Hercules XVI radials		
Maximum speed:	282 mph (454kmh) at 13,500ft (4,115m)		
Range:	1,860 miles (3,000km)		
Service ceiling:	24,000ft (7,315m)		
Armament:	8 x 0.303in (7.7mm) Browning machine guns in nose tail and dorsal turrets		
Bomb load:	13,000lb (5,897kg)		

VARIANTS:	
H.P.57	The first and second prototypes (Halifax Mk.I); Halifax B.I Series I, the first production version; series II stressed for operating at a higher gross weight; series III re-engined with Merlin XX engines, new upper turret in place of beam guns, with revised undercarriage and additional centre-section fuel tanks.
H.P.58	Halifax Mk II, projected variant with revised armament including 20 mm cannon and no tail turret. Due to problems with the new armament, the project was cancelled and the Mk II designation given to H.P.59.
H.P.59	Halifax Mk II, new variant with increased takeoff weight, fuel and weapons carriage; series I, first series of the bomber variant; series I (Special) SOE, version for the Special Operations Executive with nose armament and dorsal turret removed, the nose faired over, as well as changes to the fuel vent pipes and exhaust shrouds; series I (Special), similar to SOE aircraft used in bombing role; series IA, modified with new glazed nose section, new radiators and new "D" fin and rudder; series I Freighter, employed in the transport role in Great Britain (unmodified SOE aircraft) and in the Middle East; GR.II, Coastal Command variant; GR.II series I, aircraft converted from Series I or Special to GR.II standard, by the fitting of ASV Mk.3 radar in an H2S type fairing; GR.II series IA, definitive Coastal Command variant of the GR.II.
H.P.61	Halifax B.III, main production variant with Bristol Hercules engines with transparent nose dome with single machine gun, Boulton Paul dorsal turret with four guns and tail turret with four guns; A.III glider tug and paratroops transport aircraft; C.III transport aircraft.
H.P.63	Halifax B.V, long-range heavy-bomber, powered by four Rolls-Royce Merlin XX engines with square empennage and wing tips, armament as B.III; series I (Special); A.V glider tugs and paratroops transport aircraft; GR.V, Coastal Command variant, maritime reconnaissance aircraft; B.VI, powered by 1,615hp (1,204kW) Bristol Hercules XVI radial engines with H2S radar, no dorsal turret; C.VI military transport aircraft; GR.VI Coastal Command variant, maritime reconnaissance aircraft; B.VII, powered by 1,615hp (1,204kW) Bristol Hercules XVI radial engines with round wing tips and armament as B.III; A.VII paratroops transport and glider tug aircraft; C.VII military transport aircraft.
H.P.70	C.VIII cargo and passenger transport aircraft.
H.P.71	A.IX paratroops transport and glider tug aircraft.
H.P.70	Halton I, Interim civil transport version; post war, a number of Halifax bombers were converted into civilian transport aircraft.

Other aircraft

No.1485 (Target Towing) Flight was formed in October 1941 at Coningsby to provide gunnery training for No.5 Group units. The flight was re-numbered and re-named No.1690 Bomber Defence Training Flight at Syerston in February 1944 equipped with Spitfire, Hurricane and Martinet aircraft with detachments at most No.5 Group stations.

Three Martinet Target Tugs (based on the Miles Master) were detached to Winthorpe in March 1944 under the command of F/Lt. Baker and Spitfires and Hurricanes arrived at Winthorpe at the end of November 1944 to carry out Fighter Affiliation training.

Miles Martinet Target Tug – NAM archives

Fighter Affiliation was to train Bomber Command's pilots and air-gunners in dealing with enemy fighter attacks, familiarising them with fighter attack tactics, and providing them with flying air-gunnery opportunities using towed targets.

In March 1945 No.1661 HCU was given the role of automatic gun laying training which involved fighter affiliation , the unit saw the addition of a Spitfire Vb (W3848) and Hurricane IIc (LF423) in addition to those already with No.1690 BDTF.

Spitfire Vb W3848 'Travancore II' was built at Eastleigh and first flew on 11 September 1941; it went first to No.8 MU then to No.111 Squadron (JU-H) on 22 September 1941, Flying Accident Cat. AC (repair is beyond the unit capacity, but can be repaired on site by another unit or contractor) 29 May 1942 then No.41 Squadron (EB-) 22 August 1942, No.122 Squadron (MT-) 14 March 1943, No.222 Squadron (ZD-P) 19 May 1943, No.67 Group USAAF* 2 November 1943, Heston Aircraft Ltd** 16 June 1944, No.1661 HCU 29 November 1944 and finally it was SOC 27 December 1945.

It was one of more than 1,500 Spitfires to be 'named'; these presentation aircraft bore the name of the individual, organisation, town/city or country that donated the funds to build an aircraft. The Maharajah of Travancore (now part of modern day Kerala, India) gave £11,250 for two Spitfires (named Travancore I and II) as reported in the Straits Times of Singapore, 8th March 1941 edition, the true cost of a Spitfire was around £12,000.

The Hurricane Mk IIA Series 1 with a new and slightly longer propeller spinner and four 20mm (.79in) Hispano Mk II cannons, two per side, replacing the machine-gun armament entered service in 1940. The IIA Series 2 became the IIC in June 1941, using a slightly modified wing. The new wings also included a hard point for a 500lb (230kg) or 250lb (110kg) bomb, and later in 1941, fuel tanks. By then performance was inferior to the latest German fighters, and the Hurricane changed to the ground-attack role. 1942 saw the cannon-armed Mk IIc perform further afield in the night intruder role over occupied Europe. LF423 was from the tenth production batch of 1,357 aircraft built in 1943/44 with deliveries starting 29 September 1943 and ending 24 May 1944.

* No.67 Group USAAF operated in the photo-reconnaissance role.

** Heston Aircraft played a major role in modifying Supermarine Spitfires for the photographic reconnaissance task. The company equipped the Spitfires with vertical and oblique cameras, additional fuel tanks, and modified cockpit canopies. Many marks of Spitfire were also repaired at Heston throughout the war.

A de Havilland Mosquito NF.XIII Night Fighter was also on strength. MM617 was assembled at the de Havilland (Second Aircraft Group (SAG)) Leavesden factory in April 1944 and equipped with Merlin 25's and delivered to No.13MU on 29 April 1944, No.27MU 15 May 1944, No.10MU and RAF Hunsdon by September 1944 then to No.264 Squadron 7 September 1944 at B6/Coulombs, France.

To No.604 Squadron 2 November 1944 and to No.1661 HCU and coded KB-A, returning to No.264 Squadron prior to May 1945 but damaged 6 May 1945 after being hit by a .303" bullet fired by an unknown person whilst F/Lt. Bentley was landing at Rheine, Germany; repaired on site 31 May to 25 June 1945, to No.49MU and No.19MU. Converted to instructional use as 6028M for the CTTB (Central Trade Testing Board) RAF Chigwell 31 July 1946.

de Havilland Mosquito NF.XIII – NAM archives

The first production night fighter Mosquito's were designated NF.II. A total of 466 were built with the first entering service with No.157 Squadron in January 1942, replacing the Douglas Havoc. These aircraft were similar to the F Mk II, but were fitted with the AI Mk.IV metric wavelength radar. The herring-bone transmitting antenna was mounted on the nose and the dipole receiving antennae were carried under the outer wings. Ninety-seven NF.IIs were upgraded with AI Mk.VIII centimetric radar and these were designated NF.XII.

The NF.XIII was based on the Mosquito FB.VI, and shared that aircrafts ability to carry under wing fuel tanks; the production equivalent of the Mk.XII conversions, 270 were built. The centimetric radar sets were mounted in a solid 'thimble' radome, requiring the machine guns be dispensed with. A longer range than the Mk.XII allowed it to operate as an intruder and long range escort as well as acting as a defensive night fighter. Entering service in the autumn of 1943 it remained in service into 1945.

An Airspeed Oxford (V3574 GP-Y) was also used by the HCU.

Lancaster R5668 1661 HCU February 1944 – NAM archives

CHAPTER SEVEN

From the ORB's - 1943

N.B.: Text in italics is additional / explanatory notes and information.

1st January

No.1661 HCU reformed at RAF Winthorpe and in the anticipation of a new course arriving a training syllabus was adopted that saw each course have alternate days of flying and classroom instruction; each course was designed to last six weeks with the flying to be carried out half on Manchesters and half on Lancasters. No flying was carried out but reorganisation activities took place following the move from Waddington and Scampton.

No.1661 HCU ORB – NAM archives

2nd January

No flying was carried out but reorganisation activities took place following the move from Waddington and Scampton.

3rd January

A Flight (Manchester) - no flying; B Flight 1hr 35min due to poor serviceability; C Flight 2hr 40min flying.

4th January

A Flight 3hr 30min; B Flight 4hr 50min; C Flight 2hr 25min flying.

The ORB for 1661 HCU continues in this manner so only other details will be used.

5th to 8th January

No flying due to bad weather and Lancasters being prepared for Operations.

11th January

Owing to the soft nature of the ground off the perimeter track and runways considerable bogging [down of aircraft] took place. Practising night circuits Lancaster W4183 yawed to starboard and the wing tip dug into the ground. Following an enquiry the pilot was withdrawn from heavy bomber training.

15th January

All Lancasters grounded in preparation for Operations.

16th / 17th January

B and C Flights carried out 5 NFTs on Lancasters and landed at Swinderby prior to going on Operations. All Night Flying Tests totalled 2hr 35min – Training was cancelled as the aircraft on Operations were manned by Instructors.

Operation – Target Berlin

Lancaster 'O' W4271 crew – F/Lt. Gunter (pilot) Sgt. Stephenson, F/O Clitheroe, F/Sgt. Upton, F/Sgt. Aitken, Sgt. Black and F/O Hopps, took off at 1713 half an hour late and on reaching the Dutch Coast the pilot decided he could not reach his objective on the time laid down by No.5 Group. Returned to base landing at 2215.

Lancaster 'N' W4132 crew - F/O Cockbain (pilot), F/O Windsor, F/O Anderson, Sgt. Barker, P/O Davis, Sgt. Roberts and P/O Stuffin, was not ready in time and failed to take off.

Lancaster 'D' R5904 crew – F/Lt. Oakley(pilot), Sgt. Cowan and F/Sgts. Robertson, Murtough, Norman, Cook and Bickley, failed to take off due to the un-serviceability of the mid upper turret and the bombing up not completed for the final take off time.

Lancaster 'U' W4258 crew – P/O Fletcher (pilot), Sgt. Good, P/O Maclean, Sgt. Johnson, P/O Andrews, Sgt. Coaker and F/Sgt. Bale; airborne at 1707. Photoflash hung up [photographs of the target could not be taken]. Nothing of particular interest on trip. Flak at the target was intense as expected. Used Target Flare (Red Cascade) as [the] aiming point. Bomb aimer reported built-up area below and for a considerable distance after dropping the bombs. Navigation OK [to target and return to base] the aircraft landing at 0024.

Lancaster 'S' R5842 crew – P/O Hartley (pilot), Sgt. Airey, F/Sgt. Linklater, Sgt. Carrod, P/O Alp, Sgt. Bagley and Sgt. Loverock, failed to get airborne owing to loss of one engine on take off.

The first Bomber Command attack on Berlin since November 1941 and the first use of Target Indicator marker bombs; 201 aircraft - 190 Lancasters and 11 Halifaxes - from the Pathfinders and Nos.1, 4 and 5 Groups were dispatched. It marked the first use of an all 4 engined bombing force, Stirlings were withdrawn from the original plan so that only the higher flying Lancasters and Halifaxes participated. Most of the force was provided by No 5 Group.

The raid was a disappointment. Berlin was well beyond the range of Gee and Oboe and H2S radar was not yet ready. Thick cloud which was encountered on the way to the target hindered navigation and Berlin was found to be covered by haze. Bombing was scattered, mostly in the southern areas, with the greatest concentration in the Tempelhof district.

The RAF casualties were light with only 1 Lancaster, from No 5 Group lost. The Bomber Command report mentions the lightness of the Berlin flak defences (about half of the personnel of the Berlin flak units were away from the city, taking part in a course) and assumed that the greater altitude of the bomber force surprised the German gunners.

17th/18th January

Operation – Target Berlin

Lancaster 'S' R5842 crew – P/O Hartley (pilot), Sgt. Airey, F/Sgt. Linklater, Sgt. Carrod, P/O Alp, Sgt. Bagley and Sgt. Loverock; airborne at 1642. Successful. Landed Woodall Spa being diverted from base at 0048. Before reaching the east coast of Denmark the aircraft was three times approached to within 400-600 yards by twin engined fighter but turning and corkscrewing evasive action was taken in very this hazy cloud and contact was broken. Target approached on track at 19,000 - 20,000 feet. Searchlight concentration seen on approach but after a 15 minute search of area for flares and landmarks a large built up area was bombed at 2047 heading N 18,500 feet. Heavy accurate flak over target - small holes in aircraft.

Lancaster 'U' W4258 crew – P/O Fletcher (pilot), Sgt. Good, P/O Maclean, Sgt. Johnson, P/O Andrews, Sgt. Coaker and F/Sgt. Bale; airborne at 1636. Successful. Flak at target considerable with heavy flak accurate but negligible damage sustained. Fires at target were not under way as left, appeared to be among first to bomb. No incidents occurred on return journey. Landed at 0137.

Lancaster 'O' W4271 crew – F/Lt. Gunter (pilot) Sgt. Stephenson, F/O Clitheroe, F/Sgt. Upton, F/Sgt. Aitken, Sgt. Black and F/O Hopps; airborne at 1649. Successful. Landed at Harwell after being diverted from base at 0206. Reached 23,000 feet waited around target for ½ hour for P. F. F. and eventually bombed from 20,000 feet... A built up area believed to be SW corner of city. We observed one Ju.88 before reaching target but were not attacked.

Lancaster 'N' W4132 crew – F/O Cockbain (pilot), F/O Windsor, F/O Anderson, Sgt. Barker, P/O Davis, Sgt. Roberts and P/O Stuffin; airborne at 1655. Failed to reach minimum bombing height of 18,000 ft. and returned before reaching target. Landed Coltishall after being diverted from base at 0009.

Lancaster 'D' R5904 crew – F/Lt. Oakley(pilot), Sgt. Cowan and F/Sgts. Robertson, Murtough, Norman, Cook and Bickley; airborne at 1645. Successful. Landed Lakenheath after being diverted from base at 0001. Arrived target area during allotted bombing time on ETA spending 25 mins. in area trying to identify target. Made bombing run over target, dropping bombs 10 mins. after bombing time, the incendiaries lighting up the streets and starting a fire. Several other sticks were dropped after this. Searchlights across target, no flak was fired.

170 Lancasters and 17 Halifaxes repeated the raid. The weather was better but the Pathfinders were again unable to mark the centre of the city and again the bombing fell mainly in the southern areas. The Bomber Command report stated that the Daimler-Benz factory was hit, either during this night or during the raid the previous night but this is not confirmed by the German report; however a BMW aero-engine factory at Spandau was hit by incendiaries and slightly damaged. There was no damage of note in any part of Berlin.

The routes taken by the bombers to and from Berlin were the same as those followed on the previous night and German night fighters were able to find the bomber stream; 19 Lancasters and 3 Halifaxes were lost, 11.8% of the force. The experiments with the Lancaster/Halifax force using target indicators against Berlin, now ceased until H2S became available.

All operations on the 16th and 17th January 1943 were carried out from RAF Station Swinderby.

28th January

Lancaster R5540 crashed and caught fire at Barkston Heath, Lincolnshire.

On night circuit and landings training the aircraft 'ballooned' into the air, stalled and crashed then bursting into flames.

1st February

Sgt. B. F. Wilmot RAAF crashed immediately after an attempted overshoot, aircraft coming to rest just off the Newark-Sleaford Rd., all other members of the crew escaped with slight injuries with the exception of the Rear Gunner Sgt. H. H. Lloyd RAAF who was killed – Sgt. W. J. Fraser the mid upper Gunner was taken to Rauceby for Specialist treatment.

Lancaster L7530 had been airborne for about 20 minutes. It is believed the pilot became dazzled by floodlights. The recovery of this aircraft is told in the chapter on No.58MU.

3rd February

Sgt. F. C. Allcroft landed at Waddington on one engine and was given a green endorsement in his logbook.

Red endorsements were made in a log book if an accident was found to be caused by a pilot, for example, neglecting to keep an eye on his fuel, running out and having to force land. A Green endorsement (one of the RAF's highest accolades) would be made if a pilot dealt with a situation well, for example an engine failure caused by technical failure and the pilot then making a forced landing in difficult terrain, saving the aircraft from serious damage and himself.

19th February

P/O G. Hartley while giving dual instruction in Lancaster R5850 to Sgt. B. F. Wilmot crashed while attempting to land.

The aircraft failed to stop and overshot the runway, crashed through telephone wires and hedges after an engine lost power, hit a telegraph pole and then caught fire and burnt out, F/Sgt. M. S. Kahn RCAF the Rear Gunner was killed.

21st February

Sgt. E. A, Robbins while on a X country landed on the sea off the Isle of Wight – leading edge of the port wing blown off by explosion. All the crew rescued.

At 19,000ft an engine caught fire followed by an explosion which blew off the wing leading edge between the fuselage and the inner starboard engine followed by the loss of the engines rear cowling. The pilot ditched Lancaster R5892 5 miles off St. Albans Head Dorset.

12th March

Lancaster I R5556 of No.1661HCU took off from RAF Swinderby following a major overhaul. Ten minutes into the test flight flames were seen coming from the port outer engine enveloping the wing which broke away. The aircraft crashed at Cromwell, Nottinghamshire near to the River Trent killing all 9 personnel on board; they were F/lt. J. Cowan DFC, F/Sgt. A. Hannay, Sgts. A. Burgess, D. Lovelady, E. Hall, S. Johnson and A. Clark, LAC K. Robson and AC1 L. Rodgers.

Manchester R5838 flown by WO E. Knight crash landed at Wickenby following a planned port engine shutdown, on restart the propeller jammed in fine pitch.

15th March

Air Commodore E. I. Bussell who had been the Officer Commanding, RAF Syerston arrived to become the AOC, Swinderby Training Base and G/Capt. E. S. Butler OBE arrived from Bomber Command Headquarters to command RAF Winthorpe and S/Ldr. W. I. Deas DFC became the Chief Flying instructor.

24th March

Manchester L7453 took off from Swinderby and the port engine burst into flames. The pilot S/Ldr. Oakley flew the circuit and made a wheels-up landing. Cat B damaged the aircraft was removed and scrapped on the 1st May.

28th March

War Establishment WAR/BC/313 came into force and Wing Commander K. H. P. Beauchamp DSO DFC assumed command of this unit. Group Captain E. S. Butler was attached to RAF Sub-Station Winthorpe to command. The unit was re-organised into a three flight basis, the fourth Flight Commander, Squadron Leader W. I. Deas DFC, taking over the duties of Chief Flying Instructor.

The No.5 Group ORB for March 1943 has a list of the total output of All HCU's and for No.1661 shows 27 crews completing training with an average of 34 hours day and 11 hours night training.

9th April

Lancaster ED823 crashed at Halam, Nottinghamshire, all the crew being killed; F/O. E. Lambert and F/Sgts. L. W. Lean RAAF and R. D. Lewis and Sgts. W. S. Graham, H. Oxspring, W. G. Stephenson and F. Dunkin RAAF.

The aircraft crashed off School Lane, Halam; the Air Investigation Branch found it impossible to ascertain the reason for the crash owing to lack of evidence.

6th May

Lancaster W4775 of No.1661 HCU crashed at Swinderby after its undercarriage collapsed.

19th May

Manchester L7297 crashed at Winthorpe after an engine caught fire in flight and an emergency landing made at Winthorpe where its undercarriage collapsed

23rd May

A contingent of 48 airmen and 21 airwomen represented this station in the 'Wings for Victory' Parade in Newark. An open air Service was conducted by the Rector of Newark, Canon Parkinson, in the Square and Councillor Parlby, the Mayor of Newark took the salute at a 'March Past'.

24th May

S/Ldr./A/W/C. E. H. P. Beauchamp posted to No.9 (War) Staff College

Wing Commander Beauchamp later served with No.23 Squadron and then commanded No.157 Squadron flying intruder (night fighter) Mosquitoes until August 1945. He joined B.O.A.C. in 1946 flying amongst others, the Handley Page Hermes, the de Havilland Comet 1 and 4, Lockheed Constellation and the Vickers VC.10.

During May Rugby, Cricket and Football matches took place between Station teams and The Army OCTU, RAF Swinderby and the Royal Engineers.

15th June

No.4300 AA Flight RAF Regiment moved to RAF Station Zeals (Wiltshire). No.2 Flight of No.2776 Squadron RAF Regiment moved in from RAF Station Davidstow Moor (Cornwall).

During June Cricket matches were played between the Station and RAF Swinderby, No.58MU, RAF Syerston, Ransome and Marles and a WAAF match between the Station and Swinderby WAAF.

8th July

No.4808 Airfield Construction Flight arrived to carry out major runway repair work.

An Aircrew Dinghy Drill exhibition was held at Newark Baths for the public's benefit.

9th July

Lancaster R5889 GP-M had a starboard tyre burst during takeoff for night circuits and landings the pilot Sgt. Barnet circled for the next 2 hours and after jettisoning fuel made a good landing and the aircraft caught fire.

18th July

Lancaster W4947 GP-Z failed to return from a training flight and presumed to have crashed in the Irish Sea.

Sports during July saw Cricket, Football, Water Polo and WAAF Baseball matches.

1st August

G/Capt. E. S. Butler posted to Dunholme Lodge and G/Capt. N. C. Pleasence posted in from HQ No.93 Group to command RAF Winthorpe

5th August

Ralph Readers 'Gang Show' provided entertainment.

S/ Ldr. Ralph Reader raised twenty-four RAF Gang Show units and two female WAAF units with a total establishment of nearly four hundred serving personnel which toured nearly every theatre of war, from Iceland to Burma. By 1944, Gang Show units were estimated to have travelled 100,000 miles and entertained 3,500,000 servicemen. Some who served in the RAF Gang Shows would later become well known entertainers, such as Peter Sellers, Tony Hancock, Dick Emery and Cardew Robinson (who later in his career invented 'Cardew the Cad' complete with his Newark Magnus school cap as part of his outfit). For his services to the RAF, Reader was awarded an MBE (Military Division) in 1943.

24th August

Lancasters W4190 GP-A crashed on takeoff when the port outer engine cut out and the aircraft swung. W4381 GP-B was also lost in a takeoff crash.

W4190 was found to have a faulty carburettor. W4381 had a tyre burst in its bay damaging the hydraulics and the crew used the emergency system to lower the undercarriage, on landing the undercarriage collapsed and the aircraft swung off the runway.

28th August

Rear Gunner 2206826 Sgt. Ronald Roberts completed his training at No.1661 HCU and with the rest of his crew was posted to No.57 Squadron.

He had trained at No.2 Air Gunners School, Dalcross near Inverness and No.14 OTU at Cottesmore and Saltby flying Wellingtons.

The crew, P/O. A. R. Wangler and Sgts. S. E. Cornford, L Barker, W. T. H. Curry, F. B. Raven, B. M. Quinn and R. Roberts were shot down and all became POWs when Lancaster JA910 was shot down by a night fighter at 2137 some 2½ miles (4km) north of Raalte in Holland on an operation to Bochum on the 29th September 1943.

Date	Hour	Aircraft Type and No.	Pilot	Duty	Remarks (including results of bombing, gunnery, exercises, etc.)	Day	Night
					Time carried forward :—	54.40	36.30
1·8·43	12·00	LANCASTER T	SGT. WANGLER	R. GUNNER	EX 8	·55	
1·8·43	13·50	LANCASTER T	SEGT WANGLER	" "	EX 9 A	2·10	
4·8·43	11·00	LANCASTER A	SEGT WANGLER	" "	EX 11	·50	
4·8·43	16·55	LANCASTER A	SEGT WANGLER	" "	EX 10 AIR FIRING 500 RDS	1·10	
6·8·43	14·35	LANCASTER F	SEGT WANGLER	" "	EX 12	4·20	
7·8·43	02·30	LANCASTER S	SEGT WANGLER	" "	EX 13 - 14		2·00
7·8·43	04·30	LANCASTER S	SEGT WANGLER	" "	EX 15		1·10
12·8·43	14·11	LANCASTER T	SEGT WANGLER	" "	EX 18 FIGHTER AFFIL	1·10	
12·8·43	15·20	LANCASTER T	SEGT WANGLER	" "	EX 18 FIGHTER AFFIL	1·00	
13·8·43	02·30	LANCASTER V	SEGT WANGLER	" "	EX 16 c		2·25
14·8·43	20·30	LANCASTER H	SEGT WANGLER	" "	EX 16 A		1·30
14·8·43	23·15	LANCASTER V	SEGT WANGLER	" "	EX 20 A		2·55
14·8·43	01·00	LANCASTER Q. R.	SEGT WANGLER	" "	EX 19		3·00
22·8·43	20·50	LANCASTER T	SGT. WANGLER	" "	EX 21		6·30
25·8·43	15·30	LANCASTER O	F/LT. GREEN	" "	CROSS WIND TAKE OFF & LANDINGS	1·00	
26·8·43	20·25	LANCASTER R	SEGT WANGLER	" "	EX 21		5·15
28·8·43	21·15	LANCASTER R	SEGT WANGLER	" "	EX 21		5·10
		TOTAL FLYING TIMES FOR COURSE 42 HRS - 30 MINS			TOTAL. SIGNED. [signature] O.C. A'Flt.	12·35	24·55
					TOTAL TIME	70·15	66·25

Sgt. Roberts Log book entry – courtesy of his son Alan Roberts.

The copy of his log book page (above) showing his training at Winthorpe is courtesy of his son Alan Roberts.

3rd September

The first record of the Halifax in the ORB – flying time of 2hrs. 25 minutes

4th September

Lancaster 'N' crashed north of Exeter on Exercise 21 No survivors

On night flying exercises while the local defences practised. Caught in the beams of 5 or 6 searchlights it dived and twisted keeping its specified height of between 12,000 and 16,000 feet then it suddenly plunged, it was followed by the lights for several thousand feet but soon lost, none of the crew (4 Australian and 4 British) had time to bale out although an escape hatch was found a mile from the wreckage. The aircraft R5492 had logged in excess of 600 flying hours.

5th September

During a night cross country training flight Lancaster W4929 crashed on Rhydwenfach, S. Wales with the loss of all crew

Lancaster GP-R took off from RAF Winthorpe on a night exercise off the Scottish coast. On the return journey the aircraft ran into a heavy storm over the Brecon Beacons and crashed at 2320 at Fan Foel near Llanddensart. The crew were P/O Norman Duxbury

(Pilot), P/O Victor Folkersen RCAF (Navigator), Sgts. Leslie Holding (F/Eng.), Frank Pratt (W/Op), Roy Wilson (Bomb Aimer), John Curran (Air Gunner) and Ernest Buckby RAAF (Air Gunner) and P/O Thomas 'Boyk' Johnson (Bomb Aimer Instructor).

8th September

As a result of considerable repair work being necessary on No.1 runway it was decided that the conversion training be carried out at RAF Station Balderton and approximately 150 maintenance personnel were detached together with all serviceable aircraft.

Lancaster R5547 crashed on landing at Balderton when the brakes proved ineffective and an undercarriage leg collapsed.

Move of No.2776 Squadron RAF Regiment (Winthorpe Detachment) to RAF Filey on AA Course. A detachment of No.2772 Squadron RAF Regiment moved as replacement.

15th September

A Station Commanders Parade was held in No.1 Hangar at 0815 hours in commemoration of the Battle of Britain.

Prayers were offered up by the Rev. J. C. Whitworth, C. of E. Officiating Chaplain.

25nd September

Manchester L7467 crashed at Winthorpe

26th September

A detachment of RAF and WAAF personnel from this Station attended a combined RAF and Civil Defence Parade Service at 1100 hours in the Parish Church, Newark followed by a march past at which the salute was taken by Air Commodore E. I. Bussell, Officer Commanding No.51 Base Headquarters.

29th September

No.2772 Squadron RAF Regiment (Winthorpe Detachment) moved to Leffenham and were replaced by No.2776 Squadron RAF Regiment (Winthorpe Detachment) on return from AA Course RAF Station Locking.

Repair work to No.1 Runway continues.

3rd October

Visit of RAF Orchestra conducted by W/C. O'Donnell.

5th October

The last recorded Manchester flight in the ORB.

10th October

Re-surfacing of No.1 runway completed.

11th October

Conversion training resumed and all maintenance personnel attached to RAF Station Balderton returned together with all serviceable aircraft and equipment.

15th October

Manchester L7401 wrecked

2nd November

Lancaster W4249 was taking off when the Instructor, for reasons unknown, throttled back and as the aircraft overshot selected undercarriage up.

Following the incident the Instructor was taken to hospital with an unknown illness.

6th November

Lancaster W4258 on landing bounced and the port wing dropped, the port undercarriage was torn off and the aircraft slewed

13th November

Lancaster LM308 made a fast approach and not in line with the runway ran across the grass and struck a ditch causing the undercarriage to collapse

17th November

The clerk of works (AMWD) handed over the keys to the new Station Sick Quarters

18th November

Variety show 'Spitfires' Concert Party.

20th November

RAF Station Winthorpe has again had to accept the responsibility for the Medical service for No.58 and No.203 Maintenance Units, Newark, who are without a Medical Officer.

21st November

Variety show Nottingham Hospital Entertainers.

30th November

In the last two days of the month it became necessary through an outbreak of influenza among WAAF personnel to open the WAAF annexe (of SSQ) and there were a total of eight WAAF admitted during those two days.

Like other stations in the Group, this station has also suffered a minor epidemic of mild influenza and it has been possible to hospitalize cases requiring in-patient treatment at Newark EMS Hospital, SSQ Swinderby being unable to admit for the last two weeks in the month.

Sports during November included Football, Rugby and Netball including a WAAFs v Airmen challenge Netball match.

7th December

G/Capt. N. C. Pleasence posted to RAF Bardney replaced by G/Capt. E. L. S. Ward posted in from HQ No.5 Group as Officer Commanding RAF Winthorpe

10th December

The first flying for a Stirling recorded in the ORB.

11th December

The last Halifax flight recorded in the ORB

14th December

Station inspected by Air Commodore Bussell (Commanding No.51 Base) on behalf of AOC No.5 Group. Progress of Inspection carried out according to plan with the exception of the cancellation of parade owing to inclement weather.

16th December

At approximately 2015 hours a Lancaster crashed one mile north of South Muskham, Notts. P/O W. H. Eager DFC RCAF Pilot Instructor, P/O K. C. Hampson, F/Sgt. R. W. Baldwin RCAF and Sgts. L. B. Lawrence, W. S, Austin and R. H. Woolcock were all killed outright, the cause of death being multiple injuries and burns. Sgts. P. Dillon and East were rescued and transferred to Newark General Hospital. Sgt. Dillon was suffering from severe shock and burns of face and head and injury to chest, and died at 6 am on 17.12. 43. Sgt. East was suffering from a lunar fracture of cranial vault and lacerations of scalp.

Lancaster LM307 GP-T crashed one mile N of South Muskham, Nottinghamshire, the aircraft flew into the ground in a turn and caught fire. The chief cause was flying low and allowing attention to be distracted from instruments to look for aerodrome lights which were unserviceable; the runway flare path had been laid and the pilot found and then lost the airfield again.

William Hedley Eager was born in June 1920 in Moose Jaw, Saskatchewan, Canada the son of Harry Herbert and Johanna Eager, his father died when William was just 7 years old.

William joined the RCAF and trained at No.7 ITS, No.19 EFTS and No.10 SFTS in Canada in 1942; No.11 (Pilots) AFU November 1942 and No.19 OTU January 1943.

While training with No.1654 HCU as a Sergeant pilot, he was involved in a flying incident on 15 April 1943, taking off at 16:45 from RAF Wigsley in Avro Manchester L7294, an engine caught fire and as he headed for base the aircraft stalled and crashed, all the crew suffered some injury but there were no fatalities.

Promoted to Pilot Officer and serving with No.61 Squadron flying from RAF Syerston he was awarded the DFC, published in the London Gazette on 16 November 1943; the citation said he '... completed many successful operations against the enemy in which [he] displayed high skill, fortitude and devotion to duty'.

After completing his tour he was posted to No.1661 HCU as an instructor and promoted to Flying Officer.

William married Ada Cox, who was serving in the WAAF stationed at RAF Waddington with No.44 Squadron, shortly before he died and twin daughters were born in 1944.His widow was presented with his DFC by the King at Buckingham Palace.

The information on William Eager is courtesy of his daughter Mrs. Jane Cooper.

19th December

Lancaster ED801 was being de-bombed of its practice bombes by armourers when one exploded severely injuring AC2 Wheeler; AC1 Thompson and AC2 Humphrey received minor injuries and were detained in SSQ whilst Wheeler was transferred to RAF Hospital South Rauceby. AC1 Thompson had failed to replace safety pins.

25th December

No flying carried out

ENSA Variety Show and Station Dance

27th December

Station Dance

31st December

Cook's Dance

CHAPTER EIGHT

The story of a Lancaster - DV246 and No.617 Squadron

Many of the aircraft that served at any of the training bases during the war had had a previous life on at least one operational Squadron. Lancaster III DV246 is one such aircraft and it served with probably the most well known Squadron of them all - No.617 (Dambusters). Following the Dams raid No.617 Squadron was retained as a specialist bombing unit in No.5 Group.

Lancasters W4929 and ED437 also served with No.617 Squadron before No.1661 HCU.

W4929 also served with No.619 Squadron prior to No.1661 HCU and had accumulated 471 flying hours when it crashed at 2320 during a night cross-country exercise from Winthorpe on 5 September 1943 near Fan Foel in the Brecon Beacons with all eight crew killed. There is a memorial near the crash site.

ED437 served with No.50 Squadron prior to No.617 and No.1661 HCU, it was later with No.622 Squadron and Nos.3 and 5 LFS and ended the war as instructional airframe 5060M.

DV246 was one of a batch of 200 ordered from Metropolitan-Vickers in 1941 and delivered between May and November 1943.

From the ORB which gives details of each aircraft taking part in a mission we can give a fair representation of an aircrafts career on a Bomber Command Squadron before its arrival with an HCU, the following details DV246's 28 missions with No.617 Squadron.

11th November 1943 flown by S/Ldr. H. B. 'Micky' Martin DSO DFC with P/O I. Whittaker, F/O J. K. Stott, F/O L.W. Curtiss, F/O B.T. Foxlee, F/LT. R. C. Hay and P/O T.D. Simpson to attack the Antheor Viaduct.

This viaduct on the vital coastal rail link between Italy and the south of France was 540 feet long, 185 feet high and contained 9 arches each with a 29 foot span, this double tracked viaduct crossed the mouth of a river a few miles east from St Raphael in Southern France. 9 Lancasters (there should have been 10 but one had engine failure and had to abort) all carrying 1 x 12,000lb bombs attacked the target, most of the bombs

Antheor Viaduct – Public domain

missed but minor damage was caused. The aircraft came under fire from small ships out a sea during the raid, it was also noted that some of the aircraft attacked the wrong railway line in the adjacent bay. After the raid all the aircraft headed south to Blida and then onto Rabat in North Africa.

Harold Brownlow Morgan Martin was born on 27th February 1918 in Sydney, Australia and educated at Lindfield Public and Randwick Boys' Intermediate High schools. He left Australia in 1937 to see the world.

In 1940 he joined the Royal Air Force Volunteer Reserve in England. Trained initially as a fighter pilot, he was promoted to pilot officer in June 1941 and transferred in October to the RAAFs No.455 Squadron. After carrying out thirteen operations flying Hampden bombers he was posted to No.50 Squadron which operated Lancaster bombers. He completed another twenty-five sorties, finishing his first tour in October 1942; he was awarded the Distinguished Flying Cross the following month.

During this period 'Micky' Martin developed an effective method of penetrating enemy defences at night, flying at low level. When No.617 Squadron was formed in March 1943 Guy Gibson, aware of Martin's low-level flying technique, had him posted to the Squadron. Martin's main task was to train the aircrews in the art of low-level night flying, in preparation for the planned attack on the German dams.

On the 16th May, flying as Gibson's no.3 he was in the first wave of aircraft briefed to breach the Möhne dam. At a height of 60ft (18m) he flew over the dam three times and his aircraft was struck by anti-aircraft fire. He acted with Gibson to distract enemy guns from the other attacking aircraft and, after the dam wall had been successfully breached, flew the Lancaster safely back to base. He was awarded the Distinguished Service Order.

Martin (right) remained with No.617 Squadron, taking part in precision bombing of Italian targets in July and in September on the Dortmund-Ems Canal, Germany. The then Squadron's commanding officer was killed during the raid and Martin took over; five of the eight attacking Lancasters were lost. He was awarded a Bar to his DFC and, as acting Squadron leader, was placed in temporary command of the now heavily depleted Squadron. When Leonard Cheshire assumed command, he and Martin devised an effective low level target marking technique.

Micky Martin – Public domain Collection Database of the Australian War Memorial under the ID Number: UK0235

In March 1944 he was posted to Air Staff Headquarters and he then transferred to No.515 Squadron, flying Mosquitos, in which he undertook intruder operations in support of Bomber Command's main force attacks. When finally removed from operations late in 1944, he had completed eighty-three sorties. In November he was awarded a second Bar to his DFC. Sir Harold Brownlow Morgan "Micky" Martin KCB DSO & bar DFC & 2 bars AFC retired from the RAF in 1974 as an Air Marshal.

Cheshire considered Martin a greater operational pilot than Gibson '... *and indeed the greatest the Air Force has produced'.*

There are no records of the aircraft taking part in the Squadrons operations between November 1943 and March 1944. Operations by the Squadron and aircraft in March and April 1944 were:

2nd March flown by F/O D. J. B. Wilson to attack an aircraft factory at Albert, France

10th March flown by F/O G. S. Stout to attack St Etienne (8 crew – nose gunner included)

16th March flown by F/Lt. J. A. Edward to attack Clermont Ferrand, France

18th March flown by Lt. H. C. Knilans (USA) to attack Bergerac, France

20th March flown by F/Lt. J. E. R. Williams to attack Angouleme, France

29th March flown by F/Lt. A. W. Fearn to attack Lyons, France

22nd April flown by F/Lt. A. W. Fearn to attack Brunswick, Germany

24th April flown by F/Lt. A. W. Fearn to attack Munich, Germany

6th June 1944 flown by F/O W. R. Lee (Aus) and F/Lt. G. E. Fawke (double crew) with F/O T.A. Bennett, W/O G. H. Riley, F/Sgts. T. McKie, H. Hoyland, H. Richards, W. N. Wait, R. Hunnisette and H. G. Clarke and Sgt. W. Mason on 'Operation Taxable'.

It was designed to divert attention from Normandy by fooling the Germans into believing that a large convoy of slow-moving ships was crossing the Channel towards the Pas-de-Calais approaching the coast at Cap d'Antifer. It was completely dependent on absolute precision in flight and navigation for its execution. In tandem with Royal Navy motor gunboats (Operation Moonshine) that were actually crossing the Channel, No.617 Squadron released 'window' or 'chaff' metallic strips that would show up on radar and make it look like a large convoy was en route.

Meticulous timing was necessary, the strips had to be released every 4 seconds, if the timing was off the radar signature would no longer resemble ships at sea and the operation would fail; it was released perfectly for the entire 3½ hours of the operation. The gunboats carried equipment that amplified and repeated the German radar signals, allowing one ship to appear as many. As the last Lancaster turned for home its crew had the satisfaction of seeing the German guns open radar predicted fire on the non-existent convoy. Meanwhile the real invasion force was nearing the coast many miles away.

8th June 1944 flown by F/Lt. R.S.D. Kearns (NZ) with P/O R.J. Henderson, F/O W.J.M.L Barclay (NZ), S/Ldr. D.S. Richardson, P/O M. Ellwood, W/O W.G. Bickley, F/O R.H. Petch and F/Lt T.J. Tate (Passenger) as the crew to attack the Saumur Railway Tunnel in France.

Saumur Tunnel – saumur-jadis.pagesperso-orange.fr

The first use of the 12,000lb Tallboy bombs developed by Barnes Wallis. The railway tunnel was near Saumur, 125 miles south of the Normandy beachhead battle area. The raid was prepared hurriedly because a German Panzer unit was expected to move by train through the tunnel. The target area was illuminated with flares by 4 Lancasters of No.83 Squadron and marked at low level by 3 Mosquitoes. 25 Lancasters of No.617 Squadron then dropped their Tallboys with great accuracy. The huge bombs exploded under the ground to create miniature 'earthquakes'; one actually pierced the roof of the tunnel and brought down a huge quantity of rock and soil which blocked it for a considerable period and the Panzer unit was badly delayed. The aircraft took off at 2245 and landed back at base at 0535.

Other operations by the Squadron and aircraft mainly using Tallboys in June to August 1944 were:

14th June flown by F/Lt. R.S.D. Kearns (NZ) to attack Submarine pens at Le Havre, France

15th June flown by F/Lt. R.S.D. Kearns (NZ) to attack E boats, Boulogne, France

17th July flown by F/O F. H. A. Watts to attack V.2 site at Wizernes, France

31st July flown by F/O T. A. Carey (Aus) to attack railway tunnel at Rilly la Montagne, France

1st August flown by F/O T. A. Carey (Aus) to attack Siracourt, France (abandoned)

4th August flown by F/O F. Levy to attack the bridge at Etaples, France

5th August flown by F/O F. Levy to attack Submarine pens at Brest, France

6th August flown by F/O A. E. Kell (Aus) to attack U-boat pens at Keroman, France

9th August flown by F/O F. H. A. Watts to attack U-boat pens La Pallice (La Rochelle) France

11th August flown by F/O F. H. A. Watts to attack U-boat pens La Pallice.

12th August flown by F/O F. H. A. Watts to attack U-boat pens Brest.

13th August flown by F/O F. H. A. Watts to attack U-boat pens Brest.

14th August flown by F/O F. H. A. Watts to attack the Cruiser 'Gueydon' in Brest harbour

27th August flown by F/O F. H. A. Watts to attack shipping in Brest harbour

The final recorded mission for the aircraft on No.617 Squadron:

11th September 1944 flown by F/Lt. H. J. Pryor with P/O R. J. Telfer, F/O R. L. Pinder (Can) F/O G. Hoyland, P/O A. Hepworth, P/O A. J. Patterson and F/Sgt. A. J. Colyer to attack the Tirpitz, via Russia.

'Operation Paravane' saw 38 Lancasters of Nos.9 and 617 Squadrons set out via Lossiemouth to fly to Yagodnik airfield in Northern Russia which was to be used as a base for an attack on the battleship at anchor in KaFjord in Northern Norway. Several of the bombers, due to bad weather, were forced to crashland and only 27 aircraft took off on September 15th, 20 carrying Tallboys for the attack.

Tirpitz in ka Fjord Fjord – arcticeurope custompublish.com   Lancaster over the Tirpitz Tirpitz – www.bismarck-class.dk/tirpitz

With mountains screening the Lancasters' approach from enemy radar, the Tirpitz was caught by surprise and her smoke-screens were late in starting. One Tallboy smashed through the Tirpitz's forecastle and burst deep in her hull. The shock caused by the explosion of this bomb or possibly other bombs which were near misses, also damaged the ship's engines. All of the Lancasters returned safely to the airfield in Russia and all but one then returned safely to Lossiemouth, F/O Levy's aircraft is believed to have crashed in the mountains in Norway.

The Germans decided that it was not practical to make Tirpitz fully seaworthy again and she was moved to Tromso, further south in Norway, but only for use as a semi-static, heavy artillery battery. The Tirpitz was finally sunk when 30 Lancasters from Nos.9 and 617 Squadrons and a film unit aircraft from No.463 Squadron of the Royal Australian Air Force flew from RAF Lossiemouth on 'Operation Catechism' on November 12th 1944, each one equipped with a Tallboy bomb. At least two bombs hit the Tirpitz, which suffered a violent internal explosion. The battleship capsized and remained bottom upwards.

After Winthorpe the aircraft was used by No.1654 HCU before going No.5 MU and being SOC in August 1947.

CHAPTER NINE

Ralph Fairhead

Several efforts have been made to contact both the publisher (now apparently defunct) and the author's next of kin for permission to use the following without success; with this in mind I hope they are happy for it to be included and my apologies are given in advance if this causes any issues.

The following comes from 'An Airmen's Diary' published in 1982, the recollections and an account of one man's war, or as Ralph himself said '... a simple account of one airman's service in the RAF, before during and for a short while after the second World War'; his story is typical of many of the aircrew from Bomber Command in WW2. The extracts regarding Winthorpe are direct from Ralphs own account.

Ralph joined the RAF in 1938. Following his reporting at the London Recruiting Office in Kingsway and the necessary medical examination he was 'kitted out' at Uxbridge; then to an Initial Training Camp '... *just inland from Sunderland* 'for six weeks. Following this he was posted to RAF Manston for training as an Aero Engine Fitter (the training depot at this time) but soon he was posted again to the new RAF St. Athan to train as a flight mechanic.

On completion of training he was posted to No.43 Squadron based at RAF Tangmere. Following spells at RAF Acklington and RAF Wick the Squadron returned to Tangmere in May 1940 where it was immediately split in two, one half remained as No.43 Squadron whilst the other half, including Ralph, was sent to RAF Hawarden to form No.7 OTU to train fighter pilots; during the Battle of Britain in September 1940 it flew operational flights over North West England claiming three enemy aircraft shot down. It was re-designated No.57 OTU on the 1st November 1940 within No.10 Group using Spitfires and Masters.

Following training at RAF St. Athan as a Flight Engineer the now Sergeant Fairhead was posted in August 1942 to RAF Swinderby in No.5 Group with No.207 Squadron Conversion Flight (later part of No.1660 HCU) before he and his fellow crew were posted to the operational Squadron at RAF Bottesford and later RAF Langar.

He completed 34 'trips' totalling 225 hours on his first tour with No.207 Squadron between September 1942 and May 1943, he was awarded the DFM (Distinguished Flying Medal) which was gazetted in August 1943.

Following a period of 6 weeks leave Ralph was posted to No.1661 HCU at RAF Winthorpe.

He writes:

RAF Station Winthorpe main camp living accommodation was located off a secondary road from the town of Newark and the village of Winthorpe a short distance beyond the camp. It was on a slight rise, with the administration blocks down this incline to the airfield which ran alongside the Newark to Lincoln Road. Not being an operational aerodrome it was not dispersed but conveniently spaced. It was a temporary camp, not planned, just put up, but the better for it. The instructional block, to which I had next to report, was the nearest one to the control tower and airfield. The buildings were of the usual mixture of concrete block and wooden huts with the odd Nissen huts for personal accommodation, all connected up by concrete roads branching off from the main entrance.

Moving people about in the RAF ... as single individuals, was presumably necessary, but it was not easy to arrive at a new station alone having absolutely no idea where anything or anybody was – except that is the Guard House at the main gate. Approaching Winthorpe main entrance by transport by road from Newark station was still by nature one of caution as to what I should find. There was one difference to previous similar events, I was now a senior NCO and god help anyone who said the wrong thing and tried to come the acid! On top of this there was something else I was not aware of. My leave after posting was 6 weeks, on operations we did not get the 'official' operation week's leave every 6 weeks. It rarely happened – due to contingencies – as my log book shows, and six weeks after a first tour was not long enough to wind down, although air crews themselves had no idea it was necessary. We all thought we were normal, but I noticed in others who were posted to the station later, their pale drawn faces and touchy behaviour was a certain indication that the case hardened wall of emotional suppression had not broken away, I was I suppose no different, hence my attitude. The state I was in was described by those who had come back to normal as 'operational twitch' and some actually had a physical twitching before they recovered. I needn't have been so abrasive because allowances were made, because they were fed up with being bawled out.

Winthorpe as a training station had not long been in existence and the awful bull shine had not developed as more established training units had. The difference between the personnel and their attitude to others was so marked that Operational Station was the happiest place to be in the RAF despite the feeling that swept over it when news that so-and-so had not been heard of again. I had noticed the comradeship and goodwill on a Squadron Station, so it was not the latter bond of sympathy that held everyone together, although it increased the comradeship, it was in fact that we were, as I put it earlier, on the shrine for which the Royal Air force had been created, real live aircraft, and real live flying.

When I had left Langar I had been given, as everyone else would have a 'chitty' – what a famous word of fond memory – although at that time a confounded nuisance. This chitty was called officially a clearance certificate, and had to be taken around all the various sections to be signed off the station strength for administration purposes. Needless to say it wasn't done. Just a few phone calls and a row of signatures that all looked alike.

My first job after passing through the main entrance was to visit the adjutant who did all the paperwork necessary to receive a new member to the unit. After the transport driver had lugged my gear into the room in Senior NCOs quarters, I made my way to the mess for a drink and a meal.

After lunch I reported to Chief Flying Instructor to be allocated my duties. It mattered little to me what I would be doing for the first thing I had no idea of what any of the instructors jobs might entail, and was still on my guard in case I didn't like what would be offered if there was a choice.

Every member of the Services has a dossier on which his (or her) progress was recorded. It was confidential, only the officer commanding the Unit which that airman served had access to it. These 'records' as they were known contained a great deal of information on a serviceman's career, and according to the entries of each commander could make or break their career. This dossier would be referred to the Officer commanding the Station, the CO of the Unit (1661 Operational Conversion Unit) and the Chief Flying Instructor, and possibly his adjutant (secretary) but not me.

I was now sitting in front of the Chief Flying Instructor in silence, while he was reading everything about me that I didn't know, and was going to decide on the basis of what he was reading what I would be offered. He began to explain what the Unit was doing (I didn't remind him I had already over 2 years on one); this was to convert pilots from twin engine bombers on to four engine jobs, and as there no Lancasters available for non-operational use, Stirlings and Halifaxes were being used to train them to fly Lancasters. It couldn't be done but I didn't say so. Instructors were divided into two sections, a few for flying dates, which entailed flying in these aircraft with 'staff' pilots (or instructor pilots and navigators) as we were called, and only possibly the Flight Engineer being the last to fly as instructor before the crew passed out for dispatch to operational Squadrons. There was only one snag with this proposition, both these aircraft had larger fuselages than the Lanc. and the Engineers controls and panels were well behind and completely out of sight of the pilot and flying controls. Both these aircraft were designed to carry two pilots, whereas the Lanc. was designed to take one, the duties of second pilot being undertaken by the Flight Engineer, if necessary as well as his own job! The alternative was to lecture pilots and engineers on how to fly Lancs. while they flew completely different aircraft. Odd as this might seem, the possibility of lecturing appealed to me; I had listened to hundreds but had not given one (apart from a talk to Cadet Training Corps, where I came off worse), and the chance to learn was too good to miss. To qualify for flying pay each aircrew had to put in a given number of flying hours each month, so I was not out of touch anyway. This interview was actually a very short one and I was told to report to the office in which the lecturers rested and prepared their work. It was obvious that the matter had been decided before that short interview, and had I chosen the alternative I may not have lived up to obvious expectations.

The sergeant's mess was not a very congenial place. Most of its members were composed of NCO aircrew and most of us Flight Sergeants. Many of the ground crew NCOs did not like aircrew NCOs considering that the latter had been given three tapes without having to go through the stages as ground crews. I didn't bother to tell them that I had done it the same way, and had more service in than themselves. The vast majority of the personnel of the RAF were now composed of conscripted men and those who had volunteered to avoid conscription. Their opinion of the very few regular airmen they met was not high. They could not understand or wouldn't believe, that without the regulars there would not have been an Air Force at all. The spirit or esprit-de-corps was never as high on training stations as on operational Squadrons, as I have just said. Having just left one where it was very high indeed, the change was not encouraging. However, I was not to put up with for long.

We were not given any training on how to lecture, we had not sufficient diagrams or displays either, just allowed to sit-in on one lecture and then told to get on with it. The RAF then were forced by the urgency of replacing crews and supplying Squadrons who were having their Stirling, Halifax, and Wellington bombers replaced by Lancasters, a much more efficient bomber and capable of carrying the large 'block buster' that was so badly needed. The pupil crews were a mixed assortment. Some had already flown many operational hours on these three types – others had never seen a heavy aircraft and had not been to an operational Squadron. There was a sprinkling of very senior officers who had commanded stations which had operated on different aircraft, and who would be commanding stations with Lancasters, for these it was a refresher course, and we NCOs were to tell them their job – or at least part of it. As it happened the course I was to instruct contained two Wing Commanders and six Squadron Leaders, people we had to salute outside the lecture room.

To call our end of the block we had to use 'lecture rooms' was chronic, just a room with two windows, a small platform (which I fell off more than once), a blackboard which often did the same and a small table, without drawers. In front of me closely packed like sardines, were my 'class'.

My subjects were aircraft handling, which involved the Theory of Flight as applicable to the Lanc. The Merlin Engine – as much as they needed to know and air screws (or propellers as some insisted they should be called). All this had to be done by building up a diagram with chalk on the board as I went through their various functions. It was difficult not to talk down to Officers who knew more about flying than I ever would, and at the same time trying to drive home how important it was to know everything they could possibly find necessary later on.

It was a hell of an experience! The first one I took I rattled through in about a quarter of an hour when it should have taken one hour. The most senior officers came to my rescue by asking questions. They had been through it many times before and understood. My mouth, throat, and voice slowly returned from parched leather to normal, and I survived – but only just. We had to take a course, which lasted about a month, only once, but as they overlapped in their stages on conversion we had four or five running at the same time. We were too busy to ponder over difficulties and I soon mastered the technique (or at least I think I did), by that I mean no one complained. The hardest job was to claim enough attention to keep the class awake, it was overcrowded and stuffy. I found insults effective, and what would happen to them if later they wished they had listened more carefully.

The flying instructors consisted of pilots, navigators, and flight engineers, and to get our necessary hours in we took the latter's place; it also made a change. Not being on regular flying meant that we others had just about every evening off; this was a most welcome change, although we worked on a seven day week.

Ralph, after a couple of months at Winthorpe was promoted to Pilot Officer and after leave returns to Winthorpe in November 1943, which brought a whole new lifestyle as he continues:

By now I had made a few friends among the 'civilians' in Newark and apart from a few drinks in the Officers Mess, I had some more with them. The greatest difference it made to me was now I was being called 'sir' and saluted, although I often forgot I was wearing a different uniform and wondered what they were doing, until I got used to the idea.

There were mess duties in every mess that officers were expected to carry out, and in Training Stations flying personnel were roped in as well, not so on Operational Stations. These duties were Bar Secretary, Social Secretary, and in the case of Officers Mess, Librarian. I had always avoided such jobs before, but knowing that I was on the short list for something, I opted for Librarian. It was the easiest job I have volunteered for, the two WAAFs who did the actual work could manage without me, I just turned up to see they were there. But it meant that I could use the money allotted for books to buy the ones I wanted to read. It gave me a few days off, usually in London to browse around bookshops, commonly known as a nice little number.

Winthorpe was only a couple of easy walking miles from Newark on the river Trent. If there were more than two of us who wanted to go there we phoned for a taxi, but usually made it on foot. In any case getting our feet under a table was a solo effort, I don't know if those who extended their hospitality to us, were aware that we were really appreciating the friendship they extended to us, but we did. Someone I met in this way was a man who worked in a local Brewery*. His pride in the place where he worked and its product was well worth the visit. I also learnt something of the stuff I had been drinking for a few years. The people I met were very kind indeed, and helped to keep servicemen in touch with the world 'outside'.

The freedom I now enjoyed was to me, after years of petty restrictions, most refreshing. No longer had I to book out for instance; and the sleeping quarters allotted to junior officers were the nearest on the site to Newark. We were in Nissen Huts halfway between the Mess and the WAAFs officers' quarters. For whose protection I am not sure! Our huts were divided into two with two beds in each half. Again I was in luck I had one half to myself. Each part was heated by a very small coke burning slow combustion stove, which was in very short supply, and our allocation was one small bucketful per day. This was not enough to keep the place warm for more than a few hours. After the Batman had filled the bucket and lit the fire, we had to fend for ourselves by robbing the coke compound. We had one Batman per hut.

The only duties, apart from the lectures, were that of Orderly Officer, that came not very often. It involved accompanying the Orderly Sergeant on specified rounds, mainly to the guard room, stores, and the airmen's dining hall, to inspect and check the food stores and ask for any complaints through the orderly sergeant. It was one obligation I attended to with most concern, remembering the awful food I had been served up with in the past. It must be said that the quality and quantity was by far better.

About 12 months from my joining Winthorpe, an Airmanship section was organised in a separate building and for some reason I never understood (there was no point in asking why) I was put in charge of this. It should have been a pilot's job. As usual in the RAF if you were given a job you just got on with it. A fitter was seconded to help me build mock-ups from parts of Lancs. scrounged from 44 Maintenance Unit near the end of the main runway, which consisted of a field of crashed aircraft and workshops to recover and make serviceable from them that which could be made to work again. Not an inspiring sight for pupil crews to take off over! I couldn't get a single phase electrical supply converter to change the mains supply to the D.C. current needed to operate the 24 motors used on aircraft, and so I had to build one, from any resistances I could find. The Station Electrical Engineer nearly had a fit when he came in to inspect it, but as he could not do better he left hoping that I wouldn't burn the place down. The lectures I had to give were on handling Lancasters in the air and on the ground, and in particular engine handling.

By this time Officers of Air Rank were coming through for conversion training, and to lecture to these very experienced pilots was indeed daunting. On the whole though they were the best to deal with.

* Warwick and Richardson's on Northgate and James Holes on Albert Street were major brewers in Newark at this time.

I got the section set up and must have been satisfactory because I was left undisturbed for quite some time, until a Squadron Leader pilot was found to replace me, and leaving me after all I had put into it as second fiddle. My attitude to these circumstances, and the fact that I wanted to get back on my second tour, soon found me booked for it.

Many experienced aircrew would form themselves into a crew from amongst those return-ing to operations from an HCU or take a 'spare' place from a crew about to complete their training, Ralph took the latter option:

Although I had flown in the Stirlings, on which crews were being trained, I had not met the crew I was due to fly with, during my flights in these aircraft, and as they were all NCOs I never had much time to get to know them; still they seemed a competent lot and we hit it off. Unfortunately, possibly the weather or some other reason I was not aware of, I only had one flight with them, and that was their last before posting to an operational Squadron.

The Lancaster has been described as a bomb bay with wings, and everything else was subordinate to that aspect. Although it may have had its faults in some ways, one way it did not fail was that modern techniques were used; everything could be controlled from upfront. The Stirling however, was of a different character. The second pilot's position was provided, but the Engineers panel and controls were down in the fuselage near the main spars, and the controls were not easy to get at. The Lanc. on the other hand could be handled from the pilots position

The last training flight for a new crew was a longish one, and entailed flying up the English Channel near the enemy coast as a familiarisation exercise. We had on board a staff Navigator and the crews original Engineer. The weather was not bad on take off, nothing to suggest it might turn nasty. We flew down over the Midlands, over the coast near Brighton, and along the French coast as far as Boulogne, then turned down that coast again before heading across the Channel to cross over Littlehampton for the return trip to Winthorpe.

The trip up and down the Channel had not attracted any enemy attention, although we saw some activity inland, and flying about ten thousand feet and everything in order, we settled back for an easy run home. However, it was not to be. We had only just left Littlehampton below us when the weather turned nasty suddenly. What had been reasonable visibility was now black as ink, caused by constant heavy rain. It came down in torrents, but everything on the aircraft was in order so we just accepted that it would be over soon or we would fly out of it. It wasn't to be like that long. After what had been only ten minutes or so the port inner engine stopped, as far as could be seen for no reason at all. It could have been a sudden heavy icing block formed on the air intake, or anything. The pilot trimmed the aircraft for the loss of power and we flew on, still in total darkness, then the starboard outer engine began to show trouble, the oil pressure on it began to fall, and the temperature rose rapidly. If these conditions did not return to normal very soon the engine would seize up. We had been warned by Flight Engineer staff instructor who had flown these aircraft on operations, that under severe weather conditions this could happen to aircooled engines on the Stirling. We had flown smack into heavy icing conditions in the air in the storm clouds and they were right down to ground level. Oil systems on all aircraft engines were fitted with coolers having thermal by-passes to maintain correct temperatures and pressure, but in heavy icing we were now flying through was faster than the response from the oil temperature control. This state of affairs was known as Coreing, a rough description of what was happening within the cooler. The only recommended way out of this problem was we had been advised to do, the exact opposite to what one would have normally done, and that was to open up the engine full out and dive to warmer air temperature. Having already lost height, and to open up one engine on the side opposite to the only one on the other, would have swung the aircraft out of control into a downward spin. We could do nothing, and it jammed solid in a matter of seconds.

We had contacted base of our first engine failure and all airfields anywhere near our route had their runways and outer marking lights ready. As we passed over them we heard them giving us permission to make an emergency landing – but we saw only a fleeting glimpse of their lights in a short break in the clouds before they were once again blotted out. With a heavy aircraft with two of its four engines out of action any sudden turn on to where a runway had been seen in the hope of it showing up again, would have been fatal, we would have just dropped out of the sky, what little of it that was left to us. We flew Northwards on a track to take us over as many airfields as possible, in case we could just be in line with a lighted runway and could put down. None showed up. The instrument called an altimeter indicating our height from the ground was operated by measuring the air pressure, and at best not reliable under good conditions; under bad hopeless. Also the ground below undulated. We passed over Winthorpe without seeing it and ahead stood Lincoln Cathedral.

About a fortnight previously I had seen a Stirling circling the airfield at Winthorpe, and suddenly without warning dive into the ground. The fire engine and crash tender crashed its way through hedges, with the blood wagon (ambulance) in pursuit, but there was only one badly injured airman recovered. I remembered too seeing the two Hampdens at Acklington crashing as they tried to land, and the pilot who hit a hangar at Hawarden, and began to wonder what might happen to us. Still, we had plenty of fuel on board, and by keeping away from where we thought Lincoln Cathedral and Newark church spire should be we could circle until a clearing in the low cloud would give up to the strain? Luckily we had one either side. Unfortunately for us they didn't! The starboard engine began to overheat and failure would not be long coming. The bomb aimer was now in the second pilot's seat to give a hand with the controls, and there was nothing left for it but to crash land, in pouring rain and inky darkness on ground that couldn't be seen.

The pilot gave the order to take up crash positions. The pilot's seats and gun turrets gave the best hold, but the rest of us in the fuselage went flat down on the floor, feet forward gripping the main forward spar for dear life. The lights of hell went out!

On the 28th October 1944 Stirling EE907 (GP-K) crashed at Housham Woods, Morton near Swinderby; the aircraft was a total wreck with the loss of three crew members and five injured. Those killed were Sgt. Robert Reed aged 20 the Wireless Operator/Air Gunner, Sgt. John J. Glasgow aged 25 the Navigator and F/O James Robertson DFC aged 30 Staff Navigator (Robertson had been awarded his DFC on the 21st April 1944 whilst with No.467 Squadron). F/O Alfred W. Gayford aged 29 the Air Bomber died later on the 31st October in Lincoln Military Hospital. The survivors were F/Lt. Martin the Pilot, Sgts. Coombes and Buckminster Air Gunners along with F/O Ralph Fairhead.

Ralph was taken to an airfield sick bay (he had no idea which but probably Swinderby) and then transferred to the RAF Hospital Rauceby near Sleaford; he spent the remainder of the war in hospitals and medical rehabilitation centres. Finally discharged from hospital with some minor eye damage which prevented him returning to flying duties he retired from the RAF.

Ariel view of technical site, April 1945 – NAM archives

CHAPTER TEN

From the ORB's - 1944

N.B.: Text in italics is additional / explanatory notes and information.

5th January

All Lancaster aircraft remaining on this Station were flown away to allotted destinations leaving No.1661 Conversion Unit equipped only with Stirling aircraft.

7th January

The last record of a flight by a Lancaster in the 1661HCU ORB, Lancasters did not return to the HCU until December 1944.

The final change over to the new Officers Mess was made when anterooms were occupied. The old Mess, Coddington Hall, was turned over entirely for sleeping accommodation for Officers. Intelligence Section moved into offices in the new Aircrew Block.

18th January

Station Headquarters move to the new Station Office Block.

21st January

At 0620 hours, Stirling EF151 was on its landing approach after a three hour training sortie when the port outer engine failed. With the undercarriage only partly down the aircraft became tail heavy, hit some trees, crashed and burst into flames at Glebe Farm, Brough near Newark. Navigator F/Sgt. Munro RCAF and Sgt. Cooper the Wireless/Operator/Air Gunner were killed with the Flight Engineer Sgt. Venables dying later the same day in Newark Hospital; the other crew members suffering injuries.

27th January

An exercise to test the Station Defence against enemy paratroopers was carried out.

28th January

The new Station Post Office was opened.

31st January

Stirling EF232 of No.1660 HCU Swinderby crashed near Bassingham Bombing Range shortly after taking off from Winthorpe on a night bombing exercise. The cause was thought to be an engine fire whilst in flight. Killed were F/O Trueman RCAF, P/O Freeman, W. O. McKnight and Sgts. Appleton, Duke and Nelson; F/O Mason RCAF and Sgt. Lamb died later in hospital and F/Sgt. Martin died on the 1st February.

1st February

The day started misty but later became cloudy, with intermittent rain which lasted until mid-day. The remainder of the day being cloudy with poor visibility.

A lecture on the USA was given by Captain Kerr of US Army.

3rd February

No.60 Course arrived from RAF Aircrew School, Scampton - 128 personnel

The (No.5) Aircrew School was formed in August 1943 to instruct newly commissioned aircrew on their duties and responsibilities, an NCOs course in drill and administration was also set up. In October the School transferred to Balderton and by the end of the year had a complement of 113 Officers, 422 SNCOs, 15 other ranks and 20 WAAF other ranks.

11th February

A lecture to all drivers of MT vehicles on Tyre Economy.

20th February

No.63 Course arrived from RAF Aircrew School, Scampton - 154 personnel.

21st February

Airmen's Dining Hall was transferred to new building.

Mr. Mellors, Superintendant Engineer, No.5 Works Area visited the station in connection with runway repairs.

Repairs to No.3 Runway started by Cementation Co.

22nd February

WAAF Dining Hall closed and communal feeding began in new Airmen's Dining Hall *(pictured right).*

The Station Medical Officer reported - The diet is plentiful and well balanced. The opening of the new O.R. Mess has done much to improve the messing facilities.

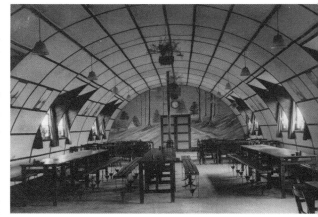

Airmen's Mess – NAM archives/Bill Taylor

23rd February

Squadron Officers Bendlebury, Haigh and Entwhistle, inspected the WAAF site on this station. The airwomen had an excellent display of handicrafts and among the articles shown were leather gloves, embroidery, knitting, toys, handbags and paintings and underclothes. It was mentioned in their report that the MT Rest Room was the best they had ever inspected.

25th February

Accident to Stirling Mark III RAF No. LN529. Crashed at 2137 hours on 25.2.44 at Port Ellen, Scotland. Fatal casualties to: - 1428549 Sgt. Sharp M. – Pilot; 1578712 Sgt. Brown, A. – F/Eng.; 1395654 Sgt. Lucha. P. – Nav.; Can R.163622 F/S Hamilton. B/A; 1576117 Sgt. Radford, K. – W/Op./A. G.; 1585086 Sgt. Widdows, M. – A.G. (M .U. G.). Injured: - 1869264 Sgt. Hamilton, G. – A.G. (Rear).

Whilst on a cross country training flight, Stirling LJ529 crashed at RAF Station Port Ellen. After 3 attempts to land with engine problems the aircraft crashed behind the watch office immediately bursting into flames with only the rear gunner Sgt. G. Hamilton surviving.

26th February

Accident to Stirling Mark III RAF No. EF127 at Edwinstowe, Nr. Mansfield, Notts. Fatal casualties to:- Aus.401986 F/Sgt. Manuel – Pilot, 1677871 Sgt. Davison, G. – F/Eng., Aus.418048 F/Sgt. Bird, G. – Nav., Aus.426127 F/Sgt. Macoun, G. – B/A, Aus.423650 F/Sgt. Christie, S. – W/Op. A. G.. Injured: - Aus.429481 F/Sgt. Plath, R. – A.G. (Mid-upper) Aus.434558 Sgt. Taylor, W. – A. G. (Rear).

Returning to base after a night training flight Stirling EF127 sent out a 'MAYDAY' which was heard by RAF Station Syerston, but they, for reasons unknown, were unable to contact the aircraft which had a suspected fuel shortage. At 0130 the aircraft hit some trees and crashed, scattering wreckage over three fields at Alby's Farm, Edwinstowe, Nottinghamshire. Five crew were killed and two seriously injured.

Repairs to No.3 Runway ceased.

27th February

Continuous sleet becoming continuous moderate snow. This lasted fourteen hours and frequent snow fell until 2400.

Snow Clearance Scheme put into operation.

A 3 page report was submitted by the Station Commander to No.51 Base Commander on the effectiveness of the operation.

W/C. Hallows DFC posted to and reported as Chief Instructor to No.1661 Conversion Unit w.e.f. 28.2.44. W/C. Woodward DFC and Bar posted to No.23 Group Headquarters w.e.f. 28.2.44.

28th February

Much moderate snow in the early hours, becoming fair or fine later with slight mist in the forenoon and cloudy with occasional moderate snow thereafter and St. Mist before midnight.

29th February

Flying hours for the month of February totalled 413 hours day and 559¼ night.

Personnel Strength: Station – 19 Officers 208 other ranks, 4 WAAF Officers, 168 WAAF other ranks including 1 Canadian, 1 Australian and 1 Rhodesian, 1 RAF Regiment Officer with 58 Regiment other ranks. No.1661 HCU - 131 Officers including 14 Canadian, 2 New Zealand, 15 Australian, 2 USA and 2 Rhodesian and 453 other ranks including 42 Canadian, 3 New Zealand, 39 Australian and 15 WAAFs.

1st March

During takeoff for an air test, Stirling EF518 GP-E veered sharply to port and struck a snow bank and reduced to Cat. B (the undercarriage being broken off).

The pilots were S/Ldr. M Crocker DFC and bar and W/Cdr. B. R. Hallows, chief flying instructor. The aircraft was deemed to be beyond economical repair (BER) and struck off charge (SOC) (scrapped).

3rd March

No.1661 HCU completed a 'Hat Trick', three Stirlings being involved in separate accidents. Stirling EF125 struck a snow bank whilst taxiing and reduced to Cat. Ac; EF965 struck a snow ridge on landing and reduced to Cat. Ac, Stirling EE956 struck a snow bank on landing and was slightly damaged.

10th March

Surfacing of No.2 Runway by Messrs. Torr and Co. Ltd commenced.

13th March

Stirling BK766 involved in accident on perimeter track with an MT vehicle. Slight damage resulted. A fresh drive to prevent such accidents inaugurated and arrangements made for station police to maintain a special watch on the airfield after dark for a period of one week. Results to be reported to the Station Commander with full details of any infringement of Station Standing Orders.

16th March

Detachment of No.1690 BDTF (Bomber (Defence) Training Flight) (HQ RAF Syerston) arrived at Station under F/Lt. Baker. With three Miles Martinet aircraft.

No.1690 (BDTF) was formed at RAF Station, Syerston from No.1485 B & G Flight, under the command of S/Ldr. E. M. Undery. All ground personnel on No.1485 B & G Flight were posted to No.1690 BDTF. During the period 15th February to 8th March, 1944 the flight personnel continued to carry the training requirements of No.1485 B & G Flight which was in the process of disbanding. All personnel were based at RAF Syerston, but detachments of servicing personnel were sent to following Bases or Stations; No.51 Base, Swinderby, No.52 Base, Coningsby, RAF Stations Winthorpe, Wigsley and East Kirkby.

18th March

Winthorpe Flight of No.2776 Squadron (RAF Regiment) withdrawn from Station on movement of Squadron to Downham Market.

19th March

F/O Matich (Air Ministry) lectured to Aircrew Trainees on his escape from Germany.

NZ414658 Nicholas Matich DSO, DFM was born in Te Kopuru, near Auckland, New Zealand on the 25th July 1917 and joined the RNZAF 17th August 1941 and qualified as a Pilot. He was awarded the Distinguished Flying Medal (DFM) 9th September 1943 when with No.35 (PFF) Squadron RAF flying the Halifax. Awarded the Distinguished Service Order (DSO) 12th June 1944, the citation reads - in air operations this officer has displayed skill and courage of the highest order.

On 27th September 1943, F/O Matich's Halifax was shot down during a raid on Hanover. He bailed out safely and successfully evaded capture. Moving by night he headed for Holland, taking nine nights to cover 100 miles to the German-Dutch border. Through taking cover by day, usually in woods and once in a haystack, he had a fairly safe journey. He reached the Dortmund-Ems canal on the seventh night only to find it securely guarded. All bridges had sentry boxes at each end, with guards also patrolling the area. Creeping into one sentry box, he overpowered the guard and safely crossed the canal. Two nights later he reached Holland and made contact with the escape and evasion organisation. After spending six weeks hiding in a cellar in a wood he was taken by train and escorted across the frontier into Belgium. From Brussels he travelled in company with another British pilot to France and eventually reached Paris. After several days there the two men were guided by a French girl to Bordeaux. They then made their way south taking three days and nights to walk across the Pyrenees into Spain, finally reaching Gibraltar, from where they were flown back to England, arriving there on 14th January 1944. He became a member of the 'Caterpillar' and 'Late Arrivals' clubs. He ended the war with the rank of Flight Lieutenant and died in Auckland on the 25th September 1992.

20th March

Stirling LK537 was extensively damaged when its undercarriage collapsed on landing. Cat. B.

The port main undercarriage failed to lock and the aircraft made a 'controlled' emergency landing, with all the crew uninjured. Further details on this and the crash of LK485 on the 7th April can be found in the book 'Riding in the Shadow of Death' by Chris Keltie which gives firsthand accounts of the events by the (same) crew.

21st March

Stirling LJ533 totally destroyed in crashing on overshoot. Crew by displaying good crash discipline, escaped injury

The port outer engine failed and would not feather. Leaving the pilot no alternative but to carry out a forced landing in a field near Syerston airfield where the aircraft unfortunately hit some trees.

Information was received from No.51 Base HQ that the Conversion Unit might be called upon to operate, probably only at night, but, in the event of the collapse of the Luftwaffe, during the day, also.

31st March

Stirling EF444 (Pilot F/Lt. A. L. Williams) overshot on landing and ran into soft ground causing damage to the nose portion of the aircraft at 2120, Cat. Ac.

EF444 was repaired on site by No.58 MU and returned to No.1661 HCU on the 6th June, 1944.

Total flying hours Day 725 hours 20 mins. Night 692 hrs 45 mins. Pool 23 hrs 40 mins.

Personnel strength: - RAF 1488, RAAF 54, RCAF 73, RNZAF 4 and USA 5.

1st April

Repair work on No.3 Runway by the Cementation Company Limited continues. Runway remains unserviceable.

4th April

Air Vice Marshal R. A. Cochrane, CB CBE AFC (Air Officer Commanding No.5 Group) visited the Station to inspect the Main Stores.

7th April

Stirling LK485 involved in accident at Ossington (engine failure in the air). Cat B.

Whilst carrying out a training flight, Stirling LK485 started to develop engine trouble. First the port inner engine failed and was feathered. There was later an oil leak in the port outer which failed and was also feathered. The aircraft then started to lose height and pilot Sgt. W. (Bill) North could not unfeather engines. A wheels' down landing was attempted but, as the undercarriage was not locked down it collapsed on landing in some small pine trees in Clipstone Forest, near Ollerton, Nottinghamshire (although Bill North's account describes the landing as being at RAF Ossington - Clipstone and Ossington are around 10 miles apart.). No injuries were sustained by the crew and Sgt. North was recommended for a Green Endorsement in his Log Book. It seemed that metal was found in the induction pipe of No.7 Cylinder of the port outer and the big end bearing in the port inner had broken up. There was also an oil leak to the CSU accounting for the inability to unfeather.

New Main Guard Room taken over from contractors. Detention cells certified fit for occupation by Station Medical Officer.

8th April

Stirling BK818 involved in accident at Winthorpe following burst tyre on landing. Cat. Ac.

11th April

Colonel Mitchell and four USAAC Officers stationed at RAF Barkston Heath (IXth Troop Carrier Command) visited Station by air for liaison purposes and were shown over the Station. G/Capt. Ward DFC and four other Officers from this unit returned the visit by air on the same day; the exchange of views and arrangements for co-operation were considered to have been of great value for both units.

Part of the US Ninth Air Force, IX Troop Carrier Command supplied air transport for the Allied airborne divisions in Europe, it consisted of three troop carrier wings, 14 troop carrier groups, and one pathfinder group, with around 1,380 operational aircraft including spares, and 2,000 gliders at its maximum strength in March 1945. Aircraft were the C-47 Skytrain and its variant, the C-53 Skytrooper, and also CG-4A Waco and Waco CG-13 gliders

On its formation in 1943 twelve airfields were designated for the new command, each to house 40 C-47s and a like number of gliders: they were Fulbeck, Langar, Bottesford, Wakerley, Balderton, North Witham, Barkston Heath, Cottesmore, North Luffenham, Saltby, Folkingham, and Woolfox Lodge.

In early 1944 gliders were reportedly stored inside hangars at Winthorpe prior to D Day.

At 1629 Stirling LK456 GP-T caught fire in the air and crashed out of control at Winthorpe, causing the death of all nine crew members (including 2 Canadians).

12th April

Again Winthorpe had a hat trick when three Stirlings were involved in minor accidents. Stirling EF447 landed off the runway at Winthorpe. Cat. Ac. Stirlings EE967 and LJ538 involved in taxiing accident at Winthorpe. Both Cat. A.

EF447 had collided with the windsock pole but the crew suffered no injuries.

16th April

Four crews of No.63 Course posted out of training to No.5 LFS.

19th April

No.72 Course arrived for conversion Training. 168 pupils including 24 Flight Engineers to be crewed up as second engineers to No.72 Course.

C.26001 P/O J. S. Sands (Tech S Radar) posted from No.3 RCAF PRC.

22nd April

Eight crews posted out of training to No.5 LFS.

Seven DFCs are awarded to Station personnel – P/Os King and Gibson, F/Os W. J. O. Grime, Simpson and Coxhill and F/Lts. J. F. Grime and J. B. Warwick.

24th April

Stirling Aircraft LK460 'O' overshot on landing and crashed on the Fosse Way, Winthorpe. The crew were treated for shock in SSQ.

It was about this time that a Post Office Engineer working at Winthorpe was reportedly told by a ground crew member that one RAF pilot had crashed that many aircraft they were thinking of making him a 'German ace'!!

27th April

G/Capt. J. H. Woodin was appointed Commanding Officer of RAF Station Winthorpe, replacing G/Capt. E. L. S. Ward DFC who was posted.

One crew of No.63 Course and eight crews of No.66 Course posted out of training to No.5 LFS

During April, No.1690 BDTF carried out Fighter Affiliation on 19 days for No.1661 HCU.

Total flying hours: - Day training 964 hrs 20 mins Night training 819 hrs 25 mins Other flying 44 hrs 35 mins Total 1828 hrs 20 mins.

The Medical Officer reported during the latter half of the month sick parades were markedly decreased in numbers. The number reporting from No.58 and No.203 MUs remained fairly high.

3rd May

One crew from No.63 Course, nine crews from No.66 Course and one crew of No.69 Course passed out to No.5 LFS on completion of Conversion Course.

6th May

No.75 Course arrived at No.1661 Conversion Unit together with 29 Flight Engineers for crewing up as second engineers to No.75 Course (203 Offs. and NCO's).

9th May

One crew of No.63 Course, one crew of No.66 Course and ten crews of No.69 Course passed out to No.5 LFS on completion of Conversion Course.

14th May

Opening of 'Salute the Soldier Week'. Contingent of RAF and WAAF personnel took part in a Parade, Church Service and March Past in Newark in support of the 140 OCTU, 'L' Coy. ATS, 11 Battn. Notts Home Guard and Army Cadet Force.

15th May

The Station Commander (G/Capt. J. H. Woodin) introduced the speaker, (Colonel J. R.T. Aldous MC) for Services Day in 'Salute the Soldier Campaign' at the Town Hall, Newark. The local target effort was £25,000 and a Special Service drive was inaugurated on the station to coincide with the Local Campaign, a total of £500 being raised.

Two crews of No.66 Course and eleven crews of No.69 Course passed out to No.5 LFS on completion of Conversion Course.

16th May

Stirling LJ575 reduced to Cat. E (burst a tyre on takeoff from RAF Waddington which resulted in the undercarriage collapsing). Stirling LK574 reduced to Cat. B (experienced failure on undercarriage system at RAF Station Woodbridge).

17th May

Stirling III EE956 reduced to Cat. E (burnt) at RAF Station Desborough. Cause of accident still under investigation. Crew of nine all killed.

At 2355 whilst on a night flying exercise, Stirling EE956 crashed and was totally destroyed with the loss of all nine crew members, at Ironstone Quarry, Rothwell, Northants., due to control being lost by icing and structural failure. During the flight the aircraft having headed south, encountered a high icing index to such severity that control of the aircraft was lost by the pilot which resulted in it spiralling out of control, it broke up and caught fire before crashing into the ground.

18th May

During the evening, S/Ldr. W. H. Orchard, Chief Technical Officer, was involved in an accident with a civilian motorcar whilst riding a service motorcycle sustaining a compound fracture of the right tibia and fibula. Admitted to Harlow Wood Hospital Mansfield.

Joseph Goodison, civilian employee admitted to Newark Hospital suffering from head injuries and 1232755 Sgt. Stebbings was admitted to SSQ with abrasions to face after being involved in a cycle collision in the camp area.

19th May

Stirling LK546 overshot with three defective engines, at RAF Culmhead, Devon, hit a tree and caught fire, with one crew member being injured.

21st May

Two crews of No.69 Course passed out to No.5 LFS on completion of Conversion Course.

26th May

25 Air Crew Cadets were posted to the Station pending absorption into the training. Arrangements were made for them to be given lectures and employed in such a way to give an insight into the various branches of Air Crew Training.

Stirling LJ558 swung on landing at Winthorpe after hitting Stirling BK776, and crashed into the station workshops. The crew members sustained only minor injuries, and the pilot 15116970 Sgt. S. Laws, being detained in SSQ suffering from shock.

No.78 Course arrived at No1661 Conversion Unit with 29 Flight Engineers to be crewed up as second engineers to No.78 Course (204 Offs. and NCO's).

30th May

Air Vice Marshal the Hon R. A. Cochrane, CB CBE AFC (AOC No.5 Group) visited the Station to discuss bombing methods. Divisional Officer Phillips (NFS Mansfield) paid liaison visit to the airfield.

31st May

The bituminous carpet being laid on the runways was nearly completed (No1 and 3 Runways 100% and No.2 practically complete).

F/O Darnton and P/Os Sergeev and Milne awarded the Distinguished Flying Cross.

Monthly Flying Hours :- Day 1072 hrs 40 mins Night 883 hrs 55 mins Other Flying 37 hrs 50 mins Total 1993 hrs 35 mins.

The Medical Officer reported the new additions to the Sewage Farm have been completed and are working satisfactorily.

During the month, the flying detachments of BDTF based at No.51 Base Stations carried out Fighter Affiliation Exercises with Nos. 1660, 1661 and 1654 HCUs. The total number of exercises carried out amounted to 812, Spitfires flying 152.40 hours, Hurricanes 313.30 hours, Martinets 202.15 hours and Tiger Moth 6.50 hours, plus target towing for ground to air firing which was carried out at Wainfleet Range for the AA School, Spilsby by the Martinet detachment from Winthorpe with a total 16.50 hours during the month.

2nd June

Twenty two crews of No.72 Course passed out to No.5 LFS on completion of conversion training.

4th June

New Station Cinema (Nissen type) was opened tonight with the presentation of 'The Life and Death of Colonel Blimp' (Roger Livesey). The general layout and acoustics of the cinema are excellent and will only be improved by the addition of better seating arrangements. New seating is on order and in the meantime, hired chairs are being used.

7th June

Stirling EE907 swung on landing and collided with a second aircraft (Stirling LK562) categorising the former Ac and the latter Cat. B.

The pilot F/Sgt. G. James was on his first night solo flight, had trouble with the starboard undercarriage and had to use the emergency system.

LK562 was salvaged and rebuilt as TS265 serving with No.190 Squadron, the aircraft failed to return from SOE Operation 'Blinkers 2' on the 15th April 1945 on its third operation.

13th June

No.81 Course (30 crews comprising 210 Offs. and NCO's with 30 'second' engineers) arrived from Scampton Aircrew School for Conversion training.

14th June

Headquarters No.51 Base under cover of their letter 51B/s.504/Trg dated 14th June 1944 indicated that Command have been giving consideration to a revised training organisation designed to reduce the bottle necks which have been making it difficult, if not impossible, to plan flying with any degree of freedom. The revised scheme, in as far as it will affect Conversion units, would involve an increase to six Flights and a reorganised input of ten crews every six days. A revision of the established Instructor personnel would also be necessary to effect the introduction of the new scheme. One of the main problems to be faced, however, would be that of accommodating the increased inputs at the peak period. A Base conference of Station Commanders and Chief Instructors has been called to discuss all angles of the plan.

10th August

LAC Francis was admitted to SSQ with first and second degree burns to face, arms and hands, received in a fire which occurred in Dispersal Nissen Hut.

12th August

No.91 Course (ten crews) arrived at Winthorpe for Conversion training.

14th August

Eight crews of No.84 Course passed out no.5 LFS on completion of Conversion Training.

18th August

No.92 Course (ten crews) arrived at Winthorpe for Conversion training.

19th August

Ten crews of No.85 Course passed out no.5 LFS on completion of Conversion Training.

21st August

The detachments of No.1690 BDTF in No.51 Base at RAF Base Station, Swinderby and sub-stations Winthorpe and Wigsley, rejoined their parent unit at No.52 Base, RAF Station Scampton. At Winthorpe transport was arranged between the Officer commanding No.1690 Flight and the Station MT Officer to report to the Martinet Dispersal Hut at 1300 to collect all aircraft components, tools and other equipment then to the living site to pick up personal kit and proceed directly to RAF Station Scampton. The Officer Commanding No.1690 Flight arranged for the three Martinet aircraft based at Winthorpe to be flown to RAF Scampton.

23rd August

Air Vice Marshal the Hon R. A. Cochrane, CB CBE AFC (AOC No.5 Group) and Mrs. Cochrane visited the Station and were entertained at lunch by the Station Commander.

24th August

No.93 Course (ten crews) arrived at Winthorpe for Conversion training.

26th August

Nine crews of No.86 Course passed out no.5 LFS on completion of Conversion Training.

27th August

Stirling III LK616 crashed at Hawton, Notts at 0155 hours. Five members of the crew killed, one placed on D. I. list and one slightly injured. Sixth member of crew died in RAF Hospital, Rauceby on 1st September. Aircraft Cat. E burnt.

On return from a cross country flight, Stirling LK616, GP-G, crashed at Hawton, near Newark at 0155 with six (1 RNZAF, 2 RCAF, 3 RAF) of the crew killed. At about 0140 the aircraft was given instructions to join the circuit and await permission land, the aircraft was heard to pass over the airfield and crashed near the AA camp at Hawton. Sgt. Solly an Air gunner survived the crash with burns to his face and hands; Sgt. Sanderson also a Gunner initially survived the crash but died from his injuries.

29th August

Cpl. E. Reid and LAC Birks were admitted to SSQ and transferred to RAF Hospital, Rauceby, suffering from severe burns of face and hands received when the Rest Room in the MT section caught fire.

30th August

No.94 Course (ten crews) arrived at Winthorpe for Conversion training.

Flying hours: Day 1094 hrs 55 mins Night 1034 hrs 30 mins Pool 106 hrs 20 mins Total 2235 hrs 45 mins.

The No.5 Group ORB noted that in the month of August 151 crews completed training and were posted to Squadrons, the highest in the Group's history, No.51 Base aircraft flew 9,000 hours despite unseasonable weather.

1st September

13 crews from Nos. 85, 86 and 87 Courses passed out to No.5 LFS on completion of Conversion training.

5th September

10 crews (with ten flight engineers) comprising No.95 Course arrived at No.1661 C. U. for Conversion Training.

7th September

12 crews of No.88 Course passed out to No.5 LFS on completion of Conversion training.

11th September

10 crews (with ten flight engineers) arrived at No.1661 C. U. to form No.96 Course for Conversion Training.

13th September

11 crews of No.89 Course passed out to No.5 LFS on completion of Conversion training.

17th September

10 crews (with 12 flight engineers) arrived at No.1661 C. U. as No.97 Course for Conversion.

Stirling III LJ523 crashed whilst making landing at Harlaxton (Cat. E). One crew member slightly injured.

On a routine training flight when it encountered bad weather, and unable to contact either the diversion airfield or base, the pilot was given a green light to land at RAF Harlaxton, Lincs. Due to bad visibility and Harlaxton being a small airfield, the Stirling overshot and collided with a Gun Post. One crew member was slightly injured and admitted to SSQ.

18th September

Miles Master aircraft from No.7 (P) AFU crashed into bungalow in Newark. Pilot 1583327 Sgt. Maynard killed. Next of Kin being resident locally, funeral arrangements carried out by this Station at the RAF Regional Cemetery, Oxford.

19th September

11 crews of No.90 Course passed out to No.5 LFS on completion of Conversion training.

24th September

Visit by ATC. One Officer and sixteen cadets visited the station and were shown round the Bombing and Gunnery sections. Flights were arranged in the afternoon.

25th September

Stirling LK547 landed 500 yards down the 1400 yard runway too fast in a light wind and overshot. The aircrafts brakes failed due to lack of air pressure – the aircraft had to be pumped up with air every alternate landing.

Stirling III LK561 developed engine trouble on cross country over Bradwell Bay, Essex. Crew forced to bale out and landed safely. Staff Pilot (P/O S. A. Hill) remained at the controls and is now reported missing.

On a night cross country training flight, firstly, the starboard outer propeller flew off and then, for no apparent reason, the port inner engine feathered. All the crew abandoned the aircraft over East Anglia, except P/O Hill, who remained at the controls; P/O Hill's body was recovered from the wreckage discovered off Point Clear, St. Osyth near Clacton-on-Sea.

30th September

The flying training programme has been maintained, fifty-five crews have passed out to Finishing School during the month. The standard of messing in the Airmen's Mess has maintained its high standard.

2nd October

No.99 Course (composed of nine crews with six spare Flight Engineers) arrived at the Unit for conversion Training to heavy bombers. Ten crews of No.92 Course passed out to No.5 LFS on completion of training.

5th October

Stirling III LK389 involved in accident, collided (with another aircraft) on parking at RAF Swinderby, and categorised Cat. E.

9th October

No.100 Course (composed of eight crews with two spare Flight Engineers) arrived at the Unit for conversion Training to heavy bombers. Eleven crews of No.93 Course passed out to No.5 LFS on completion of training.

10th October

Stirling III LK617 involved in accident, undercarriage failure at RAF Woodbridge. Categorised Cat. E.

Unable to retract its undercarriage and the dinghy blew out after takeoff from Winthorpe.

The pilot was detailed to proceed to RAF Woodbridge where the undercarriage collapsed on landing.

11th October

F/Lt. Gerrard paid a visit to the station and gave a lecture on Japan and the Far East. This was well received by a large audience.

16th October

No.101 Course (composed of eight crews with two spare flight engineers and two spare air gunners) arrived at the Unit for conversion Training to heavy bombers. Nine crews of No.94 Course passed out to No.5 LFS on completion of training.

17th October

Stirling III EF194 force landed at RAF Tatenhill near Burton-on-Trent, Staffordshire with engine trouble and categorised Cat. A (whilst carrying out a cross country flight).

19th October

S/Ldr. Woodhouse of the Royal Canadian Air Force, Overseas HQ visited the RCAF personnel.

The Assistant Chaplain-in-Chief (G/Capt. R. L. G. Wright) visited the station to confer with the Officiating C. of E. Padre (the Rev. B. Woodworth of Coddington).

23rd October

No.102 Course (composed of eight crews with twelve spare flight engineers) arrived at the Unit to commence conversion training. Ten crews of No.95 Course passed out to No.5 LFS on completion of training.

26th October

One crew of No.96 Course passed out to No.5 LFS on completion of training.

27th October

One crew of No.96 Course passed out to No.5 LFS on completion of training.

Information was received from Headquarters Bomber Command under their reference BC/S.31873/Org dated 27th October 1944 to the effect that it was proposed a) To transfer certain bases (including No.51 Base) from their respective operational groups to the newly formed No.7 Group and b) Concurrently to renumber such bases. An administrative conference to discuss the various aspects of the proposed changes has been called by HQ No.51 Base.

28th October

Three crews of No.96 Course passed out to No.5 LFS on completion of their training.

Advance information that the transfer of the base (together with No.1661 HCU) to No.7 Group has been fixed for the 3rd November, 1944 and, as from that date No.51 Base will become No.75 Base.

Sqd./Officer Entwhistle (WAAF), No.5 Group, carried out an inspection of the WAAF

Section on behalf of the AOC No.5 Group.

Stirling III EE907 crashed at Morton Village, near Swinderby. Cause of accident unknown- aircraft categorised E

At 2320 whilst on a three engined approach, Stirling EE907 crashed at Norton Disney, near Swinderby, after control was lost when the landing flaps were lowered. The aircraft was a total wreck with the loss of four crew members and four seriously injured.

For the story of the flight and the crash landing at Housham Wood see the account by Ralph Fairhead.

Stirling III LJ586 crashed at Blandford, Dorset. Cause suspected icing. Categorised E.

During a night cross country sortie the aircraft encountered heavy icing at 17,500 feet and was unable to maintain height. The aircraft broke cloud at 3,000 feet and crash landed at Iwerne Minster, Blandford, Dorset at 2240 resulting in four fatalities and three crew members injured.

Information received from Headquarters, Bomber command under their reference BC/46859/1/E.4 dated 23.10.44 that the Conversion Unit would be re-arming from 40 U.E.Stirling aircraft to 32 Mark I/III Lancaster aircraft with effect from 30th December 1944. Equipment Officer is taking action to demand spare parts for the new type aircraft, whilst a survey of existing stock of Stirling parts is being carried out by all sections concerned with a view to reducing holdings to a minimum without impairing the efficiency of operations.

30th October

Stirling III EF177 force landed at Alverston, Nr. Bristol following P. O. Engine failure and is categorised Cat. E. Crew baled out and landed safely.

At 2250 the aircraft crashed during a night cross country training flight following failure of the port outer engine. The pilot was unable to feather the faulty engine and this resulted in the propeller flying off and hitting the port inner engine and fuselage. The crew abandoned the aircraft which crashed, three crew members were injured, one with a broken leg, as a result of the parachute descent.

31st October

No.103 Course (composed of eight crews and ten spare Flight Engineers) arrived at this unit to commence conversion training. One crew of No.95 and three crews of No.97 Course passed out to No.5 LFS on completion of training.

Flying time for the month of October amounted to 988hrs 50 minutes day flying, 901hrs 20 minutes night flying, and 14hrs 45 minutes on the pool Oxford, Total 1904 hrs 55 mins.

Strength of personnel: RAF 1602, RCAF 41, RNZAF 8, RAAF 67, USA 2, Chile 2.

On the administration side, no matters of importance call for comment during October. The station continues to run smoothly.

Despite adverse weather conditions on many days. Training has progressed very

from one type of aircraft to another will probably involve a slight drop in training output during December but an extra effort from both training staff and maintenance personnel will compensate for this during the first month of all-Lancaster training in January.

Flying hours for November amounted to 732 hrs 35 mins day flying, 749hrs 05 mins, night flying and 10hrs 40 mins for the pool Oxford, Total 1492 hrs 20 mins.

The total strength of the station amounted to: RAF1580, RCAF 24, RNZAF 6, RAAF 23, Rhodesian 1, USA 1, and South African 1.

2nd December

No.107 Course (six crews with ten Flight Engineers) arrived at Winthorpe to commence conversion training.

Stirling III LK462 collided with Stirling III LK429 whilst taxiing. LK462 rendered Cat. Ac LK429 Cat. A.

LK462 was taxiing in slight rain when it swung to avoid a lorry seen at the last moment and hit the other aircraft.

3rd December

Stirling III BK818 rendered Cat. Ac following collapse of tail wheel subsequent to landing and running into overshoot area.

At 0045 Stirling BK818 landed on the short runway on three engines after trouble in the port outer due to displacement of a blanking plate on the air cooler. Further trouble was suspected so the pilot F/O H. R. Andrews taxied into the uneven overshoot area to clear an aircraft following him in and the tail wheel collapsed, the seven crew were uninjured. Repairs were carried out on site by No.58 MU and the aircraft returned to No.1661 HCU on 19th February 1945.

4th December

Seven crews of No.100 Course passed out to No.5 LFS on completion of conversion course.

Stirling III EF186 Cat. E (burnt) following crash through causes unknown.

On a night training exercise to practice recovery from unusual flight attitudes and after entering cumulonimbus cloud the aircraft crashed out of control at Breeders Hill near Grantham, Lincs, at 0140 with the loss of all nine crew members. The crew were F/O G. R. Campbell RAAF Staff Pilot (Instructor), F/Sgt. D. J. Standring Pilot, Sgts. L. G. Diggins Flight Engineer, E. W, Heaton Navigator, A. L. Terry Air Bomber, A. Winn Wireless Operator/Air Gunner, B. Stowe Rear Gunner, K.C. Glinz RCAF Mid-upper Gunner and W. L. Howarth Flight Engineer.

The crew and aircraft GP-V are remembered as part of the RAF Winthorpe/No.1661 HCU Memorial. Nine weeping cherry trees are planted around the memorial to commemorate each of the nine aircrew with each tree marked with the name of an individual aircrew member.

7th December

Stirling III LJ527 landed safely (at Glatton, Hunts) following icing of controls at 5,000 feet. Two members of crew baled out, one landing safely, one killed in descent.

Sgt. C. A. Cuany (Bomb Aimer) was admitted to Ely Hospital where he died on the 9th December from injuries received.

8th December

Course No.108 (six crews with one Flight Engineer) arrived at Winthorpe for conversion training.

9th December

Stirling III EF208 rendered Cat. E after force landing (at Wiggenhall St. Peter) following inability to maintain height on three engines. No casualties.

10th December

Eight crews of No.101 Course passed out to No.5 LFS on completion of training.

Air Commodore E. I. Bussell and W/Cdr. E. F. Wilde, both from No.75 Base visited the station during the afternoon and inspected the Technical Site.

11th December

Inputs of Courses temporarily suspended until the end of month during change-over period from Stirling aircraft to Lancasters.

18th December

Seven crews of No.102 Course passed out to No.5 LFS on completion of training together with two crews of No.103 Course and one crew of No.98 Course.

25th December

Christmas day was celebrated in the traditional manner. Dense fog prevented any flying during the day or night and a skeleton staff maintained the services for the station. Dinner was served to the airmen and airwomen by Officers and Senior NCOs in the Airmens Dining Hall whilst music was provided by the Station Dance Band.

The Station Commander spoke briefly at the conclusion of dinner, thanking all ranks for their efforts during the past year and calling for unslackened efforts in the year to come. Weather conditions prevented the usual football match in the afternoon, but an All-Ranks Dance in the evening was pronounced a great success, and a

AIRMEN'S MESS
R.A.F. STATION, WINTHORPE

Christmas Dinner

MONDAY, 25th DECEMBER 1944

MENU

SOUP
CREAM OF TOMATO

—

ROAST
ROAST TURKEY   ROAST PORK   YORK HAM
FORCEMEAT STUFFING   APPLE SAUCE   GRAVY
CHIPOLATA SAUSAGES   BREAD SAUCE
ROAST POTATOES   CREAMED POTATOES
BRUSSELS SPROUTS   GREEN PEAS

SWEET
CHRISTMAS PUDDING   MINCE PIES
CUSTARD SAUCE

—

SAVOURY
CHEESE AND BISCUITS

—

DESSERT
ORANGES   APPLES   NUTS   DATES

BEER   LEMONADE   CIGARETTES

Christmas Dinner Menu - NAM archives/Bill Taylor

fitting conclusion to the day's activities.

The station Orderly Officer for the day was Canadian James (Sandy) Sands whose story is told in the next chapter.

31st December

The departure of the old year was celebrated with a Station Dance.

Training has been considerably handicapped by weather conditions, aircraft being grounded by fog for days on end. The standard of crews passed out, however, continues to maintain a high standard. Lancaster aircraft are still arriving at Swinderby as part of the change over from Stirlings to Lancasters and the training syllabus for the new type has been received and is being closely studied by all Instructors.

We shall go forward into the New Year with the same spirit that had marked our work in 1944 and in the high hope that 1945 will see our efforts rewarded by final victory.

Monthly flying hours: Day 507 hrs 25 mins, Night 405 hrs 5 mins.

CHAPTER ELEVEN

James Sands RCAF

The following includes extracts from the books Footprints in the Sands of Time and Airborne Radar 1944/1945 Heavy Conversion Units 1661 & 1668 and additional anecdotes by James and are used with his permission.

James 'Jim' or 'Sandy' Sands (right) joined the RCAF in July 1942. After being first rejected for being colour blind he was accepted after retesting. His records showed he weighed 108lbs (7stone 10lbs) and *'Should gain weight after a period of time in the Air Force'*; he gained 3lbs in 3 ½ years - and with wartime rationing!

Basic training was in Toronto, Ontario followed by technical training with the rank of AC2 at the University of Toronto whilst living in university accommodation. Following this he was transferred to the Radar School at Clinton, Ontario where *'... we were introduced to the new development and top secrets of RADAR. We were all sworn to secrecy and every one of us had been investigated by the RCMP before we arrived'*. This came with advancement to LAC.

James Sands

On completion of training Jim was commissioned (one of six on his course) and on the Officers course learnt how to destroy the equipment to prevent its capture. He was given a uniform allowance of C$150 of which he spent C$8.50 on his hat.

He was posted to the US Naval base, Corpus Christi, Texas for two months in July and August 1943 where he trained on the American equipment in preparation for a possible Far East posting; he was back at Clinton for September and October setting up training courses on American transponders. Then to Nassau, Bahamas for November and December awaiting an aircraft to go to India or Burma flying the South Atlantic Ferry route (which actually ended in Cairo, Egypt after crossing sub-Saharan Africa), he spent some of this time flying with OTU training flights on Liberators which used a Radar called 'George' which Jim had trained on in Texas. All set to fly out between Xmas & New Year a telegram arrived to say I was to now go to Britain. Busy time eh - Jim (Sandy).

On New Year's Eve 1943 Jim began the journey back to Canada and following embarkation leave at home in Peterborough, Ontario he went on to Moncton, New Brunswick to await a ship to the UK. With no ship ready Jim applied for leave to marry and was given 7 days. His bride to be said there was not enough time for a wedding but when he arrived home he found he had been granted an extra 7 days. He married Evelyn and they celebrated their 70th anniversary early in 2014.

On the 28th January, Jim had arrived in the UK and was at Bournemouth (No.3 Personnel Receiving Centre RCAF Bournemouth) awaiting his posting.

P/O James Sands RCAF was posted to Winthorpe as the Station Radar Officer (Radar Technical Officer).

I was met at the Newark train station by a young WAAF in a truck who took me to the airfield where I signed in as the first Radar Officer to be at Winthorpe. I was now billeted in one quarter of a Nissen hut. The first thing to do now was to go to the Radar

James Sands

Section and see what I was in for. This was my first command position. Up to my arrival the section was in the charge of a Canadian Sergeant named Dave Galbraith.

I had a great staff (pictured left are some of the Radar Mechanics with James Sands at Winthorpe, Dave Galbraith is on the right in the second row), this included RAF, RCAF and one South African and the later addition of two WAAFs.

The following are tales of Jim's life at Winthorpe:

It's all in how you Word It!

There comes a time when a young Technical Officer is faced with his first time laying a charge against one of the men under his command. My time arrived after a couple of months at RAF Winthorpe. Every so often it was necessary to return some Radar equipment to the Morton Stores and to pick up replacements. One of my best corporals, a young Yorkshireman named Alex Ainley, accompanied me to exchange some equipment at Morton Hall, HQ No.5 Group.

We returned to Winthorpe where Alex was scheduled to finish his night duty. He had the next day off and was to spend it at his home on the outskirts of Newark. The next day I received a phone call from Group Headquarters asking me if we had been to Morton Hall the previous day. My answer was, of course, yes. They then advised me that a box of green spot Radar crystals was missing. I was told to take immediate action and look into the matter. I drove to Alex's home and asked him if he knew anything about the missing crystals and he said, "Yes Sir. I picked up a box and put them into our stores." We were having some problems getting these parts and when Alex saw all the boxes at Morton, he felt they wouldn't miss one and we really needed them at Winthorpe.

In actual fact, he had picked the only box of Green spot crystals that had been set aside for No.617 Squadron! Group was notified and we flew them to their proper destination.

Now came the matter of laying the charge. How do you word it so you do minimal damage to Alex? If you say he stole them then it would be a court martial offense. I really was in a spot!

Fortunately, the Motor Transport pool was located next to my Radar shack. The officer in charge was a new Pilot Officer named Walter Star who had been in the RAF for a number of years and knew the ropes. I explained my problem to Walter and in a matter of minutes he pulled out a charge form and filled in the following.

'Corporal A. Ainley, while on active duty, did use improper stores procedure in transferring 50 Green spot crystals from Morton Hall stores to RAF Winthorpe stores.' I told Walter he was a genius, thanked him and signed the form. Alex would appear before the Chief Technical Officer, W/Cdr. Hazel, for his hearing and his punishment, whatever that may be. I went to see the Wing Commander and explained what had happened and I asked him if he could make the sentence as light as possible. He smiled and said he would see what he could do.

Shortly after, the SP's arrived and marched Alex off to meet his Waterloo. Sgt. David Galbraith, another RCAF member of my group, sat across from me as we waited for the return of Alex. It was not long before we looked up and saw Alex standing at my office door with a wide grin on his face. I asked him what happened. Alex replied, "Well Sir, he said naughty, naughty!" As Alex was saying this he was slapping his wrist. Dave and I had a really good laugh and Alex went back to work out on the flights.

That evening at the Officers Mess I thanked the Wing Commander for the way he handled the matter. The W/C was a very fine gentleman and I liked and respected him a great deal.

Before I was transferred from RAF Winthorpe to RAF Bottesford, I signed the application forms recommending Cpl. Ainley and Cpl. Brown for Officers Training. A short time after being at Bottesford both Corporals came to see me to tell me that they had been accepted and were leaving for their course.

Orderly Officer Duty can be fun

Part of the daily routine of an Orderly Officer was to visit the Airman's Mess along with the Orderly Sgt.; the sergeant would stand beside me and call out in a loud voice, 'Any complaints?' I could never recall anyone having a complaint.

One day I thought we could change the routine and call in on the WAAF Mess as well as the Airman's Mess. I was reminded by the Sgt. that it was usual for the WAAF Officers to do the check in the WAAF Mess. However, we decided that it would be fun for a change and we headed to their mess.

Upon arrival, the Sgt. gave the clarion call, 'Any complaints?' It was expected that, as usual, nothing would happen. However, knowing a good moment when she saw one, a cute young WAAF with a gleam in her eye decided she would test me. She stood up and said 'Yes, I have a complaint.' I asked her what her problem was and she replied, 'The sweet's too sweet'. All eyes were now on the Sgt. and myself and I knew I had to take some action.

Their Mess Sgt. was nearby and I called her over and asked her if by any chance she would have a grapefruit. Strangely enough she did and I asked her to cut one in half and give it to the young lady as is, with no sugar. I stood there as she gamely ate it and it was very difficult not to laugh at her facial expressions. Later the same day I visited the Signals Section where she worked and she told me what a rotten trick I had pulled on her. However, she was a good sport and it was the topic of conversation for a day or two.

Winthorpe, as I'm sure did all stations, had wonderful WAAF's.

Christmas 1944

I was asked to be the Orderly Officer over the Christmas time period as, being Canadian, my family was 3,000 miles away and I would not be going home for the holiday. During Christmas 1944, England received a heavy snowfall that left us grounded for a short while.

We had a special Christmas dinner in the Officer's Mess, which was attended by all the officers on the station as well as many of the wives of the senior officers. As there were no missions being flown due to the snow, one of our gunnery officers, Scotty, had "hoisted a few" before dinner and arrived at the door to the mess with a bottle under each arm. I finally convinced him that the bottles would have to remain outside and I had him sit beside me so I could keep an eye on him.

The dinner went very well until it came time for the toast to the King (and just about anyone else that came to mind). Scotty decided he would like to toast our Station Commander. We all waited with baited breath as Scotty extolled the virtues of the Group Captain. Finally, we all stood and raised our glasses as he said, "To Group Captain..." - he could not remember his name.

In desperation he leaned down to me an in a deafening whisper said, "What's the old bastard's name?" There was dead silence as I told him it was G/Cpt. Woodin, and we all toasted our C.O.

I apologized to the C.O. after the dinner, but in his usual way he told me not to worry and in fact, it had provided the best laugh of the evening.

Appreciation for a Station Commander

I made many friends at Winthorpe. Shortly before I arrived at RAF Winthorpe as the new Radar Tech Officer, Group Captain Jack Woodin had also arrived to take on his posting as the new station commander. At that time, radar was a top secret system and not familiar to those who didn't work with this new technology. Upon my first meeting with the CO. he told me that I could work more or less on my own, without interference from him. He was indeed true to his word and I had great admiration for his support.

Jim also became the Canadian Liaison Officer for all the RCAF personnel at Winthorpe and would handle any complaints they had with the RAF.

Radar as you know was wrapped in secret and now the story can be told. (James Sands March 2013).

During his time at Winthorpe Jim created a number of sketches showing the details of the Radar Equipment and illustrating how it was used. His booklet based on these sketches, with detailed explanations of the equipment and its use covers Airborne Night fighter gear, Gee navigation, H2S navigation and bombing gear, Fishpond and the American Loran system.

The Gee system was based on transmissions from strategically based ground stations which provided navigators with extremely accurate fixes, they loved Gee because even with solid cloud cover when coming home from a raid it would get you to your home base and with the coordinates set when the blips lined up you were there.

The earlier Gee radar had a limited range because of its high frequency and was basically limited to British soil. Loran operated at 1.9 MHz and was well able to cover enemy territory; the operating distance from each ground station pair was 500 nautical miles using ground wave charts and 1,200 nautical miles using sky wave charts. However Loran was not as convenient to use as Gee.

Loran was an American development, of the Gee radio navigation system. While Gee had a range of about 400 miles (644km), initial Loran systems had a range of 1,200 miles (1,930km). Loran systems were developed at the Massachusetts Institute of Technology (MIT) Radiation Laboratory.

A special radar training section was created at Winthorpe to train navigators and technicians on the use of the Loran system in No.5 Group and was set up by Jim.

H2S was the first airborne, ground scanning radar system. It was developed during World War II and was used by Bomber Command aircraft from 1943 through to the 1990s. It was designed to identify targets on the ground for night and all-weather bombing.

Jim wrote of this sketch: *The Scanner shown should have been drawn in the upside down view. The scanner hung down inside of a large blister under the belly. The Radar mechanics soon found out that they could warm their hands on a cold day by holding them in front of the wave guide and the RF energy would warm them. We did not realize it at the time but it worked like our modern day microwave ovens.*

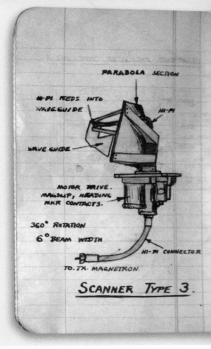

James Sands

Fishpond, a side benefit of the H2S radar, was set up at the Wireless Operators position and allowed radar coverage directly under the aircraft – a favourite attack position by the German night fighters; with a range of 30 miles (48.2km) it gave the crew warning and allowed the aircraft to elude the fighter.

The following photographs were all taken by or on behalf of Jim whilst at Winthorpe:

With Signals Officer Bert Cooper – James Sands

With F/Lt. Tom Smart DFC (a Scotsman) the head of Flying Training Section – James Sands

F/Lt. Harry Darnton DFC (another Scot) navigation section – James Sands

This is the only known photograph of a Stirling aircraft landing at Winthorpe taken by Jim – James Sands

One day I was informed that I was being moved to RAF Station Bottesford (No.1668 HCU). When I asked why I was told that they were having problems with the Canadian Radar Officer. The men under him were complaining and they moved him out and I was moving in. I wasn't too happy about it but you go where they want you.

I would have been sent to the Far East but the A bomb changed the set up and I headed home to my wife and discharge in Ottawa in early December 1945.

CHAPTER TWELVE

James Brown Warwick DFC

James Brown Warwick was born on the 10th October 1921 in Belfast, N. Ireland and attended the City's Boys Model School.

On leaving school he joined the Civil Service in Belfast and was employed at the Air Ministry in 1938.

He enlisted in the RAF in August 1941 and was sent to Canada and then to Miami, Florida, USA and trained as a navigator under the British Commonwealth Air Training Plan.

After completing his training he was posted, in April 1943, to No.49 Squadron flying Lancasters based at RAF Fiskerton and briefly at Dunholme Lodge, Lincolnshire where he and his fellow crew members, piloted by P/O Reginald Hales RCAF (who went on to No.1654 HCU Wigsley as an instructor), completed a tour of 27 operations including missions to the Ruhr, Hamburg, Peenemunde and Berlin, with the Squadron. He was

1393272 James Brown Warwick DFC RAFVR
– bomberhistory.co.uk

commissioned in August 1943 and also awarded the DFC (Gazetted in February 1944).

In January 1944 he was posted to No.1485 Bombing and Gunnery Flight at RAF Syerston and then almost immediately to No.1661 Heavy Conversion Unit at Winthorpe in February 1944 where he helped establish the radar navigation

No.49 Squadron Ops board for 18/19 November 1943, target Berlin. Hales is 5th down in C Charlie – bomberhistory.co.uk section (right - F/Lt. J. B. 'Paddy' Warwick DFC Radar/Nav Instructor outside his 'office'), then on the 25th August 1944 he was promoted to Squadron Leader and posted to be the Station Navigation Officer (screened off operational duties or a non-flying posting) at No.54 Base, RAF Coningsby where he and his girlfriend were planning to get engaged.

S/Ldr. Jim 'Paddy' Warwick was killed on 19th September 1944 flying as the Navigator with W/Cdr. Guy Gibson in a Mosquito XX, KB267 AZ-E, of No.627 Squadron on a raid to Rheydt, near Mönchengladbach, Germany.

No.627 Squadron had originally formed as part of the Light Night Striking Force in No.8 Group at Oakington in November 1943 and was 'loaned' to No.5 Group in April 1944 and based at Woodhall Spa as a Pathfinder marker Squadron using techniques previously developed by W/Cdr. Leonard Cheshire and No.617 Squadron.

James Warwick – James Sands/Bill Taylor

Gibson had asked Jim Warwick if he would be his navigator for just this one trip. On Wednesday the 20th September, the world learned the news that the famous 'Dambuster' leader, Guy Gibson, was missing from air operations.

Days later it was confirmed that he and Jim 'Paddy' Warwick were dead. Their Mosquito had crashed on Walcheren in Holland after the Rheydt raid on the night of the 19th.

Grave site – NAM archives

S/Ldr. Warwick DFC and W/Cdr. Gibson VC DSO DFC rest together in Steenbergen-en-Kruisland Cemetery, Noord-Brabant Holland.

CHAPTER THIRTEEN

From the ORB's - 1945

N.B.: Text in italics is additional / explanatory notes and information.

1st January

Fog persisting throughout the day. Surface wind light SW.

3rd January

Eight crews of No.103 Course passed out to No.5 LFS on completion of training.

5th January

Eight crews, comprising No.1 Lancaster Course arrived from RAF Balderton for Conversion training.

10th January

Five crews of No.104 Course passed out to No.5 LFS on completion of training.

12th January

Eight crews comprising No.2 Lancaster Course arrived from RAF Balderton for training.

14th January

At 1100, a telephone message was received that Stirling EH688 had crashed at Annesley Park, Nr. Mansfield. Station Medical Officer and ambulance proceeded to the scene of the crash. The entire crew were killed instantly.

The aircraft was being ferried to Northern Ireland for disposal and was only crewed by five personnel; S/Ldr. S. L. Cockbain DFC Pilot, F/Sgts. E. C. Barton Navigator and T. A. Balls Flight Engineer, Sgts. J. Littlemore trainee Wireless Operator and K. Harris Air Gunner. Early in the flight the aircraft suffered a loss of power from at first one then two engines, the pilot attempted to reach Hucknall airfield but continued to lose height and crashed out of control after starboard engine fire.

At 2330 Station Medical Officer and ambulance proceeded to scene of crash at Barnby Village (Barnby-in-the-Willows), Lincolnshire. Of the seven of the crew, five were killed instantly, the rear A/G suffered from shock and abrasions of scalp and was treated at SSQ Winthorpe. The pilot (F/Sgt. Holditch) RAF Wigsley received very extensive injuries, following treatment at SSQ Winthorpe his condition improved and at 0430 15th January transferred to RAF Hospital, Rauceby.

Stirling EF204 from No.1654 HCU RAF Wigsley had been on a 'Bullseye' exercise when it flew into the ground whilst descending in low cloud and poor visibility.

19th January

Eight crews comprising No.3 Lancaster Course arrived from RAF Balderton for training.

One Officer and two Airwomen were admitted to SSQ suffering from shock and slight injuries received in a transport accident on the Fosse Way.

21st January

Six crews of No.105 Course passed out to No.5 LFS on completion of training.

27th January

The RAF Gang Show visited the Station. The Base Commander and Mrs. E. I. Bussell attended the performance which was of the usual high standard.

29th January

Following a breakdown in the Newark Corporation reservoir, insufficient pressure was delivered to pump up water to the high level tanks in the camp. Emergency measures were taken to obtain supplies for essential services, water being drawn from RAF Stations Swinderby and Wigsley.

30th January

The water shortage remains acute but emergency services still operate satisfactorily.

31st January

No improvement in the shortage of water. Every effort is still being made to restore the reservoir to full power, but in the meantime only essential services can be maintained, and this only by drawing from other stations to supplement the meagre supplies filtering through. Strict rationing for domestic purposes continues.

On the instructions of the Base Commander, this unit has been selected to carry out, over a period of three months, an investigation into mean of improving bombing technique. This has been taken up enthusiastically by all members of the staff and a Bombing Officer has been appointed in each Flight to co-ordinate bombing methods both in the air and on the ground. With the co-operation of the Flying Staff and the Station Armament and Electrical Officers it is hoped that this investigation will produce constructive results.

Inclement weather has again hindered the flying programme.

Flying times: Day 477 hrs 40 mins, Night 175 hrs 30 mins, Total 653 hrs 10 mins.

1st February

Breakdown in Newark Corporation reservoir repaired and normal supplies of water reached this camp during the latter part of the afternoon.

Squadron Officer W. Edrich, of No.7 Group paid a visit to the station and carried out an inspection of the WAAF site.

4th February

The last Stirling crew passed out from HCU to No.5 LFS on completion of training. In future, crews completing training will pass out direct to their Squadrons and, towards the end of the month, the last Stirling/Lancaster training crew will pass out leaving the Conversion Unit completely given over to Lancaster training.

5th February

One crew passed out to No.218 Squadron.

Lancaster I PB865 flying on a cross country exercise converged on a Flying Fortress and damaged port outer propeller blades. Aircraft Cat. A. The pilot, F/O A. G. Edgar to be charged at General Court Martial with dangerous flying.

12th February

One crew passed out to No.195 Squadron, two to No.218 Squadron and one to No.44 Squadron.

13th February

One crew passed out to No.195 Squadron.

14th February

One crew passed out to No.622 Squadron and one to No.90 Squadron.

16th February

Twelve crews (ten from ACS Balderton and two from ACS Dalton) arrived at Winthorpe to commence training as Course No.7c.

The No.7 Group Aircrew School strength was listed at the end of February as 508 RAF and 21 WAAF.

One crew passed out to No.44 Squadron.

17th February

The American high intensity lighting has now been in operation for two months and a report has been submitted to higher authority.

The report stated – 'Although the system has advantages over Mark II Drem the report recommends that the instillation should not be installed permanently at a training unit, damage to the fittings is much more likely to occur ... they are expensive items and difficult to replace'.

20th February

One crew passed out to No.186 Squadron.

21st February

Lancaster III ND862 swung off runway on landing at Swinderby. Cat. Ac.

22nd February

One crew passed out to No.90 Squadron and one to No.248 Squadron.

23rd February

One crew passed out to No.463 Squadron and one to No.166 Squadron.

24th February

One crew passed out to No.149 Squadron.

26th February

Two crews passed out to No.44 Squadron and one to No.622 Squadron.

27th February

One crew passed out to No.44 Squadron, one to No.106 Squadron, two crews to No.90 Squadron and two crews to No.550 Squadron.

28th February

Two crews passed out to No.90 Squadron, one to No.106 Squadron and one to No.195 Squadron.

Flying times: Lancaster Day 929 hrs 55 mins, Lancaster Night 860 hrs 50 mins, Oxford 1 hr 25 mins, Fighter types 86 hrs 35 mins, Total 1878 hrs 45 mins.

The Medical Officer reported that the period of inclement weather during the first week of February placed a severe strain on the sanitary arrangements and water supply. Emergency Elsan's were put into use for a short period. The water supply was restricted for several days owing to havoc caused by frost.

2nd March

Ten crews, comprising No.9c Course arrived at Winthorpe for training.

3rd March

The crash ambulance and Medical Officer were called to the scene of an aircraft accident at Stapleford Village. The remains of three charred bodies were recovered from the wreckage and identification established. This aircraft belonged to No.1654 HCU Wigsley and was shot down by an enemy aircraft.

This aircraft was Lancaster LM748 with the loss of all crew.

In 'Unternehmen (Operation) Gisela', some 200 Junkers JU.88 night fighters of the Luftwaffe Nachtjagdeschwafer Gruppen (Night Fighter destroyer Group) had been deployed to intercept the allied bombers returning to base at their most vulnerable point, just before landing. The marauding aircraft crossed the North Sea at points stretching between the Thames Estuary and up the east coast to the North Yorkshire Moors. The fact these intruders were able to cross the North Sea coast without being picked up by English radar operators would seem to have been a result of a degree of complacency that had set in amongst Bomber Command, as the Luftwaffe appeared to be subdued.

The Bomber Command mission scheduled for that evening was a dual attack on the synthetic oil producing plant at Kamen and a raid on the Dortmund-Ems canal. 234 aircraft from No.4 & 6 Groups took on the first mission, with 222 bombers from No.5 Group tackling the canal, departing at around 10.00pm on the 3rd. The mission ran smoothly, until the return, when they ran into trouble in the form of 'Operation Gisela'. On this clear night, some of the early returning aircraft had inexplicably switched on their navigation lights much earlier than usual, despite warnings of the dangers of possible predators, which was copied by those following. This gave the circling intruders a clear, enticing target.

The attack lasted just two and a half hours, and during that time 13 Halifaxes, 9 Lancasters, one Fortress and a Mosquito had been shot down. Whilst over England, the Germans had strafed anything that moved on the ground; as a result 17 civilians had been killed and 12 seriously wounded. The night had served as a timely reminder that the enemy was still a capable and deadly opponent.

7th March

One crew passed out to No.467 Squadron on completion of training.

8th March

One crew posted out to No.44 Squadron, two crews to No.103 Squadron, two crews to No.218 Squadron and one to No.115 Squadron on completion of training.

9th March

One crew posted to No.514 Squadron, one to No.103 Squadron, one to No.44 Squadron and one to No.195 Squadron on completion of training.

F/O A. G. Edgar was found not guilty at his court-martial on the charge of damaging one of His Majesty's aircraft on February 5th.

10th March

Twelve crews, comprising No.10c Course arrived at Winthorpe for training. One crew posted to No.227 Squadron and one to No.153 Squadron on completion of training.

12th March

One crew posted to No.106 Squadron, one to No.153 Squadron and one to No.625 Squadron on completion of training.

13th March

One crew posted to No.630 Squadron on completion of training.

14th March

One crew posted to No.101 Squadron on completion of training.

16th March

One crew posted to No.103 Squadron and one to No.227 Squadron on completion of training.

19th March

One crew posted to No.12 Squadron and one to No.57 Squadron on completion of training.

Air Vice Marshal E. B. A. Rice CB CBE MC (AOC No.7 Group) visited the Station and inspected the Training and Technical Sections.

20th March

Instructions received from Air Ministry Z. A. that the American high intensity lighting on the station was to be dismantled. Superintendant Engineer, No.5 Works Area contacted to make the necessary arrangements.

21st March

One crew posted to No.431 Squadron and one to No.227 Squadron on completion of training.

22nd March

Eleven crews, comprising No.12c Course arrived at Winthorpe for conversion training. One crew posted to No.419 Squadron on completion of training.

No.4794 A. C. Flight attached to Winthorpe to carry out works services on the station.

23rd March

Seven crews, comprising No.13c Course arrived at Winthorpe for conversion training. Twenty-two Flight Engineers arrived at Winthorpe for crewing up.

No.5 Air Crew School closed down and all U/T crews proceeded to HCU's. From 30th March, crews for HCU Training were to proceed direct from OTU to HCU's but still remained on the posting strength of No.57 Base.

The Balderton ORB on the 15th March '... No.5 Aircrew School is no longer required for the reception of aircrews awaiting Heavy Conversion Unit training... it has been decided to disband this unit w.e.f. from 23rd March 1945 ...'

24th March

One crew posted to No.460 Squadron on completion of training.

Lancaster I HK738 crashed near Langford, Notts. Following failure of flaps to retract when carrying out a three engine overshoot. Cat. E. No casualties.

At 2020 the Lancaster crashed about one mile from the airfield. The fuselage broke in half just forward of the mid-upper turret and the aircraft caught fire. Eight members of the crew escaped without injury and helped to release the rear gunner, Sgt. P. McArdle who was trapped in his turret and admitted to SSQ suffering from minor injuries.
The C-in-C Bomber Command, Sir Arthur T. (Bomber) Harris commended the crew and highly commended the pilot instructor F/O Lett who having taken over control of the aircraft belly landed in a field short of a row of houses.

26th March

One crew posted to No.186 Squadron, one to No.12 Squadron, one to No.101 Squadron, one to No.207 Squadron, one to No.463 Squadron and one to No.150 Squadron on completion of training.

27th March

One crew posted to No.625 Squadron on completion of training.

28th March

One crew posted to No.107 Squadron on completion of training.

29th March

One crew posted to No.50 Squadron on completion of training.

30th March

Nine crews, comprising No.14c Course arrived at Winthorpe for conversion training. One Staff Pilot and crew joined Course. One crew posted to No.189 Squadron and one to No.431 Squadron on completion of training.

31st March

The month of March completed the re-equipping of Nos.1661, 1654 and 1660 HCU's with Lancaster aircraft.

One crew posted to No.101 Squadron, one to No.103 Squadron, one to No.419 Squadron, one to No.467 Squadron, one to No.630 Squadron, one to No.150 Squadron and one to No.166 Squadron on completion of training.

March proved another exemplary good month for flying, the full commitment being met and passed. The standard of crews passed out remained at a high level. Crews now reported to the unit direct from their OTU and on completion of their training, proceeded direct to the Squadrons. Some minor snags resulted from this change in policy but were satisfactorily met.

A special drive to improve the bombing technique being carried out by the unit is producing good results.

Maintenance was kept at a very high level and the aircraft accident rate continues to decline. During the month of March there were fewer minor accidents than the previous month.

Flying Times: Day 1173 hrs 55 mins, Night 981 hrs 40 mins, Oxford 9hrs 45 mins, Fighter types 118 hrs 30 mins Total 2283 hrs 50 mins.

5th April

12 crews, (No.15 Course) arrived at Winthorpe for conversion training.

6th April

Two crews posted out to No.170 Squadron on completion of conversion training.

8th April

Lancaster PB758 on landing after dual circuits and landings overshot, the pilot swung the aircraft to avoid a totem pole and ran into a four feet deep ditch and the port undercarriage was torn off. The aircraft had been landed at excessive speed.

9th April

One crew posted to No.463 Squadron, two crews to No.460 Squadron, one to No.626 Squadron and one to No.424 Squadron on completion of training.

11th April

One crew posted to No.626 Squadron on completion of training.

12th April

11 crews, (No.16 Course) arrived from OTU together with one crew made up from Staff Instructors to enter conversion training. Two crews posted to No.75 Squadron and one to No.433 Squadron on completion of training.

13th April

One crew posted to No.467 Squadron on completion of training.

15th April

One crew posted to No.50 Squadron on completion of training.

Lancaster III PB213 crashed at Oxton, Nr. Southwell Notts at 0025 hrs. Three members of the crew were killed and a fourth died later in hospital.

At 0025 a 15 year old boy, Derek Fearn, of Private Road, Southwell, was walking home from a dance at Oxton, when he was struck by debris from a crashing bomber at the top of Oxton Hill. He ran to a nearby farmhouse for help, and Dr. Snell, of Southwell, was soon on the scene, followed by Inspector Arnold and PC Schofield of Southwell and PC Stirland from Oxton. The aircraft was approaching Epperstone bombing range from the north. Flying very low, it struck the brow of the hill just east of Hill Farm, at the top of Oxton Hill on the Southwell Road. The Lancaster skidded some distance across a field before coming to rest with its fuselage broken in two, the front part catching fire and burning out. Four members of the crew were injured, Sgt. G. A. Martin the Flight Engineer died on the 28th April in Nottingham General hospital.

16th April

One crew posted to No.33 Base on completion of training.

17th April

Two crews posted out to No.630 Squadron, one to No.428 Squadron, one to No.460 Squadron, one to No.49 Squadron and one to No.429 Squadron on completion of training.

18th April

One crew posted to No.427 Squadron, one to No.207 Squadron and one to No.50 Squadron on completion of training.

19th April

One crew posted to No.630 Squadron on completion of training.

20th April

Ten crews, (No.17 Course) arrived at Winthorpe for conversion training together with two crews made up from Staff Instructors

The station ambulance and Medical Officer were called out at 1650 to an aircraft crash at Claypole involving Lancaster HK598 from No.1660 HCU Swinderby. Control of the aircraft was lost whilst flying on two engines; three of the crew were killed and four suffered injuries.

21st April

One crew posted to No.75 Squadron and one to No.15 Squadron on completion of training.

22nd April

Two crews posted out to No.431 Squadron and one to No.61 Squadron on completion of training.

In order to assist personnel in answering their queries and solving their many problems, a Committee on Release and Resettlement Advice has been set up. This Committee will endeavour to answer all questions relating to release from the service and resettlement in civilian life, together with any E. V. T. Problems which may be raised. It is hoped that personnel will take full advantage of this service and will feel that they can bring their queries to the Committee for solution.

23rd April

One crew posted to No.75 Squadron and one to No.57 Squadron on completion of training.

24th April

One crew posted to No.49 Squadron and one to No.433 Squadron on completion of training.

The Principal Medical Officer, Bomber Command, Air Vice Marshal Cawton visited the Station.

25th April

Two crews posted out to No.630 Squadron on completion of conversion training.

27th April

Ten crews, (No.18 Course) arrived from OTU and one crew of Staff Instructors arrived at Winthorpe for conversion training.

28th April

One crew posted out to No.106 Squadron on completion of training. One crew posted to No.431 Squadron.

29th April

Eleven Pilot/F/Engs and Flight Engineers arrived at Winthorpe from No.4 S. Of T. T. One crew posted out to No.227 Squadron on completion of training.

30th April

One crew posted to No.227 Squadron, one to No.419 Squadron and one to No.9 Squadron on completion of training.

Flying hours: Day 1161 hrs 5 mins, Night 906 hrs 40 mins, Pool flying 4 hrs 30 mins, Fighter types 92 hrs, Total 2164 hrs 15 mins.

2nd May

The ambulance was summoned to the scene of an accident on the airfield. Of the ten members of the crew only one F/O R. Hubbard (Staff Pilot) received minor injuries and was detained in SSQ for a short period.

The aircraft, Lancaster PB733, had been on night circuit practice and coming in to land the pilot misjudged his height and levelled off too high. The aircraft hit the runway heavily and the undercarriage collapsed.

4th May

Ten crews with eight Flight Engineers arrived at Winthorpe to form No.19c Course.

7th May

Eight crews passed out to Squadrons on completion of Conversion Training.

8th May 1945

Cloudy with moderate visibility. Slight thunderstorm in afternoon. Surface wind light and variable.

Today has been declared Victory in Europe Day. The news was received throughout the station rather with a sense of relief than of exuberance. A Station Parade was held at 1000 hours at which a short service of thanksgiving was celebrated by the Station Padre. The Station Commander addressed the station and announced that a special V-E Day 48 hour pass had been granted to all ranks. A Station Dance was held in the evening for all ranks and similar celebrations were organised in the Sergeants and Officers Messes.

12th May

Eight crews also 17 Flight Engineers arrived at Winthorpe to form No.20c Course.

17th May

Three crews passed out to Squadrons on completion of Conversion Training.

18th May

Stirling EF146 from No.1660 HCU, Swinderby was involved in a wheels up landing at Coddington. The Stirling was Struck off Charge and removed by No.58 MU.

19th May

Seven crews with one spare P/F/E arrived at Winthorpe to commence training on No.21c Course. Two crews passed out to Squadrons on completion of Conversion Training.

25th May

Six crews with two Flight Engineers arrived at Winthorpe to commence training on

No.22c Course.

S/Ldr. J. Reynolds (A. M.) visited the station for two days to deliver lectures to all personnel on the Governments Release Scheme and Resettlement Plans. These lectures were attended by a large proportion of the station and many personnel availed themselves of the opportunities of addressing personal queries to S/Ldr. Reynolds.

At 2355 the ambulance was called to the scene of a road accident. Private Kennedy of the OCTU Beckingham was admitted to SSQ suffering from concussion and laceration of the head and shoulder.

26th May

At 0005 the ambulance was summoned to the scene of an aircraft accident on the airfield. No injuries were sustained by members of the crew.

The aircraft, Lancaster PB227, swung violently to port on landing and the undercarriage collapsed.

28th May

Air Vice Marshal, E. B. A. Bryce CB CBE MC (AOC No.7 Group) visited the Station with the Base Commander (A/Cdr. E. I. Bussell) to discus training.

31st May

Eight crews arrived at Winthorpe for training on No.23c Course.

Satisfactory progress was maintained during the month although a slight fall in flying hours was noticed mainly due to poor weather and the general stand down during VE Day.

AGLT Training has proved slightly disappointing owing, mainly, to unserviceability of equipment and shortage of aircraft, but a general improvement is expected during the coming month. The drive to improve bombing technique continues and all courses are receiving intensive instruction in the need for accuracy and adhering rigidly to laid down principles.

Station Strength: RAF 1766, RCAF 26, RNZAF 8, RAAF 58, USA 1, Rhodesia 2, BWI 17.

4th June

A Lancaster aircraft crash landed near the aerodrome. No injuries sustained by any member of the crew who were treated in SSQ for shock.

Lancaster JA909 from No.467 Squadron RAAF was on a training flight from Waddington when on a 3 engined approach to Winthorpe, the pupil pilot in bumpy conditions had the aircraft on the port side of the runway, the instructor realising the error took over and opened the throttles to clear the control tower and hangar and the aircraft belly landed in a field at Langford, near Winthorpe.

7th June

Mr. Creighdon a civilian employee received a gunshot wound in the left foot whilst working on the perimeter track. He was given treatment at SSQ and transferred to Newark General Hospital.

11th June

Four crews passed out to No.50 Squadron on completion of training.

14th June

Five crews passed out to No.619 Sqn., two to No.61 Sqn. and two to No.630 Sqn. on completion of training.

15th June

Six crews arrived at Winthorpe to form No.25 Course for conversion training.

18th June

Three crews passed out to No.35 Sqn., six crews to No.156 Sqn., two to No.635 Sqn. on completion of conversion training.

21st June

Seven crews arrived at Winthorpe to form No.26 Course with 17 P/F/E awaiting crewing.

23rd June

Two crews passed out to No.115 Sqn., three to No.582 Sqn., four to No.635 Sqn. and two to No.550 Sqn. on completion of conversion training.

25th June

One crew passed out to No.115 Sqn., two to No.625 Sqn., three to No.12 Sqn. and four to No.550 Sqn. on completion of conversion training.

Celebration of the 6th Anniversary of the WAAF was held today.

Photographs of the WAAF personnel were taken before tea served in the Airmen's Mess. The Station Commander and Senior Officers of the station were present. In the evening a dance was held for all ranks in the WAAF NAAFI.

27th June

Two crews passed out to No.150 Sqn., two to No.50 Sqn., one to No.101 Sqn. and one to No.62 Sqn. on completion of conversion training.

28th June

One crew passed out to No.619 Sqn. and one to No.61 Squadron on completion of conversion training.

29th June

Seven crew arrived at Winthorpe to form Course No.27. Two crews passed out to No.61 Sqn., two to No.62 Sqn. and one to No.166 Sqn. on completion of conversion training.

30th June

Air Vice Marshal Izycki (AOC Polish Air Force) visited Newark to inspect the graves of fallen Polish Airmen and visited the Station for lunch.

This has been a month of changes and the building up of firm foundations for the commencement of Phase Two Training. New Instructors have arrived with new methods and a general re-organisation and improvement in the ground section has been carried out from which it is hoped to reap the full benefit in the coming months. Special mention should be made of the improvement in bombing method during the month, on which the station has received the congratulations of the Base Commander.

Total hours: Day 924 hrs 40 mins, Night 683 hrs, Pool 3 hrs 25 mins, Total 1611 hrs 05 mins.

Strength: RAF 1516, RCAF 13, RNZAF 1, RAAF 66 USA 1, Rhodesia 2, BWI 17.

1st July

F/lt. H. Rogers (GD) awarded AFC.

3rd July

A Lancaster aircraft crashed on the airfield on taking off. No serious damage was sustained and members of the crew were treated for shock in SSQ but none were detained.

The port tyre burst on takeoff when the aircraft, PD381, was travelling at speed, it swung to port and the port undercarriage collapsed. Fire broke out in one engine but was extinguished.

4th July

One crew passed out to No.576 Squadron on completion of training.

7th July

Two crews passed out to No.622 Squadron on completion of training.

16th July

One crew passed out to No.49 Squadron on completion of training.

17th July

Two crews passed out to No.622 Squadron on completion of training.

21st July

Station Sports Day. A full programme was carried out in reasonably good weather, marred only by occasional rain showers. The Station Challenge Cup was won by Station Headquarters with Maintenance Wing in second place and Training Wing third. Some excellent times were recorded by both station personnel and visitors. The prizes were presented at the close of the meeting by Mrs. E. B. A. Rice, wife of the Air Officer Commanding No.7 Group.

23rd July

One crew passed out to No.102 Squadron on completion of training.

24th July

Information has been received from Headquarters, Bomber Command in their BC/S.25546/Org to the effect that No.1661 Heavy Conversion Unit will be disbanded with effect from 24th August 1945. Preliminary instructions have been prepared for the disbandment of the Unit in conjunction with B.C.A.I. No.2.

In No.7 Group letter 7G/S.12159/Org. dated the 4th August, paragraph 2b states 'This airfield is very close to the town of Newark and the noise of the aircraft has been the subject of acrimonious complaint in the past. The perimeter track is poor and runways are not in first class condition. It is, therefore, recommended for transfer to Maintenance Command.'

July

Rat infestation of airmen's Mess and Station Cinema successfully blitzed. Total of 58 bodies were found.

Training on the unit is drawing to a close. No crews have arrived during the month and the last of the crews under training are now preparing for the last stages. Training is scheduled to cease here on the 10th August when the Conversion Unit will be disbanded.

Flying hours: Day 667 hrs 25 mins, Night 359 hrs 15 mins, Pool 5 hrs 5 mins, Total 1031 hrs 45 mins.

The station strength: RAF 1315, RCAF 5, RNZAF 11, RAAF 1, USA 1 and BWI 8.

August

The Meteorological Section has despatched all its records to higher authority. It is not possible therefore to include a detailed weather report in this month's form 540. Generally the weather has been fair to fine during the early part of the month, but has deteriorated towards the end with some rain and cold winds.

Flying has been restricted to the completion of a few outstanding crews at the beginning of the month, all of which were disposed of during the first ten days. Subsequently flying has been confined to the despatch of aircraft to other Units on disbandment of the Conversion Unit. All aircraft have been disposed of without incident.

The Lancasters left during August and their destinations can be seen in appendix two.

1st August

Arrangements are in hand for the closing of the Station and Conversion Unit in accordance with Bomber Command and Base instructions. It is anticipated that all Conversion Unit personnel will be posted away from the from the Unit by 24th August 1945, trainees as soon as possible after completion of training (on or about the 10th August 1945) and Base personnel by approximately 10th September 1945.

7th August

Squadron Leader Skinner visited the station to lecture on Release and Resettlement plans and was available for private interview. A large number of personnel availed themselves of the opportunity offered by his visit to clear up personal problems and obtain information.

10th August

Farewell Party held in the Officers Mess.

13th August

S/Ldr. R. O. Lane assumed command of RAF Station Winthorpe, vice Group Captain J. H. Woodin (posted).

21st August

Farewell Dance for all ranks held in Tech. Site Hangar.

28th August

Strength: RAF 768, RCAF 5, RNZAF 1, RAAF 3, Rhodesia 2, BWI 8.

The closing down of the station is proceeding as rapidly as possible. No major problems in this connection have been encountered.

During August there were no casualties resulting from aircraft accidents.

September

In the absence of Meteorological personnel on this Unit which is at present in a state of transition from Bomber to Transport commands, no detailed statement of weather conditions can be given. The weather generally during the month has been poor for the season of the year. Cold winds and rain have persisted during the first half; the latter half has been fair to moderately fine with fog in early morning.

No flying or training has been carried out during the month.

1st September

The main activity on the Station during the month has been centred around the closing down of No.1661 HCU, the date for which has now been advanced to 10th September, 1945 and the transfer of SHQ from Bomber to Transport Command. It is anticipated that this latter transfer will take place on approximately the 15th October 1945 but the exact date and function of the station under its new command are still to be notified.

The majority of Conversion Unit personnel have already been posted and most sections have now completed the return of the equipment and final closing of their sections. Remaining personnel are being accommodated on one living site to enable other sites to be cleared and handed over. Sites 5 and 6 (WAAF?) have already been evacuated and marching out inspections carried out.

10th September

No.1661 HCU is officially disbanded.

11th September

Marching out inspection of No.1 Site completed. Air Commodore E. I. Bussell (No.75 Base) visited the Station to discuss disbandment.

19th September

Ambulance and Medical Officer summoned to the scene of a lorry crash in Stapleford Woods. Mr. T. Shea, the driver, received first aid treatment having been pinned under an overturned lorry.

20th September

Marching out inspection of No.4 Site carried out. All personnel are now accommodated on No.2 Site and Officers in Coddington Hall.

WAAF personnel were accommodated at RAF Swinderby; in November 1945 the Swinderby ORB notes that 10 airwomen employed at Winthorpe are accommodated there.

G/Capt. Freeman (HQTC) visited the Station re the transfer of Winthorpe to Transport Command.

29th September

The closing down of No.1661 HCU and the transfer of the station to Transport Command has fully occupied the entire month. No major problems have been encountered. Conversion Unit personnel are now all now earmarked for posting and the majority have already left.

Station personnel are standing by pending the receipt of final instructions for the disposal of the station. It is now anticipated that the unit will be reduced to a Care and Maintenance basis to await the arrival of whatever unit of Transport Command is allocated to it.

Strength: RAF 249, BWI 4, Australian 1.

On the 20th October Winthorpe becomes a satellite of RAF Syerston in No.4 Group Transport Command.

The RAF base began in 1940 as a station with some huts alongside the A46 road. Later these original huts were vacated for accommodation on the east side of the airfield; they were reportedly occupied by Italian Prisoners of War sometime in 1944/5 although no evidence has been found to substantiate this. Many POW camps 'dispersed' personnel to work on farms in the later stages of the war and very few records were kept.

CHAPTER FOURTEEN

Stanley Bray
Experiences of a WW2 wireless operator

The following is based upon an article by Howard Heeley first published in FlyPast magazine in the April 2004 edition and used with permission.

Howard wrote *'I first met Stan Bray during the filming of a video interview for Newark Air Museum's Virtual Museum CD ROM project. Stan flew with No.1661 HCU as both a student and an instructor and during the meeting in March 2003 I was moved by the deep sense of honour and compassion that he still carried from his time in the Royal Air Force during the Second World War.'*

1232381 Stanley Bray was born in Sheffield in 1921 and joined the RAF in 1941. Having completed his basic training at Cardington, Bedfordshire and Boscombe near Bournemouth he was given the option of moving straight onto general duties or waiting to be called up for a course. Stan volunteered for general duties and actually worked on gas protection duties for a number of months.

Between August 6 1942 and August 23 1942 Stan experienced his first flying with 'Q' Flight, No.1 Anti-Aircraft Co-operation Unit [AACU] at Aberporth, on the Cardigan Bay coast in Wales where he completed 18hrs 55mins on Henleys. Whilst there Stan qualified as a target tug operator controlling targets as they were flown across the bay for the ground based anti-aircraft guns to fire at.

His next posting was to Blackpool where he completed his initial wireless training. Having attained the required speed of 10-12 words per minute, he passed out to Air Operations Section No.2 Signals School, Madley, Herefordshire where between September 2 1942 and October 6 1942 he completed 14hrs 10mins on de Havilland Dominies. Despite passing out from here as a proficient wireless operator even then he did not move onto full flying duties but was posted to Aldershot for a brief spell as a ground wireless operator.

Another flying course followed with No.1 Air Gunnery School [AGS] Pembrey, near Carmarthen between November 1 1942 and December 12 1942, where Stan logged 9hrs for the course on Blenheims. Course notes from his Observer's and Air Gunner's Flying

Sighting Instruction was given in accordance with the addendes 7 25 Group.

Time carried forward :—

| RESULTS OF AB-INITIO GUNNERY COURSE | | | | Flying Times Night |
| (including results of bombing, gunnery, exercises, etc.) | | | | |

Station held   NO. 1 A.G.S., PEMBREY
Period of Course   1·11·42 to 12·12·42

Exercise	Rounds fired	% Hits	Type of Aircraft
25 yds. range /10 " 200 " M/T.	400-540 14 280	} N.A.	V.G. of BROWNING REVOLVER BROWNING (TURRET)
GROUND No. of G. 28 films. Cine footage.	25' 25 ft.	64 N.A.	POLE MODEL. BLENHEIM
Air to Ground	250	N/A	"
Beam	200	8·5	"
Beam R.S.	200	6·5	"
Under Tail	250	4·0	"
Quarter	—	—	
AIR TRACER DEM	200	N/A	
Night	—	—	

Exam. Marks 83 %   Course Flying Time   9 Hrs. 00

REMARKS: PASS/FAIL
Finished 2nd on the Course. Has been an excellent pupil.

C.I.

12·12·42   TOTAL TIME ...

NAM archives/Howard Heeley

Log Book (left) provide an insight into the course content which included: Ground Firing, Air to Ground, Beam, Beam R.S., Under Tail, Quarter and Air Tracer. A hand written entry in the Log Book states, 'Sighting instruction was given in accordance with 25 Group standards'. Stan's exam marks were noted at 83%, with the final average number of hits to rounds fired being 6.33%. The final Course Remarks stated, 'Finished 2nd on the Course. Has been an excellent pupil.'

The top three on the course were shown the list of postings and could select their own. Stan chose Lindholme near Doncaster and was offered fourteen days leave. On the second day at home he received a telegram to report to North Luffenham immediately. As it turned out Stan viewed this as his first bit of luck, because from Lindholme he would have gone on to fly Halifaxes not Lancasters.

On January 27 1943 Stan commenced what he considered to be his 'first true flying experience' with No.29 Operational Training Unit [OTU]. Flying Wellington IIIs from Bruntingthorpe (and satellite stations Woolfox Lodge and North Luffenham), this phase of Stan's training lasted until April 9 1943. During this period Stan recorded a total Course Flying Hours of 50hrs 20mins [day] and 44hrs 55mins [night], with the following individual monthly totals:

January   3hrs [day]
February   15hrs 25mins [day]; 6hrs 25mins [night]
March   23hrs 55mins [day]; 21hrs 45mins [night]
April   8hrs [day]; 16hrs 45mins [night]

Stan fondly recalled the time at No.29 OTU as being the first real time where people started to 'Crew Up' and he considered himself very lucky to have formed the bonds that he did. Different categories of aircrew went to an OTU, pilots, navigators, wireless operators, bomb aimers and air gunners most of who had never seen each other before. Billeted next to a pilot, Neale McClelland, Stan quickly became friendly with the Australian Flight Sergeant and during crewing up Stan was asked to become his Wireless Operator. The bond having been established, Neale McClelland remained Stan's pilot for the next eleven months; also he was the best man at Stan's wedding in August 1944.

Only hours after Stan and Neale McClelland had decided to stay together, they undertook the crewing-up process, during which everyone on the Course was placed in a hangar and left to sort themselves out. First to approach Neale McClelland was a 30-year-old Navigator, Sgt. Booth, who wanted to join his crew, he was told that he would have to check with Stan first, before deciding. Stan agreed and felt that this could be considered his second lucky break, as he was a 'bloody good navigator'. Such personal consideration highlights, that already, those special bonds had started to form with someone who Stan had only known for three days. The rest of the crew were collected together to start their training.

After their OTU Course Stan and the other 4 crew members (pilot, navigator, air bomber, wireless operator and rear gunner) moved to RAF Winthorpe and commenced their next spell of flying training on Course 8 1943 with No.1661 HCU on May 11 1943. A sixth crew member, a mid-upper gunner was allocated to the crew a week before the Winthorpe posting.

Their first flight training at Winthorpe was completed on the twin-engined Manchester, and Log Book entries note Manchester Flying Hours of 8hrs 5mins [day], of which most flights consisted of circuits and landings. Before moving on to Lancasters the crew were allocated a Flight Engineer. Sgt. Martin had completed six operational sorties before falling ill; whilst his crew carried on he came back to Winthorpe for re-crewing. He fitted in well and Stan believes that his operational experience helped them with the early part of their later operational tour.

Having attained the full Lancaster crew of seven, they flew their first Lancaster sortie on May 22 1943. The initial flights were circuits and landings, flown on a duel control basis with a screen pilot instructor who had completed a tour of operations. When he was happy that the pilot was competent the crew went solo. As the Course progressed they started to do cross country

NAM archives/Howard Heeley

exercises of varying lengths, a typical flight Stan recalls was from Winthorpe to a point near Newcastle, across to Blackpool, down to Swansea and back to Winthorpe. By the end of their Course on June 12 1943 they had recorded Lancaster Flying Hours of 18hrs 50mins [day] and 18hrs 40mins [night] (see log book previous page).

Such was the intensity of the Conversion Course in little over a month they had completed total Flying Hours for their Course of 26hrs 55mins [day] and 18hrs 40mins [night].

As an Australian pilot led their crew, they were posted to 'B' Flight No.467 Squadron RAAF at Bottesford, where they flew their first Squadron training sortie on June 17 1943. Only five days later on June 22 1943 they were flying their first operational [Ops] sortie, a 4hrs 55mins night-time raid on Mulheim. The Operations Record Book for No.467 Squadron RAAF for the crew's first Op records the crew of Lancaster III ED500 as: Captain - F/Sgt. N. M. McClelland; F/Engineer – Sgt. A. W. Martin; Navigator – Sgt. W. Booth; A/Bomber – Sgt. H. Griffin; W/Operator – Sgt. S. Bray; M/U. A/G. – Sgt. S. G. W. Bethell; Rear A/G. – Sgt. K. L. Worden; they took off at 2315 hours and landed at 0411 hours and the recorded details of the Op were as follows.

"Bombing – MULHEIM – sortie completed. Scattered broken cloud, vis. moderate. Bombed red T1 from 20000 at 156½ [1 x 4000HC, 1 x 500MC 37 Mk4 pistol, 3 x 500MC, 540 x 4lb inc, 56 x 4lb]. Numerous small fires. PFF went down on time, but only reds visible in target area. Plenty of light flak but not much heavy, appeared to be barrage fire. Evasive action – diving turn to port and stbd and climbing turns. Flak hole in front of MU turret."

Left to right back row: Booth; Bethell; Worden; Martin. Front row: Griffin; McClelland; Bray. - NAM archives/Howard Heeley

Two further Ops quickly followed to Wuppertal and Gelsenkirchen on June 24 and 25 respectively. Stan explained that the reason their new crew more or less went straight onto Ops, with three sorties in five nights was in itself a little unusual at that time. This was due to some of the other Squadron crews participating in a long-range raid where they flew on into North Africa. On their return these crew then bombed the Leghorn Docks. With limited crew availability the new crews were immediately called into action. In June 1943 Stan's Log Book records 5hrs 45mins [day] and 29hrs 10mins [night], amongst this total were 4 Ops.

The Squadron moved to Waddington in November and by December 16, 1943, the crew had completed their remaining 21 sorties and first tour. These were broken down into the following monthly Flying Hours Totals.

July	5hrs 15mins [day] and 20hrs 35mins [night], this included 4 Ops
August	6hrs 20mins [day] and 35hrs 30mins [night], this included 5 Ops
September	5hrs 20mins [day] and 34hrs 45mins [night], this included 5 Ops
October	30mins [day] and 13hrs 20mins [night], this included 2 Ops
November	3hrs 55mins [day] and 25hrs [night], this included 4 Ops
December	1hr [day] and 7hrs 20mins [night], this included 1 Op

OPERATIONS RECORD BOOK

DETAIL OF WORK CARRIED OUT

By No. 467 (RAAF) Squadron

FOR THE MONTH OF December 1943

APPENDIX A

SECRET

A.F. FORM 541.

PAGE No. 7

DATE	AIRCRAFT TYPE & NUMBER	CREW	DUTY	TIME UP	TIME DOWN	DETAILS OF SORTIE OR FLIGHT	REFERENCES
16/17 Dec	Lancaster III RD.547	P/O A.B.Simpson Sgt Curl O.P. F/Sgt Manson K.W. W/O R.G.Watts F/Sgt Dyson A.W. F/Sgt Campbell O.A. Sgt Doncaster P.H.	Bombing – BERLIN.	1637	0014	Sortie completed. 10/10ths cloud. Bombed green TI from 20500 at 2002 (1 x 4000lb HC, 48 x 30lb inc., 950 x 4lb and 100 x 4lb XIB's). Results unobserved owing to cloud. PFF good. Everything O.K. except return to base very grim. Vis. poor.	
16/17 Dec	Lancaster III RD.803	P/O R.N.Stanford Sgt Juison E. F/Sgt Clarke O.K. F/Sgt Butler N.T. F/L D.A.G.Andrews Sgt Griffiths L.D. F/Sgt Aitken J.R. W/O A.Rushton. P/O A.D.McDonald (2nd Pilot)	Bombing – BERLIN.	1638	2348	Sortie completed. 10/10ths cloud (low). Bombed centre of Approx. 12 sky markers from 20000 at 2002 (1 x 4000lb HC, 48 x 30lb inc., 950 x 4lb and 100 x 4lb XIB's). Results unobserved owing to cloud, but several glows from fires could be seen which seemed to develop as aircraft left area. Broadcast winds and navigation a good idea. Route in and out good.	
16/17 Dec	Lancaster III LM.372	P/O N.K.McClelland F/Sgt Martin A.W. P/O H.Griffin P/O W.Booth F/Sgt Bray E. Sgt Bethell B.O.W. F/Sgt Norden K.L. S/L A.W.Doubleday (2nd Pilot)	Bombing – BERLIN.	1627	2345	Sortie completed. 9/10ths cloud, tops 5000 ft. Bombed centre of concentration of green TIs from 20000 at 2002½ (1 x 4000lb HC, 48 x 30lb inc., 950 x 4lb and 100 x 4lb XIB's). Green TIs well concentrated but nothing observed owing to cloud over target. Jerry continually dropping red flares and red with green stars from about 50 miles inland to BERLIN area. Lanes of fighter flares dropped by Jerry to N. of target but well to port. Defences medium over target but appeared to be foxed.	
16/17 Dec	Lancaster III RD.994	F/L D.S.Symonds Sgt Sykes E. F/Sgt Twitchett H.E. P/O R.G.Gilson F/Sgt Noble G. Sgt Sanford E.A.B. F/Sgt Manley B.M. F/Sgt O'Brien C. (2nd Pilot)	Bombing – BERLIN.	1620	2332	Sortie completed. 10/10ths cloud, tops about 10/12000 ft. Bombed glow of 3 green TIs from 21000 at 2003 (1 x 4000lb HC, 48 x 30lb inc., 950 x 4lb and 100 x 4lb XIB's). PFF TIs and flares seemed well concentrated. Results unobserved owing to cloud, but glow of fires could be seen after leaving target. Defences not up to standard except for fighter activity on DUTCH coast. This was probably due to early arrival of PFF. Broadcast winds excellent and proved invaluable to navigation.	
16/17 Dec	Lancaster I DV.277	F/Sgt Gibbs D.L. Sgt Middlemast K. F/Sgt Sugg P.A. Sgt Tong G.L. F/Sgt Green E.A. Sgt Stone J. Sgt Bird L.W.	Bombing – BERLIN.	1631	2358	Sortie completed. 10/10ths cloud, tops 10-12000 ft. Bombed centre of concentration of sky markers (red with green stars) from 21000 at 2003 (1 x 4000lb HC, 48 x 30lb inc., and 100 x 4lb XIB's). Trip uneventful. Results unobserved. No fighters seen, flak over target moderate and bursting about 20000 ft. Return trip also uneventful. Flak and S/ls apparently from ships about 150 miles from enemy coast on way home.	

NAM archives/Howard Heeley

The Squadron Operations Record Book (above), for the crew's last Op, records on the 16/17 December the crew (the same as for their first Op) of Lancaster III LM372, with the exception that they had a second Pilot on board, S/Ldr. A. W. Doubleday, the new Squadron Commanding Officer. Duty: Bombing – BERLIN, they took off at 1627 hours and landed at 2345 hours and the recorded details of the Op were as follows.

"Sortie completed. 9/10ths cloud, tops 500 ft. Bombed centre of concentration of green TIs from 20000 at 2002½ [1 x 400lb HC, 48 x 30 lb inc., 950 x 4lb and 100 x 4lb XIB's]. Green TIs well concentrated but nothing observed owing to cloud over target. Jerry continually dropping red flares and red with green stars from about 50 miles inland to BERLIN area. Lanes of fighter flares dropped by Jerry to N. of target but well to port. Defences medium over target but appeared to be foxed".

What was not noted in this report was the crew's near miss as they approached the

English North Sea coast in the Grimsby area. They became aware of problem when their Bomb Aimer called out and told to pilot to get up higher as they were flying at just over house top level. Fortunately he was able to climb to a safe height and flew on to land safely.

For many years afterwards Stan blamed himself for the close call, believing that he had miss-heard the QFE figures (Altimeter Settings - atmospheric pressure at sea level, corrected for temperature and adjusted to a specified datum such as airfield elevation). When set on the altimeter it reads height. However he later found out heavy losses that evening were caused by a combination of atrocious weather conditions and that some aircraft had been given incorrect QFE readings.

NAM archives/Howard Heeley

Not only did the crew live to tell their tale, but also in autumn 1943 they flew five Ops on perhaps one of the Squadron's most famous Lancasters, R5868 'S for Sugar' (left), which is now on display in the Bomber Command Museum at the RAF Museum in Hendon.

The aircraft had completed nearly 80 Ops with No.83 Squadron as 'Q Queenie' before arriving in November 1943 with No.467! The aircraft completed a total of 137 sorties.

Stan however noted that R5868 was not famous at the time but was actually considered an old airframe because it had completed so many flying hours – but it never let them down!

Stan admitted to initially being puzzled as to why after their 'First Tour' they were taken off Ops. Only after the war did they realise that at that time RAF was desperate for Instructors. Experienced crews were constantly being lost, and whilst they had plenty of aircraft to train on and fly Ops, they did not have sufficient crew to fly them hence the reason why experienced crews were transferred to become Instructors with the HCUs.

Stan Bray was promoted to Flight Sergeant and posted back to Winthorpe as an Instructor in January 1944, a commission for which he was recommended whilst on the Squadron came through six weeks later. Stan commented that he found Winthorpe little different from when he had left less than a year before, however this time he was an Instructor not a student, but as he noted *'as both you were treated with respect and what's more the food was good'*.

One aspect that was different related to rank. In his new role as an Instructor Stan could be teaching a student of a higher rank. He stated that he never found this a problem and he believed that 'respect' was the order of the day and very often the higher the rank of the student the more eager he was to learn, appreciating that what was learnt could be the difference between staying alive and not.

The type of training provided at an HCU was different to the traditional skills based training programmes the students had previously encountered. Having already passed exams for their particular trade, the HCU training aimed to let the pilot become accustomed to a different aircraft and for the crew to develop into a team, and not just seven individuals without a common aim. With so many crew members coming from such varied backgrounds Stan wonders how it all managed to work out so well. Even though it usually did Stan highlighted one particular part of signals training he helped to resolve.

With such a varied cross section of students and even of varied nationalities many of them had different accents. An important part of their wireless/intercom training stressed the need to use standard phrases and encouraged plain speaking. With today's modern communications technology it is perhaps hard to imagine that in the Second World War very few people had used a telephone other than an occasional call from a phone box.

To help overcome this problem Stan built a recording studio at Winthorpe, with eight operating points in it, one for each crew member and one for the Instructor. Stan had been on a speech training course held in London by the BBC (British Broadcasting Corporation training staff). Using skills gained from this course Stan would encourage students to speak in such a way that everyone understood what was being said and why.

In addition to the ground based instruction Stan maintained a steady number of flying hours in his Log Book. Between February 2 1944 and July 24 1945 Stan accumulated 95hrs and 40mins flying time on 64 flights with No.1661 HCU.

What these flying hours do not represent are the dangers inherent in HCU operations. Like many others have also stated Stan believes flying on the HCUs was in some ways more dangerous than flying on Ops. Instructor and students had to undertake high intensity flying at many different times of the day and night, often flying during indifferent weather conditions, and in some cases on old aircraft. This is illustrated by a series of entries in Stan's Log Book, which highlight the true life on 1661 HCU.

February 9, 1944; Hour – 23.10; Stirling EF444; Pilot - F/S Dechastel; Stan's Duty – W/Op; Remarks – Radar Ex 13 returned early U/C U/S. This entry is immediately followed by: February 9, 1944; Hour – 01.15; Stirling EF444; Pilot - F/S Dechastel; Stan's Duty – W/Op; Remarks – Radar Ex 13 returned early U/C still U/S.

May 31, 1944; Hour – 16.30; Stirling 'X'; Pilot – F/Sgt Cowan; Stan's Duty – Staff W/ Op; Remarks – Ex 10, Force landed Little Stourton, Stb. Inn. U/S, Prt. Inn. & Stb. Out over heating.

Date	Hour	Aircraft Type and No.	Pilot	Duty	Remarks (including results of bombing, gunnery, exercises, etc.)	Flying Times Day	Night
					Time carried forward :—	16035	205·30
17/7/44	0945	E	F/Sgt Billing	Staff	Ex 5 & Ex 10 BALED OUT 3 ENSINES U/S F/E KILLED	3·35	
20/7/44	0930	K EF444	Sgt Bowden	Staff	Ex 10. PILOT CRASH LANDED ALONE	1·00	
					TOTAL FOR JULY	4·35	
					J. Rogers F/L for W/CMDR OC 1661 C.U.		
9/8/44	17.35	T	F/Lt Handcock	W/OP	AIR TEST	·25	
11/8/44	17.10	O	F/Lt Webster DFM	W/OP	STAFF C & L	·55	
16/8/44	16.00	O	F/O Lett	W/OP	SWINDERBY TO WINTHORPE AIR TEST	·45	
29/8/44	11.35	C	F/Lt Webster DFM	W/OP	AIR TEST	·50	
					TOTAL FOR AUGUST	2·55	
					W/CMDR OC 1661 C.U.		
					TOTAL TIME ...	168·05	205·30

NAM archives/Howard Heeley

Just two months later and the 20th July entry in Stan's Log Book (above) greatly under plays the events surrounding another flight.

July 20, 1944; Hour – 09.30; Stirling 'K' EF444; Pilot – Sgt. Bowden; Duty – Staff; Remarks – Ex 10, Baled out 3 engines U/S, pilot crash landed alone, F/E killed.

Stirling EF444 was detailed for Exercise 10 – a daylight cross-country aircrew training flight. Stan was flying as Staff Wireless Operator. His role was to assess the crew, which was nearly ready to pass out of the course. Also with a seasoned Wireless Op on board if for any reason they got lost, they had a good chance to get back to base.

Stan recalled the day's events in more detail:

After a good breakfast, Stan joined the crew of seven at the dispersal point. Here he found the Flight Engineer on the wing, dipping the fuel tanks, when he asked why, Stan was informed that on a night flight a few days earlier they had an engine cut out, with the fuel tank empty even when the gauge showed a quarter full.

Led by their skipper Sgt. Bowden, they took off at 0930hrs. The first leg of the flight was uneventful. Having been airborne for about an hour Sgt. Bowden noticed that the Stirling had developed a serious oil leak in the port outer engine giving him no alternative but to feather the propeller. Further problems followed when the starboard inner engine also developed an oil leak, this engine was also feathered. Luck was certainly against them that day because the starboard outer now began to show signs of trouble, and the artificial horizon was also unserviceable!

They put out a Mayday call but received no response so Sgt. Bowden gave the order to abandon the aircraft. Six crew members baled out leaving just Stan and the pilot, after Stan baled out Sgt. Bowden opted to remain with the aircraft, in part because he was now too low but also because he was close to some built up areas of Leeds. Sgt. Bowden subsequently crash-landed the Stirling in Dawson's Corner Field at Stanningley, near Pudsey, Leeds.

Stan recalled a violent jerk just after leaving the stricken aircraft, and his first thought was that the parachute had caught on the tail plane, but thankfully, it was his parachute opening. Looking down he could see houses, gardens and greenhouses in his likely landing area. Fortunately he landed safely in someone's back garden on a local council housing estate.

A crowd had gathered but no one offered to help. Stan gathered up his parachute and enquired where was the nearest telephone, having been told 'round the corner!' Stan set off to find it. Whilst walking down the road Stan was approached by a local who shook his hand and exclaimed, "Does tha' know lad, I paid half a crown before war to see a chap jump out of a plane and I've seen five of you this morning for nowt!"

Stan contacted the Police and an Inspector came and picked him up and then took him out to the crashed aircraft. Stan was informed that Sgt. Bowden had been taken to hospital in Bradford and with the Fire Brigade adopting a watching brief and despite fuel soaking the ground all around the crashed aircraft Stan was allowed to enter it to retrieve the code books and maps.

They then went to collect all of the other surviving crew members, before visiting the pilot in hospital. Unfortunately the only person not to survive abandoning the aircraft was the diligent Flight Engineer, Sgt. Alfred Keith Moncur, whose chute had failed to open. As Stan remarked 'what justice?'

The Inspector took the crew back to his house, in those days Police Officers of such rank lived at the station that they were in charge of. From here Stan telephoned Winthorpe and transport was sent to take them all back to base. The following morning having received a check up in the sick bay, Stan had breakfast with the Station Commander where he explained what had happened. Stan was then granted 48 hours leave and he travelled back to his mother's house in Sheffield.

Of the seven survivors only Stan and Sgt. Bowden flew again after the Stanningley crash, the others were transferred to other duties. Sgt. Bowden was later killed during a raid over Hamburg.

On the 11th November 1944, No.57 Squadron Avro Lancaster I LL939 (DX-H) took off at 16:54 from East Kirkby. The aircraft was hit by flak and crashed at about 19:27 near Beckdorf, 8km SSW from Buxtehude. On the first impact one engine and the rear turret were torn away, the rest of the Lancaster bouncing back into the air and flew on for over a kilometre before smashing back to earth, five crew members were killed and two survived and became POWs.

Back at Winthorpe Stan became Assistant Chief Ground Instructor to an Australian Squadron Leader and he really enjoyed the job, which involved a lot of organising but still gave Stan the chance to occasionally fly. In the ground instructional role the crews were trained using a variety of different exercises, but this had to be organised around when they were not flying.

By the end of 1944 the No.1661 HCU's Stirlings were being replaced by Lancasters and the Stirlings were being placed into storage prior to scrapping. Instructors were ferrying most of the aircraft to Maghaberry in Northern Ireland and on December 30 1944 Stan flew as Wireless Op with Flying Officer Edy DFC when they ferried Stirling 'O' to the storage facility across the Irish Sea.

For these flights the aircraft were stripped of all but essential flying kit and as they approached their destination they noted a loss of brake pressure. Faced with a long return flight back to land on the longer runway at Winthorpe they opted to land in Northern Ireland. As expected after touching down they were unable to stop, so at the end of the runway the pilot just kicked the rudder over and pulled the aircraft clear of the runway. Fortunately no one was hurt, so they literally left the crashed aircraft just off the end of the runway and climbed into the aircraft that had been sent over to return them to Winthorpe.

Normally on these trips to Northern Ireland only three crew operated the aircraft, a screened pilot who offered to take the aircraft and he in turn engaged a Flight Engineer and Wireless Operator. These were usually two people who had flown with him pretty frequently.

On January 14 1945 Stan was invited to fly on another such sortie to deliver Stirling EH988 to Maghaberry but was not happy about the pilot, who had been a first class pilot and well decorated, but who had completed a very difficult operational tour which left him very nervous and he had done very little flying since. With this in mind Stan refused the offer, as did other screened Wireless Operators later approached. As he could not fly without a Wireless Operator a volunteer was requested from a class of students, many offered and a Sgt. Littlemore was selected. Shortly after takeoff the Stirling developed engine problems and a starboard engine caught fire and the aircraft crashed near Annesley Woodhouse, Mansfield Notts. killing all on board.

The aircraft was being ferried to Northern Ireland and was only crewed by five personnel; S/Ldr. S. L. Cockbain DFC Pilot, F/Sgt. E. C. Barton Navigator, F/Sgt. T. A. Balls

Date	Hour	Aircraft Type and No.	Pilot	Duty	Remarks (including results of bombing, gunnery, exercises, etc.)	Flying Times Day	Night
					Time carried forward :—	266·30	
25/61/45	0630	LANCASTER YN - Y	F/LT SPRIGGS DFC	W/OP	BASE TO TIBENHAM	·35	
"	0800	YN - Y	" " "	"	TIBENHAM TO GATOW (BERLIN)		
					TOUR OF BOMB DAMAGE ETC	2·30	
26/61/45	1130	YN · Y	" " "	"	GATOW (BERLIN) TO TIBENHAM		
					DIVERTED TO POLEBROOK	4·00	
27/61/45	1030	YN · Y	" " "	"	POLEBROOK TO BASE	·25	
30/61/45	1435	YN · V	F/LT SPRIGGS DFC	PASSENGER	BASE TO ST ATHEN	1·15	
30/61/45	1645	ZX744	P/O LETT DFC	W/OP	ST ATHEN TO BASE	1·00	
					Total Time ...		

NAM archives/Howard Heeley

Flight Engineer, Sgt. J. Littlemore Wireless Operator and Sgt. K. Harris Air Gunner. Early in the flight the aircraft suffered a loss of power from at first one then two engines, the pilot attempted to reach Hucknall airfield but continued to lose height and crashed.

Stan completed his time with No.1661 HCU in July 1945. Before being demobbed he went on to complete No.72 W/Op Air Course at No.14 Radio School RAF St. Athan, between September 7 and September 28 1945, flying 12hrs and 15mins on Ansons.

He then also completed 17hrs 25mins on Lancasters with No.1660 HCU at RAF Swinderby, between October 25 and November 8 1945. Ironically this was a course for Instructors only and as Stan remarked 'a bit late in the day, but typical RAF'.

In total Stan recorded a total Flying Time in his Observer's & Air Gunner's Flying Log Book of 263hrs and 55mins [day] and 212hrs and 30mins [night].

In civilian life Stan became a salesman and during the 1970s he and the fellow members of his No.467 RAAF Squadron crew who had served on Lancaster, R5868, 'S for Sugar', were frequently invited to special events for the aircraft at the RAF Museum in Hendon.

CHAPTER FIFTEEN

Airmens memories

The following stories and recollections (in no particular order) are from items held in Newark Air Museum's Archive.

June 1944 - The Arrival - P. P. Cockerton

Having just completed an aero-engine course at RAF Halton (No.1 School of Technical Training) I was posted to No.1661 HCU at Winthorpe. A couple of us arrived at the LNER station in Newark after a very roundabout route - Wendover, Aylesbury, Nottingham (Victoria), Grantham and Newark.

We enquired of the station staff regarding RAF transport to the camp and were told that a lorry would call on the hour. However, our most urgent enquiry was to the effect of the ownership of a Stirling, which could be seen on the hill behind the [Ransome and Marles] Ball Bearing factory. *"Oh that will have come from Winthorpe"*, the porter replied, *"Watch out they are more dangerous than the Luftwaffe".**

This information sent us into a deep state of depression. It was common knowledge that the Stirling was known for the many design faults and the difficulties and general unreliability of the aircraft.

When we reported to the Guardroom we were put in a hut near the main gate for the night, directed to the cookhouse, and told to report to the Orderly Office at 0900 the next morning. In the mess hail we met some 'erks' from Repair and Inspection (R & I), and it was obvious that moral was very low. The main reasons being (A) the worn out Stirlings they were expected to patch up (B) the terrible living conditions and environment and (C) The long hours and working conditions (10 hour days – 7 days a week then 1 day off on a continuous roster). This had the effect that we left our huts at 0615hrs and returned about 1900hrs.

We decided to cheer ourselves up after this shock, so decided to sample the delights of Newark. We walked around the town, had a fish and chip supper and then as it was

*Checking records there are no details of a Stirling crashing in the locality around this date.

almost dark made our way back to camp. Some 30 minutes later it was obvious that we had picked the Lincoln Road, not the Sleaford Road. The [A46] highway, which abutted onto the aerodrome and along its entire length, was protected by three high rolls of barbed wire.

As we started to walk back to Newark, two 'erks' enquired where we were going and as we explained what had happened burst out into laughter, *"Don't worry"*, they said, *"There are more holes in the wire defences of Winthorpe than rabbit holes"*.

As we walked round the a/c taxiway we met 3 Home Guards, in the 60+ year's range guarding the aerodrome, they at that time were the only defence I can remember.

This was my introduction to the crazy world of No.1661 HCU, and the war which ranged between the station personnel and the technical personnel in all ranks. Any preconceptions of the life on a station were shattered within a week, thus destroying the 'Biggles' saga forever.

Ray Darney and the 'Goon Palace'

This account was written in the 1990s and is largely unaltered with the exception of the added photographs.

At last I can put pen to paper and come up with something about the hut I was billeted in at RAF Winthorpe.

"Goon Palace" was situated on No.4 site adjacent to the cart track that connected Beaconfield Farm to the Coddington to Newark road. Constructed of a wooden frame erected on a concrete base it was clad in an asbestos/cement sheet with an apex roof. Windows were plentiful with a door centrally positioned on both end walls giving access.

Internally, one corner was partitioned off to provide quarters for the NCO I/C. Midway along length and width was a coke stove with its accompanying steel bin holding the ration of coke (only issued during winter months). Other furniture consisted of a table and two forms, all collapsible. Of beds, I can't give an exact figure. In my mind, there were no more than 28. Others have thought the figure to be 24. So on that score it is best not to be too precise.

The beds were a heavy cast type where the bottom half slid into the top half. Not the best of beds to sleep in and cursed by all as a support strut mid length would strike the middle of the back and be most uncomfortable. The mattress was the well-known 3 biscuits and with a pillow comprised ones sleeping set up, with four army blankets.

For all its faults this type of bed was better than having bunks that had problems of its own, especially the doubling of personnel to a point of almost being overcrowded. Each bed space had a small wooden shelf and two coat hooks for storage of kit. The billet also had a wireless (radio) issued by the P.S.I.

Near to the billet was a small latrine block containing about 3 W.C.s, a urinal and one coldwater tap. The coldwater tap, meant as a water source for cleaning only, was the favoured place for a morning wash that most people used. The main ablutions were on the communal site and that was quite some distance away.

It is not known for sure how or why "Goon Palace" got its name. Possibly it came from one of the many wireless variety shows that were vogue at the time. In my own mind I rather suspect that Teddy Cockburn was instrumental in it somewhere. Even to this day "Goon Palace" is remembered and spoken of with affection by people it billeted.

Sgt. Addison occupied the NCO's room and both Cpl's slept in the dormitory. The rest were LAC's, the highest rank possible for our trade of Flight Mechanic engines that we all were; our place of work being 3 Site.

Billet names that can be recalled; NCO's first, other ranks by alphabetical order of surname.

Sgt. Addison	Cpl. Haggar	Cpl. Noake

Other Ranks:-

Cape, Stan	Davies, Taff	Munday, Ken
Chace, Charlie	East, Joe	Nichols, Harry
Clarkson, Don	Eccles, Harry	Powell, Eric
Cockburn, Teddy	Harding, Jeff	Sammons, Bill
Darney, Taff	Heap, Jimmy	Shelton, Derek
Daubney, Tiny	Millar, Jock	Watson, Paddy

'Goon Palace' Residents in 1944 (pictures from 'Tiny' Daubney's album donated to NAM) – NAM archives

This billet contained a mix of different people from various walks of life and age groups; and the range of occupations stretched from a colliery worker to a bank manager.

Fred, a married man with family, was in the newspaper printing industry with a wage packet in excess of £10 per week and that was a lot of money pre-war. Harry was a bank manager and married with family. I can recall him telling me that it was unlikely he would return to banking after the war. So sheltered was his life pre RAF that he didn't know how other people lived. This experience, to use his words, "a revelation."

Stan was also married with family and a grocery store manager (a pipe smoker). Cpl Noake, married with family, was in the motor trade and ran a small car repair garage. Teddy Cockburn, a Geordie and single, was the joker in the pack and life and soul of the party. Laughter and he were never far away from one another. Had the ability to make light of matters. Liked to sing and in fairness had a good voice. Somehow he acquired the nickname 'Cobanski' and it is he, I'm almost sure, came up with the "Goon Palace" tag. It was sad to hear he died from meningitis in 1950 aged 50, leaving a widow and 3 year old son.

These were some of the older members of the billet who were a good calming influence on us younger lot who often required pointing in a direction away from trouble.

James Daubney (from his father's albums) and Bill Taylor and NAM archives

Some friendships created in the billet are still in existence today. There is Stan Cape and Harry Noake. Don Clarkson and, until he died 12 months ago, Bill Sammons. Ken Munday, Tiny Daubney and Taff Darney were a threesome that got on well together (pictured in both l-r Kenneth 'Smoothie' Munday Ray 'Taff' Darney and Albert 'Tiny' Daubney) (from Tiny Daubney's album). Though somehow after Winthorpe closed Ken drifted away.

Camaraderie was high and a willingness to help colleagues did exist. It was recognised practice that anybody unexpectedly having to work late and going out would arrive in the billet to find buttons and footwear cleaned ready for a quick getaway. Beds would also be made up. There was tomfoolery and plenty of it! French beds were common. More troublesome though was to find ones biscuits had been removed and hidden. There wasn't any comfort or sleep with just a blanket to cover bed springs! Boots would be tucked away under a bed elsewhere. So one would be mindful of these things after a night out and perhaps a few beers. These things did happen and I suppose one-upmanship to go one better was very much to the fore. Malice was never part of it.

What makes a good billet? Why should one be known as "Goon Palace" and the inmates as "Goons?" A difficult question to answer. But that was a billet that was different to others, and more to the point, was a fact known to all. A good billet, smashing people and is the place that I look back on with fond memories as the place where I came of age. This is the testimony I ascribe to "Goon Palace".

Photograph left: eight engine fitters, all LACs, all from B Flight and all billeted in Hut 107 (known as Goon Palace) at RAF Winthorpe. Pictured during a reunion, they are: back row, from left, Stan Cape, Ken Munday, Harry Eccles, Albert Daubney and Bill Sammonds; front, Ray Darney, Charlie Chase and Don Clarkson – NAM archives. Photograph right: 'Goon Palace' fitters at Newark Air Museum during the 1991 reunion – NAM archives

Stan Cape, Teddy Cockburn, Paddy Watson, Charlie Chace, Jeff Harding, Taff Davies and Joe East, all billet members, were the advance party and founders of 1661 HCU. They lived on iron rations until catering facilities were set up. Winthorpe at that time was known as RAF Coddington Hall.

The camp was without a boundary fence of a barrier nature, so there were many 'ways in' and many 'ways out'. Only when having to collect a leave pass or whatever at the guardroom would we 'book in and out'. This made for easier living and gave access to Newark via the dirt cart track adjacent to the billet as we were about the third billet from the road.

Stan Matthews

My introduction to Winthorpe was not a happy one. I had been on leave for two days ... when I received a telegram to report back to camp. On arriving back at camp I was told I was posted to Winthorpe. I spent all day running around to get my clearance chit signed and left the same evening with an all night journey to London and then another train to Newark and arrived at a small station (not the main one).

We [3 of us] asked the railway bod the way to Winthorpe, he told us, and we asked about transport and was told we would have to walk. After trudging up the hill, with full kit we finally arrived at the main gate and the guardroom, where we encountered a snotty S. P. Who said 'Where have you been, you are late', however he took us to a billet and at the other end of the hut there was as couple of erks and a corporal playing pontoon.

I don't know why the panic to be recalled from leave, I was an armourers assistant on the bomb dump, a posh name for a labourer. The next day we went to the bomb dump and our first job was unloading a lorry load of American 1,000lb bombs, the tail board was dropped and the bombs rolled off onto the ground, frightened the life out of me, but after a couple of days we were taking no notice of it.

I don't know the dates but it was probably January or February *(the end of February 1944)*, we had quite a bad winter and one night we were told that we had to go snow clearing on the runway, however my pal Joe Fox and I got on our bikes and went to the Land Army Girls hostel a couple of miles along the Sleaford road, we used to go there playing table tennis. The next morning our boss Cpl. Foster said 'where were you last night?', we told him the truth, he said it was not fair that you should leave the other chaps to do all the work, anyone else we would have been on a 252 (charge), he was a good NCO and not long after was promoted sergeant.

On another occasion we were walking round the bomb dump when a Stirling was heading our way, its port outer engine on fire with bits falling off. We thought he was heading for the runway when he suddenly banked to port, the flames shot up the wing and into the cockpit, the plane turned over and straight into the ground, there was an explosion and a great ball red ball of fire and a huge cloud of black smoke. We jumped a couple of fences and were the first people there, a terrible mess but no survivors, just a big crater with ammo popping off and flames.

This was probably Stirling EF232 of No.1660 HCU Swinderby which crashed near Bassingham Bombing Range shortly after taking off from Winthorpe on a night bombing exercise on the 31st January 1944.

One day we were told that there was going to be a Rook shoot, the bomb dump was quite wooded in parts; I could not believe it, a war going on and a lot of civvies on a bomb dump shooting Rooks. However it did happen and they has a good bag.

There was another time when we had to bomb up a Stirling using some new equipment, instead of using hand winches this new gear consisted of hydraulics and rubber pipes connected inside the aircraft, when the exercise started we ended up with oil all over the place and leaking pipes and so we finished the job in the usual way by hand. I don't know if the new kit ever took off, I was long gone.

Shortly before D Day a directive came round asking for volunteers for the Guards Armoured Division. After that I saw my Sgt. and said I wanted to remuster to Air Sea Rescue, so I went to SHQ and did the necessary after cycling a long way from the bomb dump and then cycled back again. After a few minutes the sergeant received

THE ROOK SHOOT

THE NEW KIT

Cartoons by Stan Mathews – NAM archives

144

a phone call to report back to SHQ. Any remustering had been cancelled and I was going in the army. Duly posted to Huyton in Liverpool where I finished up in the Royal Artillery and demobbed in October 1947.

John Hyman

John arrived at Winthorpe in 1943 from the RAF Hospital at Rauceby near Sleaford, the '... *station was full of mud and potholes*'. The SSQ was a large hut, the M.Os. were Paddy Dunn and Doc. Brown, anybody that passed out sick was sent to another station, RAF Swinderby for lice etc. and we used Newark Hawtonville Hospital. We did our stint on the airfield at night and standby during the day. I can recall a time when two bods from Jamaica went on strike because there was no rice on the camp and on the menu. How it was resolved I cannot remember.

I met my wife in May 1943 and we were married in Coddington Church in June 1944, my wife's family owned Coddington Hall which was the Officers Mess. I went to look it over just after the war, it had had the lead stolen off its roof, the rain had got in and it was thus pulled down because it was said the cost of restoration was too great.

Keith Slade

These are condensed extracts of Keith's story of his time in the RAF in the UK from 1941-45.

Joining the RAF in 1941 as a Flight Mechanic/Engines and first posted to Padgate to be kitted out and on to Blackpool and 159 Entry, No.3 School of Technical Training at

Squires Gate then posted to Waterbeach as an LAC and looking after the Trolley Accs. for Stirlings. In September 1942 posted again to a conversion flight at Waddington and then arrived at Winthorpe as part of the HCU.

At Winthorpe he worked a shift system comprising, day one 6am to 10pm (late finish), day two 6am to 6pm (early finish), day three 6am to 6am (next day) 'night flying'; the next day was one's own unless on guard duty, fire picket etc. etc. It really was a hard life and this went on, day in day out – Saturdays and Sundays were ignored.

Keith went on a course at No.5 School of TT at Innsworth and returned to Winthorpe as a Group 1 Engine Fitter in March 1944. He became part of a group of around ten men who travelled to other airfields to repair aircraft that had landed with some problem or other to sort out.

Winthorpe was unusual in that it had civilians actually living within the camp area. These people had probably lived there before the camp was built *(Beaconfield Farm?)* so they worked on the airfield, and we knew some of them. I asked one family if Peggy *(his girlfriend, they married in March 1945)* could come and stay with them for a week in the summer and this was agreed, so Peg and I were able to be together for a few marvellous days. We went out in the evenings, down to Newark and went dancing at the Corn Exchange.

In late 1943 the RAF Regiment seemed to appear. It was decided by the powers that be, or were, that that there ought to be some 'back up' for the Regiment in the event of an invasion. The chances were that the ground crews had little or no knowledge of fighting on the beaches or the airfields as suggested by Winston Churchill, so a group of valuable Fitters and Riggers were selected to go up to Filey Bay in November to practice

Flight Sergeant Ronald William Bridgland, I/C Electrical Section, RAF Winthorpe 26 June 1944 to 9 July 1945 – NAM archives

Commando Tactics. We had ten days of torture, scaling cliffs in heavy rain and high wind, scrambling under nets and creeping through the wet grass with the training staff firing live rounds over our heads. I cannot remember what the food was like I am glad to say. They must have been potty to send trained engineers on such a course. It was more dangerous than flying.

Almost immediately on my return to Winthorpe, I found I had been posted to Bottesford another Bomber Station not far from Newark. This was to be No.1669 Conversion Unit with Lancasters.

Ronald W. Bridgland

He wrote in 1998 – Winthorpe had an important role in providing war-time aircrews for Bomber

Command and I support the recording of all the material available for historical reasons. I suspect that much of the anecdotal information has been lost after this period of time. I also regret that my own contribution was in the nature of a supporting role and not of front line interest.

From the outbreak of war the RAF had limited numbers of personnel and resources. Consequently the emphasis was, at that time, upon training. Having some qualifications in Electrical Engineering, I spent the first three and a half years or so in Training Command, at Hereford and Melksham.

Joining the RAF in 1940 at No.2 Reception Centre Cardington and Drill Training at No.7 Reception Centre, Morecombe and training at Henlow on an Electrical Course; posted to No.2 Army Co-Operation Squadron at Sawbridgeworth operating Lysanders. In December to No.11 School of TT at Hereford and in April 1941 to Halton for an Instructors Course and posted as a Corporal to Hereford as an Electrical Instructor.

Promoted to Sergeant on 1st November 1941 and following a course at Plessey's in London posted to No.12 School of TT at Melksham in June 1942 training RAF and Fleet Air Arm Electricians and setting up the School for WAAF Charging Board Operators. Again promoted (to F/Sgt.) in December 1943 and posted as NCO I/C Electrical Section at East Kirkby in February 1944 responsible for 44 Lancasters (of Nos. 57 and 630 Squadrons) and 96 Electrical Fitters.

On the 26 June 1944 again posted, this time to No.1661 HCU at RAF Winthorpe as NCO I/C Electrical Section.

The aircraft complement of 1661 HCU was at that time forty Stirlings which were scheduled to be replaced at a later date with thirty-two Lancasters. During my stay of some thirteen months, eighteen Stirlings and five Lancasters were involved in crashes. I visited many of the incidents within a short radius of the station. The first priority was to disconnect the aircraft batteries in order to make safe the equipment and armaments.

Because the Stirlings were due to be replaced, the holding of equipment and spares was being reduced to a minimum or below. To keep the aircraft air-worthy, it was necessary to find somewhat unofficial solutions. A number of sorties were made to a local graveyard for wrecked airframes in order to reclaim suitable spares.

Giving rise to particular problems were the large motors used to lower, and retract, the Stirling undercarriage. An appreciable number of the Stirling incidents were due to collapsed undercarriages.

The squeeze was felt in other ways, apart from the shortage of equipment. Transport had been commandeered to support the invasion of France and an electric vehicle was built in the Section utilizing an old Morgan three wheeled chassis. The power unit was a three hp Stirling undercarriage motor, supplied by two trolley accumulators slung under the chassis. For visiting Dispersals it proved adequate, although the motor had a history of overheating.

The DOOFA MT was built by Ronald Bridgland (on the left) with Sgt. Stone (on the right) and members of the Electrical Section.

A number of other devices were born in the Electrical Section. One of these was the Bridgland Mousetrap. It was built to combat a plague of mice inhabiting the workshop area. They had resisted

Ron Bridgland and Sgt. Stone – NAM archives

all other attempts, using mechanical traps and cheese. The principle was for the mouse to step onto a metal plate in order to get to the cheese and for the plate to complete an electrical connection. This allowed the practice bomb release to drop the house brick. The method was both clean and effective.

Of more practical importance was a mock-up of a Lancaster bomb panel and circuits (below), which I built with the help of the Electrical Section, in January and February 1945 from instructions from the Base Commander to investigate means if improving

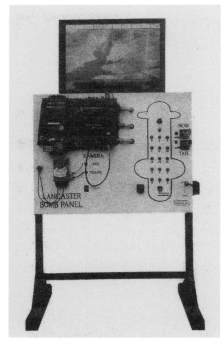

NAM archives

bombing techniques. It was intended to simulate the sequence of photographic and bombing operations during a flight to the target. Ten events are covered, with the position of the aircraft shown illuminated on the coloured map. Operation of the camera control, bomb doors, selection fusing and the 'Mickey Mouse' etc. advanced each stage, showing an illuminated typical photograph taken. Errors in operation locked out the panel.

The Electrical Section also had responsibilities for other items of training equipment. The AML bombing trainer was located in a two storey building. On the upper floor, the bomb aimer lay prone with his computer and bomb sight. He looked down on a realistic, coloured, moving map of the Ruhr which could be steered to present the target. Upon release of the bombs, the trajectory was calculated from the height and speed etc. The point of impact was then shown as a point of light on the frozen map.

Another training aid was in the building which housed a number of link trainers. I spent many off duty hours with these and the sensation of flying was quite realistic. It was particularly so when night flying by instruments with the hood down. The aircraft movements were plotted by a moving spider on the instructors table. Although I felt fairly proficient with the Link Trainers, I suffered from air-sickness when actually on air-test etc. The worst scenario was weaving (taking evasive action).

Third, a gunnery trainer was housed in a darkened domed building, which I never visited. I assumed it held a turret and a projector.

I cannot remember the living quarters in detail but I remember sharing a hut near the Coddington Road with Sgt. Bob Reading (Engine Fitter) and Sgt. Bourne. The latter came from a family of Organ builders and was passionately fond of classical music.

I remember walking down the farm lane during the very cold winter. The power lines at the side of the lane were coated with four inches or more of ice and the light breeze was causing them to dance in the sunlight.

I remember serving the airmen with Christmas Dinner in 1944. I served on the left side of the Mess but I cannot remember the Commanding Officers speech. I also remember that I was possibly the only Orderly NCO on duty that Christmas.

Victory in Europe was declared on the 8 May 1945 (VE Day) much to the relief of the whole station. I missed out on the Station celebrations having obtained a week's leave. Within a fortnight of returning from leave, I received my posting from Winthorpe actually departing on the 9 July 1945. I was very sorry to leave what had proved a very happy station.

The following poem was written during the Second World war and passed to the Museum by an ex-RAF Winthorpe airman. Author unknown.

Ode to the Armourers

He wears a suit of faded blue, no brevet on his chest,

You'll find more blisters on his hands, than medals on his chest,

He doesn't sit behind the guns of multi-engined planes,

'Nor steer a graceful fighter high above the clouds and rain,

He wields a wire toggle, and a piece of oily rag,

While other fellows 'shoot a line' and boast about their bag.

continued over...

He works in mud, and sleet and rain, cursing the senseless war,

And wonders ninety times a day what he joined the Air Force for,

He's just an AC/Armourer, nothing more and nothing less

With his greasy suit of faded blue in place of battledress,

But he strikes a blow at the filthy hun with honest British skill,

As sure as he who aims the bombs or the gunner who makes the kill.

He doesn't ask for glory – it's not the armourer's way,

All he wants is the pilots cheery smile – 'the guns are all ok.'

So when you read of bombing raids, and Messerschmitts shot down,

When you've covered flying heroes with honour and renown,

When you've handed out the D.F.C. and D.F.M. and such,

Have a thought for the armourer who doesn't ask for much,

Just shake him by the hand and think that he did lots,

To make those spitting Brownings safe for the man who fires the shots.

L/AC G.H.Davis

CHAPTER SIXTEEN

Aircrew memories

The following stories and recollections (in no particular order) are from items held in Newark Air Museum's Archive.

Stan Jolly

Stan Jolly and his fellow crew members pictured in front of a Stirling at Winthorpe in March 1944; they are from l-r, Stan Jolly Bomb Aimer, Hilton Forden Rear Gunner, Col Dickson Pilot (all Australians), Horace Skellorn Mid-upper Gunner, Oscar Furness Navigator, Bob Hunter Wireless Operator (both Australian) and Philip Weaver Flight Engineer.

They were posted to No.467 RAAF Squadron at Waddington in April and shot down on the 3/4 May 1944 on their fourth trip

NAM archives

flying Lancaster JA901 PO-N after bombing Mailly-le-Camp. Stan and Bob Hunter were the only survivors and evaded capture, their fellow crew members are buried in France.

Roy Hill

The following appears in Roy's self-published book 'Survivor' and is used with permission.

It was May '44 and the fledgling crew of which I was Wireless Op. had just finished its OTU stint flying Wellingtons out of Silverstone. We were six in number and arrived at 1661 HCU Winthorpe to collect a Flight Engineer and to do our four engined conversion on Short Stirlings.

On arrival at Winthorpe, we were greeted by the rather unusual sight of a one-legged Stirling circling the airfield. Apparently the crew had done all they could to either retract the leg which dangled (some 14 feet in length!) or lower its mate, but all to no avail, so they were circling to lose fuel thus reducing the risk of fire when the inevitable crash landing occurred. About two hours later the pilot brought off just about the most brilliant piece of flying I ever witnessed. He brought his huge, ungainly charge in at minimum flying speed, the port undercart leg which was lowered, on the extreme starboard side of the runway, and the aircraft, on losing speed, swung gently onto the grass, digging its wingtip into the soft surface and bending its starboard outer prop. The crew were unscathed, (at least physically) and the pilot was given an ovation by an appreciative audience.

On the 20th March (!!) Stirling LK537 was extensively damaged when its undercarriage collapsed on landing. Cat. B. The port main undercarriage failed to lock and the aircraft made a 'controlled' emergency landing, with all the crew uninjured.

Having collected our Flight Engineer, we duly had our crew photo taken for the one and only time, unfortunately with a Nissen hut in the background and not a Stirling. The crew had quite an international flavour, being comprised of three Aussies, a Scot and three English lads. All were NCOs apart from yours truly, who had been instructing on Ansons prior to crewing up. The three Aussie crew members were eventually all commissioned after we had completed five Ops.

(Back row left to right), Bill Turner Rear gunner, George Wall RAAF Pilot, Roy Hill W/Op. (Front row left to right) Eric Dunn Flight Engineer, Jock Sweeney Mid-upper gunner, A. Clarke RAAF Navigator and Bill Wulff RAAF Bomb Aimer
– NAM archives

The Stirling was a large, well constructed, but rather unwieldy machine. Although relatively well appointed by WW2 bomber standards, it was unpopular with many of its crews, (although some thought very highly of it) owing to its inability to fly as high or fast, with or without a full load, as the Lancs and Halis which comprised the remainder, and majority of the four- engined bomber force.

However speaking as a Wop, it was luxury after flying Wimpys. The radio compartment was roomy and had a window with a view, and most reassuringly, a swivel chair with armour-plating underneath and at the back of it. No other plane that I know of was so equipped, the extra weight being deemed too great a price to pay. One Wop I got to know at a later date, who almost survived a tour on Stirlings, told me that whenever flak was flying around he would swivel his chair so that the armour-plating was between him and it – makes sense to me.

Our sojourn at Winthorpe lasted only about six weeks and on completion of the course we moved down the road to No.5 LFS (Lancaster Finishing School) at Syerston. During our stay at Winthorpe we had really gelled as a team,

Roy in November 1944 ...and two weeks later his POW photographs – NAM archives

enjoyed flying the much maligned Stirling but we were rather glad we weren't going to fly it on Ops! We had enjoyed getting to know Newark and its friendly people.

...After Syerston ...we joined No.207 Squadron at Spilsby. We were shot down in Lancaster PB765 EM-B on our 18th Op, a trip to Heilbronn in the Rhur. Three of our 'band of brothers' were killed while the four survivors spent the last six months of the war as POWs. (Jock Sweeney was not on this Op; Ted Sharpe replaced him and was one of those killed).

E. G. 'Nobby' Clark

Our crew, Captain F/Lt. Wally Hunter, Bomb Aimer F/O E. G. Nobby Clark, on 11 March 1945 during Exercise 14 were detailed on a 6hr 10 min Cross Country (Night) which included bombing at the Epperstone Range. After dropping our 6 bombs the error was converted to 20,000 ft, the result being 84 yds.

It was the ambition of all captains to see their names displayed on the board outside of Station Headquarters showing the lowest error for a stick of six bombs. You can imagine our captain's pleasure when the next morning we had taken first place.

We were posted to No.227 Squadron at Balderton.

Harry Le Marchant

March 43 to April 43 – advanced training and conversion course on 4 engined aircraft using Manchesters then Lancasters. On completion posted to No.57 Squadron RAF Scampton.

Jan 44 to Jan 45 – having finished my first tour of operations I was then a Radar Navigator Instructor at Winthorpe. I helped to set up the Radar Navigation Section with my friend F/Lt. Warwick who was later killed in action with W/Cdr. Guy Gibson.

From my log book I Note:-

On 3/3/44 whilst with a pupil crew, our Stirling pranged on return from a x-country flight when landing in the snow.

3/7/44, pranged on takeoff with pupil crew in Stirling aircraft which broke in half. Aircraft written off. Cuts, aircrew OK.

A friend of mine who was a Flight Commander at Winthorpe (S/Ldr. S. Cockbain DFC) was ferrying one of the elderly Stirlings back to Short Bros. Factory in N. Ireland. It caught fire on takeoff. We had planned to fly over together but training duties intervened. Regrettably all the crew were killed

On the14th January 1945 Stirling EH688 crashed at Annesley Park, Nr. Mansfield. Early in the flight the aircraft suffered a loss of power from at first one then two engines, the pilot attempted to reach Hucknall airfield but continued to lose height and crashed out of control.

My own skipper of my first tour of operations (S/Ldr. M. Crocker DFC and bar) was a Flight Commander at Winthorpe. He managed to get all our crew together as instructors with a view to doing a second tour together. He was an American who learned to fly as a civilian in the USA and worked his own passage to join the RAF. In early summer of 1944 he was promoted and posted as CO of No.44 Squadron. Before all of us could join him he was shot down and killed along with 2 other old crew members (F/O J. Mathews and F/O Worthington) when doing a quick operation to get his hand in.

John F. Grime

I first arrived at Winthorpe on the 13 April 1943 as a pupil. I converted there from twin to four engined, flying Manchesters and then Lancasters. At the time the Commanding Officer was G/Capt. Pleasance and the Chief Flying Instructor Bill Deas and my Flight Commander was S/Ldr. McKenzie. I left for No.207 Squadron at Langar on the 15 May 1943 ... having completed a tour with No.207 I was posted back to Winthorpe as a Flying Instructor on the 22 Jan. 1944.

G/Capt. Pleasance was still Commanding Officer but was replaced by G/Capt. Woodin about the middle of 1944. He was the last CO before the airfield closed. I stayed until very nearly the end of the Stations life and was posted to RAF Blyton on the 20 August 1945, where I was helping re-organise the lives of the many aircrews, who at that time, were made redundant. I subsequently went to Swinderby and was Acting CFI when I was demobilised in May 1946.

By the time I returned to Winthorpe all the Lancasters had been sent to operational Squadrons and we were teaching pilots to fly Stirlings. After the course the crews had completed they went to Syerston to the Lancaster Finishing School for about 10 hours experience before they went to Squadrons. By September 1944 we were being re-equipped with Lancasters fortunately. Stirlings were not our favourite aircraft and I have entries in my log book that I flew to Longkesh and Maghaberry, N. Ireland where we were delivering the Stirlings for scrapping.

When I arrived back at Winthorpe, W/Cdr. Brian Hallows was the Chief Instructor. He was followed, at the end of 1944 by W/Cdr. R. Shields and from the middle of 1945 until we closed by W/Cdr. J. Molesworth. I instructed in B Flight under S/Ldr. G. Hall until August, when I became OC A Flight and then in 1945 C Flight.

Winthorpe was a hard working, but happy station and after the end of the war (in Europe) were still training crews to join the Tiger Force, which was meant to go to the Far East to help finish the war in Japan.

I fortunately met my wife when she was a Watch Keeper in Winthorpe and we were married in September 1944.

S. E. Liddicoat

I was posted to 1661 CU Winthorpe from 29 OTU (Bruntingthorpe/Bitteswell) at the end of April 1944 and left for No.5 LFS Syerston at the end of May 1944, some 4 weeks later. I was the Wireless Operator with Sgt. L. L. Goffs crew and sporting the fairly new 'S' brevet!!

The first sight of the Stirling was quite a shock – the size of it!; having not even been close to one before.

Our flying time on 1661 CU amounted to 19.35 hours by day and 18.45 by night, consisting of a familiarisation flight 55 mins, circuits and (bumps) landings, fighter affiliation (camera), a cross country with a high level bombing exercise of 5 hours and more fighter affiliation (corkscrews) and a radius of action which completed the day flying.

The night training consisted of 4 hours, on one night only, of circuits and bumps, 4 cross country exercises of roughly 3 hours duration, a high level bombing exercise (infra- red light) – at Goole I seem to remember. The skipper did well and on our last fighter affiliation flight (day) was throwing the Stirling into corkscrews in good style, much to the discomfort of my stomach!!

I'm not too sure how many hours of instruction (2nd Pilot hours) with training instructors we had but it wasn't long before we had the Stirling all to ourselves! I seem to remember the skipper liked to do 'wheely' landings with the rear gunner shouting 'let me down' which he did with a big bump. Overshoots ended up with a Stirling across the main road at times, but not us thankfully.

The only problem we had during the conversion course was on returning from one of the night time exercises we had a spot of bother getting our undercarriage down and locked Green. This involved several circuits selecting up and down, shining Aldis thro' the cabin side to try see if the port leg showed any signs of not being fully down. Eventually we had undercarriage down and locked and got back on Winthorpe in one piece.

On reflection the exercises consisted of a simulation of conditions of flight expected on operations i.e. climbing on track, arriving at given point at a given height, conserving fuel usage (engineer training being new to crew and flying conditions) finally being limited to fuel load enough to cover ex. as would be experienced on 'ops' etc. The fighter affiliation was with a real fighter which we called playmates from a nearby fighter base, using camera. The high level bombing I seem to remember were tied up with an infra-red target, not too sure about this.

I have told the story over the years of during our many circuits we wandered a bit and got close to Newark Church spire which sported a red light and a cockerel. On our last circuit the cockerel got so agitated that it flapped its wings and 'crowed'. Just a story ... but it raised a laugh or two over the years.

After Lancaster Finishing School at Syerston we were posted to No.207 Squadron at Spilsby and after 13 trips, transferred to No.227 Squadron (a new Lanc Squadron formed at Bardney Nov. 1944) and operated from Balderton, completing tour March 1945.

Colin Ewen

I was stationed at Winthorpe in early 1943. After completing my basic training at Skegness I was posted as a Flight Mechanic U/T. I had volunteered for Flight Engineer while at Skegness and had been posted to Winthorpe prior to going on a Flight Mechanics course. Not having the fitting experience I was used as a bit of a dogsbody, doing whatever the Flight Sergeant chose – helping to get aircraft out of the mud, collecting spares from Swinderby, crating engines to be despatched, changing plugs etc. etc. working only out of a big marquee.

Tony Morley / NAM archives

I must have gone to Winthorpe during the week commencing 11 January 1943 – 10 days after it (No.1661 HCU) was formed which I didn't realise at the time. Although I was only there until April-May I was very keen and enjoyed doing whatever was necessary around the Lancs.

Bob Morley

These photographs along with copies of his log book entries were sent to Newark Air Museum by Bob's son Tony and show the crew at Winthorpe and Bob in front of Hut 174, a Nissen hut described as an airmen's accommodation hut and inscribed 'The Nest'. Pictured are from L-R; F/Sgt. Neville Lund RAAF (Navigator), F/Sgt. Reg Francis (Bomb Aimer), Sgt. Alan Cassidy (MU Gunner), P/O Allan Elliott RAAF (Pilot), F/Sgt. Bob Morley (Flight Engineer) and Sgt. Bob Craigs (Rear Gunner). The Wireless Operator, Sgt. Dennis Scully, is presumed to be the crew member missing from this group. The crew trained at Winthorpe between November 1944 and February 1945 and were posted to No.455 Squadron at North Killingholme on operations. The log book entries show that their training started flying Stirlings but the course was completed on Lancasters.

Tony Morley / NAM archives

Stan R. Liversedge

Stan trained as a Navigator and was at Winthorpe between 12 September and 12 October 1944 before proceeding to No.5 LFS at Syerston. The copied page of his logbook is representative of all those aircrew that followed this training path. He and his crew then went to No.467 RAAF Squadron at Waddington.

NAM archives

No. 5 L.F.S. SYERSTON. NOTTS.

Date	Hour	Aircraft Type and No.	Pilot	Duty	Remarks (Including results of bombing, gunnery, exercises, etc.)	Flying Times Day	Night
					Time Carried Forward:—	136·50	96·05
1944.							
Nov. 2.		LANC. Z.	F/LT. JONES.	NAVIGATOR	Ex 1	2·00	
" 2		" "	P/O MORRIS	"	Ex 2	·40	
" 6		" E	F/LT. JONES.	"	Ex 3	1·48	
" 6		" "	P/O MORRIS.	"	Ex 4	·50	
" 7		" B	F/LT. JONES.	"	Ex 5		1·05
" 7		" B	P/O JONES	"	Ex 6		1·05
" 9		" E	P/O MORRIS	"	Ex 7 RADIUS OF ACTION·BASE·SHAFTSBURY		3·15
" 10		" E	P/O MORRIS	"	RETURN FROM WOODBRIDGE.	1·00	
					TOTALS.	6·15	6·25
		SUMMARY FOR 23RD OCT 13TH NOV 1944.	1 LANCASTER III			6·15	6·25
		UNIT. N° 5 L.F.S. AIRCRAFT	2				
		DATE 11TH NOV. 1944. TYPES	3				
		SIGNATURE S.R. Liversedge	4				
					TOTAL TIME....		

SIGNED .... S/LDR.
O.C. "C" FLIGHT

SIGNED .... W/CDR.
C.I. S.L.S. SYERSTON

Winthorpe was a generally well liked and popular station although one newly arrived aircrew trainee (writing in what must have been spring 1944) saw things a little differently as his letter home records...

Dear Folks,

Just landed in last night and I must say that this must be the grimmest place in England. Dad says he slept up to the eyes in s--- in France, well we are <u>living</u> in it! The billets are corrugated iron Nissen huts, damp and cold, the lavatories are dry ones! which stink like blazes and to get a wash you have to walk across a couple of fields to the Sgts Mess (which is a fancy name for a wooden hut) and the food just about tops it all, the last place was supposed to be a Commando School but it was a paradise compared to this joint. After 3 weeks there is a miserable 48hr pass and no leave until after 5 'ops'. What I want to know is, how do they know a bloke is going to get as far as five? There are some crews who have been here 18 weeks, I certainly hope that I'm not here that long. Anyway that's enough complaining; now for a bit of gen. This place is about 35 mins walk from Newark, and the bus service is practically negligible, the town is full of Yanks incidentally. This morning we had a dental inspection and I was passed fit, the last dentist evidently knew his stuff. I am writing to that photographers in Lincoln today to send my photos along, otherwise I'll never get them as I don't look like going there again. Well I must close now so I will close with love to all.

Cheerio

CHAPTER SEVENTEEN

No.5 Bomber Group

All of the crews trained at the HCUs of No.51 Base either Swinderby, Wigsley or Winthorpe was destined to serve with No.5 Group as had the majority of crews trained under these individual HCUs since their introduction in 1941. In so doing they took part in all of the bomber campaigns of WW2 from their inception to the end of hostilities.

No.5 Group was formed on the 1st September 1937 with headquarters at RAF Mildenhall, Suffolk and in October 1937 moved to St. Vincents House in Grantham, Lincolnshire and finally to Morton Hall near Swinderby, Lincolnshire in November 1943. During the war the Group was mainly concentrated in and around South Lincolnshire.

The Group began the war in 1939 with five stations (Scampton, Waddington, Hemswell, Finningley and Cottesmore) and ten Squadrons, all equipped with the Handley-Page Hampden. During the winter of 1940-1941 it began to convert to the new Avro Manchester and in early 1942 to the four-engined Avro Lancaster, No.44 (Rhodesia) Squadron was the first to receive the Lancaster and by March 1943 the Group was equipped entirely with the aircraft as the main operational bomber (training and some other units retained the Wellington and Stirling alongside other aircraft types).

It not only contributed to the heavy bombing offensive, but was responsible for many of the most dramatic and specialised attacks of the war. These included the successful breaching of the Dortmund-Ems Canal; the destruction of the Möhne and Eder Dams and the Kembs Dam on the upper Rhine; the sinking of the Tirpitz and Lützow; and the shuttle bombing of Friedrichshafen and Spezia flying between bases in England and North Africa.

Some notable operations carried out by the Group were:

In March and April 1941, the Group played its part in the daring daylight attacks on the Scharnhorst and Gneisenau at Brest, France then the most heavily defended target of all.

12/13th October 1941, the Group despatched 118 aircraft on the night attack of Hüls and Bremen in Germany or diversionary objectives in what was its biggest effort up to then.

In December an aircraft from No.50 Squadron laid the smoke screens for the Commando raid on Vaagsö and Maaloy in Norway.

The first operation undertaken by Lancasters was a minelaying operation in the Heligoland Bight on 3rd/4th March 1942.

17th April 1942, the daylight raid on Augsburg, Germany took place, led by S/Ldr. Nettleton of No.44 Squadron from Waddington (who also took part in the previously mentioned mine-laying op). Twelve aircraft from Nos.44 and 97 Squadrons flew out at tree-top height to attack the MAN Diesel engine factory.

30th May 1942 the group contributed 162 aircraft and 286 tons of bombs as part of the first 'thousand bomber' attack on Cologne, Germany. For his part in the attack, Flying Officer L.T. Manser, a pilot stationed at Swinderby, was awarded a posthumous VC.

17th October 1942, 86 Lancasters (without fighter escort) flew deep into occupied France to attack the Schneider armaments works at Le Creusot and the associated electrical station at Montchanin.

Möhne Dam – Public domain Photograph of the breached Möhne Dam taken by Flying Officer Jerry Fray of No. 542 Squadron from his Spitfire PR IX

On the night of the 22/23rd October 1942, 85 Lancasters attacked Genoa, Italy without a single loss.

24th October 1942, 74 Lancasters delivered a daylight attack on Milan, Italy.

16/17th May 1943 Operation Chastise, the Dams raid, No.617 Squadron breached two of the Ruhr dams in Germany, the Mohne (left) and Eder.

From November 1943 and all through the winter to the spring of 1944, during the Battle of Berlin the Group played a full part.

In April 1944 in the lead up to D-Day the Commanding Officer of No.5 Group, AVM Cochrane, an advocate of precision low level marking, lobbied heavily to be allowed to operationally prove the principle, arguing that No.5 Group could attempt targets and techniques that No.8 (Pathfinder) Group would not. New systems of target marking were developed and were successfully trialled by No.617 Squadron and its Commanding Officer, Wing Commander Leonard Cheshire using the de Havilland Mosquito and later the North American P-51 Mustang.

6th June 1944 No.617 Squadron took part in 'Operation Taxable' simulating an invasion force approaching Cap d'Antifer.

Following D-Day in June No.5 Group flew more than 3,000 sorties for the first time in its history.

8th June 1944 No.617 Squadron dropped the first 12,000lb Tallboy bombs and blocked the Saumur Tunnel in France.

17th July 1944, using SABS (Stabilizing Automatic Bomb Sight) and the 12,000lb Tallboy bomb, No.617 Squadron achieved a bombing error of only 94 yards at the 'V' Weapon launch site at Wizernes near Abbeville, France.

9th - 14th August aircraft attacked the U-boat bases at La Pallice (La Rochelle), Lorient and Brest in France and later in the month the uncompleted hull of the battleship Clemenceau and the cruiser Gueydon were sunk.

12th November the Tirpitz was sunk in Tromsö fjord, Norway by aircraft from Bardney and Woodhall Spa (Nos.9 and 617 Squadrons), which made a round trip of more than 2,000 miles from an advanced base (RAF Lossiemouth) in Scotland. A No.9 Squadron aircraft is believed to have actually caused the sinking.

13th February 1945 the group formed part of the attack on Dresden.

14th March 1945 the first 22,000lb 'Grand Slam' bomb attack on the Bielefeld (Schildesche) viaduct, (right) in all seven bridges or viaducts were put out of action in ten days.

23rd March 1945 as part of 'Operation Plunder' the crossing of the Rhine at 2100 hours bombers from Nos. 463 and 467 RAAF Squadrons each dropped a 22,000lb 'Grand Slam' bomb on Wesel, Field Marshal Montgomery said, *'The bombing of Wesel last night was a masterpiece and was a decisive factor in making possible our entry into the town before midnight.'*

During WWII No.5 Group flew 70,357 sorties and lost 1,888 aircraft of which 1,389 were Lancasters.

Bielefeld Viaduct – www.bomberhistory.co.uk

Commanding Officers (date appointed):
Air Commodore W. B. Calloway 17th Aug. 1937
Air Vice-Marshal A. T. Harris 11th Sept. 1939
Air Vice-Marshal N. R. Bottomley 22nd Nov. 1940
Air Vice-Marshal J. C. Slessor 12th May 1941

Air Vice-Marshal W. A. Coryton 25th Apr. 1942

Air Vice-Marshal the Hon. R. A. Cochrane 28th Feb. 1943

Air Vice-Marshal H. A. Constantine 16th Jan. 1945

Most of the Group's main airfields were around Lincoln. The following were part of No.5 Group at some point during the war, Swinderby, Winthorpe, Wigsley, Syerston (to 30th October 1944), Barkston Heath, Scampton (to No.1 Group 30th October 1944), Fiskerton, Dunholme Lodge (October 1944 only), Waddington, Finningley, Cottesmore, Hemswell, Skellingthorpe, Bardney, Coningsby, Woodhall Spa, Metheringham, East Kirkby, Spilsby, Strubby , Syerston, Fulbeck and Balderton.

In 1945 under No.5 Group command was No.9, No.44, No.49, No.50, No.61, No.83, No.97, No.106, No.189, No.207, No.227, No.463 RAAF, No.467 RAAF, No.617, No.619, No.627 and No.630 squadrons, and other units.

The Group had some of the most effective Squadrons of Bomber Command, led by No.617 Squadron (the Dambusters) formed from No.5 Group aircrew in March 1943 especially for Operation Chastise and then retained as a specialist bombing Squadron.

Noted for high accuracy bombing by both Nos.9 and 617 Squadrons the Group introduced new weapons and tactics operationally, including Barnes Wallis's 'bouncing bomb' and his Tallboy and Grand Slam 'earthquake' bombs.

The Group was disbanded on the 15th December 1945.

CHAPTER EIGHTEEN

Nos.58 and 203 Maintenance Units

No. 58 MU

No.58 Maintenance Unit Badge –
Mike Smith/Newark Town Hall Museum

Although not strictly based at RAF Winthorpe No.58 Maintenance Unit used the airfield for storage so that it warrants inclusion in the Winthorpe story.

Before WW2 military aircraft crashes were normally the task of the nearest RAF station; as the aircraft were relatively small and flimsy recovery was not a major problem. However due to the number and increasing complexity of aircraft and the amount of salvageable items specialist units were created to handle them.

The need to recover parts that could be re-used was important but also the need to prevent morale being affected by the sight of crashed aircraft led to recovery being carried out quickly and efficiently. As Flight Magazine reported in May 1940:–

In Salvage work, the principle laid down is to remove a crash quickly. Nobody wants it to remain on the spot a moment longer than necessary. The farmer does not want it in his field, and it is bad for public moral to leave it about. If the crash is repairable, it is hurried to the repair hangars; if it is a write-off, then it is removed and "reduced to produce" also with celerity.

The Group is itself building up an understanding with civil firms, mostly in the motor trade, whereby they undertake the removal of crashes, and this has been working very well. But the Salvage Centre has a number of mobile sections which are self-contained. They sometimes vanish into the moors and are lost to human ken for a couple of nights, but they eventually turn up, quite happily, having either effected repairs in situ and had the machine flown away, or having brought it in for the Repair Section to deal with, or having dealt appropriately with a write-off.

Wednesday 3rd - Working at Beacon Hill

Thursday 4th - Working at Beacon Hill, Remove starboard mainplane and disconnect centre section conduits etc.

Friday 5th - Working at Beacon Hill, Disconnect hydraulics etc. on centre section.

Saturday 6th - Working at Beacon Hill all morning and afternoon until 3.15pm

Sunday 7th - Working at Beacon Hill all morning

Monday 8th - Working at Beacon Hill all day taking bomb doors off and loosening nose section.

Tuesday 9th - Beacon Hill all day loosening Lancaster nose section.

Wednesday 10th - Beacon Hill all day, Remove nose section and split trailing edge off. Send them into base at Newark.

Thursday 11th - Beacon Hill all day, remove rear fuselage, tail unit and odd bits out of field at rear of houses.

Friday 12th - we finish at Beacon Hill and arrive back at 58MU at 3.30pm.

An unnamed airman dismantling a crashed aircraft – NAM archives

On the 1st February 1943, Lancaster L7530 piloted by Sgt. B. F. Wilmot crashed immediately after an attempted overshoot; the aircraft had been airborne for about 20 minutes. The aircraft came to rest just off the Newark - Sleaford Rd., all the members of the crew escaped with slight injuries with the exception of the Rear Gunner Sgt. H. H. Lloyd who was killed and Sgt. W. J. Fraser the mid upper Gunner who was taken to RAF Hospital Rauceby for treatment. The aircraft was a write off and scrapped.

A typical recovery team of around ten airmen was led by a Sergeant and included airframe and engine fitters and electricians, with armourers included when needed, along with MT drivers around 50 personnel in total were involved in every salvage and each MU had a number of such teams; No.58 MU had twenty RAF and four civilian teams. One team led by Sgt. C. R. Machin carried out over 60 recoveries whilst based at Newark from Tiger Moths to the four engined heavy bombers; these are listed in appendix five.

In July 1944 the personnel of the MU were 25 RAF, 1 WAAF and 4 Polish Officers with 720 RAF, 110 WAAF and 53 Polish other ranks. The unit recorded 106,761 MT miles in the month.

166

Photograph left: On the 30th July 1943 Lancaster I R5845 of No.1660 HCU RAF Langar took off at 1230 for a familiarisation flight, after 45 minutes the aircraft made a wheels-up landing at Winthorpe and the aircraft was recovered by No.58 MU. The aircraft was SOC (scrapped) in September 1945 – NAM archives. Photograph right: Lancaster II DS763 of No.1668 HCU RAF Swinderby crashed on the 13th October 1944 and was recovered by No.58 MU. The aircraft was deemed BER (beyond economical repair) and SOC – NAM archives

On the 27/29th November 1945 the unit relocated to RAF Skellingthorpe and the ORB reports '... *the move was undertaken in sections and was completed quickly, efficiently and without any hitch whatsoever*'.

No. 203 MU

No.203 Maintenance Unit, March 1945 – NAM archives

Replacing No.58 MU at the Castle Station was No.203 MU, a transport unit which distributed equipment to a range of stations and units throughout the area.

The unit was formed in Newark in January 1942 and disbanded in December 1945.

NAM archives

LACW Eileen Hitchman (on the right in the photograph) donated some of her photographs and records to Newark Air Museum otherwise this unit would be almost totally forgotten.

Eileen had joined the WAAF in 1942 aged 19 and was discharged at Newark in August 1945, her discharge certificate states '... most trustworthy and conscientious worker and a most satisfactory MT Driver.'

The places visited by Eileen Hitchman in her duties included places as far south as Peterborough and airfields throughout Leicestershire, Lincolnshire and Nottinghamshire.

CHAPTER NINETEEN

Post War Usage

Following the disbanding of No.1661 HCU, on the 10th September 1945 Winthorpe was transferred from Bomber Command to Transport Command and placed on a 'Care and Maintenance' basis (the airfield is not in current use although it is kept in good condition to enable it to be quickly brought into service if there is demand). On the 20th October 1945 Winthorpe became a satellite of RAF Syerston in No.4 Group Transport Command when it too transferred from No.5 Group to Transport Command.

Transport Training

No 107 (Transport) Operational Training Unit formed, initially as a half OTU, on the 3rd May 1943 at RAF Leicester East, under the control of No 46 Group Transport Command to train both glider tug and transport crews. The unit was disbanded by being redesignated No.1333 (Transport Support) Conversion Unit on 12th March 1945.

No.1333 Conversion Unit arrived at RAF Syerston in October 1945 with its Dakota and Halifax tugs plus Horsa gliders and Oxfords. However, the glider training was slowly running down, after which crews would be trained purely in the air transport aspect. In December 1946 the unit transferred to RAF North Luffenham but part of it stayed behind and formed into No.1331 Heavy Transport Conversion Unit in December 1946 mainly equipped with Dakotas although it also possessed a few Wellingtons. It remained until disbanding on the 5th of January 1948 becoming part of No.241 OCU when the few remaining trainees transferred to RAF Dishforth.

During this period Winthorpe was used as a dropping zone for No.1333 Conversion Unit (from November 1945 to July 1947) and No.1331 Heavy Transport Conversion Unit (from December 1946 to January 1948). The No.1333 ORB for the 19th and 20th August 1946 records Halifaxes dropping containers over Winthorpe, although a note in the Syerston ORB for March 1946 stated that '... *Orston Dropping Zone having been given up ... efforts are being made to find a suitable alternative. All possible areas except Newton five miles away are too remote for practical purposes'*.

Winthorpe at this time was used as a billet for Royal Army Service Corps personnel.

Air Dispatchers' badge – www.pathfindergroupuk.com

There were two different units No.1 Air Training Wing and 749 Company Air Despatch RASC.

749 Coy. RASC was formed in 1942 as a General Transport Unit and the Air Despatch Group, Royal Army Service Corps was formed in April 1944 and within a couple of months had a strength of over 5000 men. It was to provide maintenance & supply by air to units that may be cut off during the forthcoming Normandy Invasion & ensuing campaign in North West Europe. RASC Air Despatchers in RAF Transport Command aircraft were to drop ammunition, fuel & other supplies by parachute (the Dakota Flash worn by all Air Despatchers was awarded in recognition of the part played by Air Despatch personnel during Operation Market Garden).

Sid Coles was billeted at Winthorpe and involved in drops over Winthorpe with army air despatch. He lived in huts just inside the main gate to the left of the guardroom (Site No.2). Arriving just after the bad winter of 1946/7 he trained with the Air Training Wing where the course lasted 12 weeks. Following a Parachutists course it was one of his jobs as Regiment Police to go by Jeep and make sure Newark was kept 'nice and quiet'. Sid was only with 749 a short time but long enough to wear the blue square with the yellow Dakota on the sleeve and he says *'I won my Red Beret, and you could wear that forever, but lost your arm badge, when you were not with the unit'*.

Sid enjoyed ice skating at Nottingham ice rink and visiting Newark when allowed to; he used to like having fish and chips on the Square in Newark. He met an ATS Girl who was stationed at REOCTU nearby but *'... had to go - got too serious'*.

Subsequently the airfield was transferred to Maintenance Command.

Maintenance Units

The majority of RAF Maintenance Units (MU) started out as Aircraft Storage Units (ASU).

RAF Maintenance Command was responsible for controlling maintenance for all UK based units from its formation on the 1st April 1938 and ultimately comprised a network of over 300 maintenance units at home and overseas; No.40 Group was formed within the command on 3rd January 1939, and responsible for all equipment except bombs and explosives. No.42 Group was made responsible for fuel and ammunition storage. As of 1940 the Command was organised into four Groups:

1. No.40 Equipment Group (responsible for all equipment except bombs and explosives)
2. No.41 Aircraft Group (the supply and allocation of aircraft)
3. No.42 Armament and Fuel Group
4. No.43 Repair and Salvage Group.

Aerial map - NAM archives Bill Taylor

17

Many of the maintenance units within the RAF were located on a multiple of airfields depending on the work that they carried out.

Classed as a 'Universal Stores' depot No.61 MU opened in 1939 based at RAF Handforth near Wilmslow Cheshire, it stored and dispatched every conceivable item that the RAF would use in wartime; from knives and forks to aircraft engines. The site was served by a large, internal railway system which left the Manchester to Crewe mainline with exchange sidings and junction; the depot had its own shunting locomotives.

No.61 MU (Universal Equipment Depot) used several airfields post war to store massive amounts of equipment. Winthorpe (pictured previous page with equipment stored on the dispersals) became a sub-site of No.61 MU from the 15th February 1946 until the 26th October 1948.

No.54 MU briefly used Winthorpe (from 30th March 1953 to the 15th September 1953). Their work at this time was to carry out Category 3 engineering repairs* on site at any eastern region airfield in the counties of Huntingdon, Northampton, Nottingham, Lincoln, Rutland and Leicester.

The parent unit, CSDE, had begun arriving in February with the MU completing its move on the 30th March with 5 Officers, 11 SNCOs and 73 other ranks under the command of F/Lt. S. R. Murray, a detachment of personnel was at RAF Binbrook. The units ORB however noted that accommodation was critical with only 94 airmen capable of being accommodated on site; further accommodation was available with 80 beds being allocated to a former (half) dining hall. S/Ldr. G. C. Turner assumed command on the 30th April.

Around 20 airmen from the unit were to take part in the Coronation celebrations in Newark on the 2nd June.

During August amongst 45 recorded incidents a Sycamore helicopter assisted in the recovery of a de Havilland Venom (left) which had crashed at the coast near Holbeach; this was deemed a successful operation. The MU moved to RAF North Coates during September with the exception of 26 personnel (5 SNCOs and 21 airmen) detached at Newton, Worksop, Scampton and Upwood.

412044 J/Tech. Geoff Lewis arrived in June 1953, he writes:-

Helicopter recovery – AIR 29/2037 National Archives

I shall never forget it; they were in the process of opening it up again. I was put in a Nissen hut which had been refurbished. I was the only one in there at the time. It had a resident Owl, which I did not know of when I moved in. The Station headquarters was being refurbished; it had been used as a cowshed. Most of the buildings had been used by the farmer.

54 MU was being formed from 60 MU which was at RAF Rufforth. The only other unit that was there was CSDE which had been there some time. Being an MU I spent most of my time on detachment to other RAF camps doing Cat. 3 repairs on whatever a/c that needed repairing. I spent a lot of time at RAF Worksop which was 211 Advanced training school flying Meteor 8 and 7 a/c.

When back at base we spent quite a lot of time shooting Rooks with a .22 rifle and a .410 shotgun which the farmer supplied us with. I was 17 and half at the time so this was great fun. Eventually we were all moved to RAF North Coates being right on the Humber estuary which was very desolate in the winter.

Another, John Dean writes; *I was in the first wave of re-opening a very run down and overgrown wartime base... Our billets, old Nissen huts, literally must have been left derelict since the war. If it hadn't been summertime and warm it would have been unusable. Saturday night dancing in the Town Hall comes to mind, I liked Newark.*

*RAF Repair/Damage categories from 1952 – 1961:

Cat.1 Undamaged and can remain in service.

Cat.2 Aircraft can be repaired within second line servicing capability of the parent or nearest unit.

Cat.3 The repair is beyond the capabilities of the parent or nearest unit, and will be carried out as indicated by the following suffixes:

Cat.3 (Rep) C The aircraft is repairable on site by a contractor's working party.

Cat.3 (Rep) S The aircraft is repairable on site by a suitably qualified Service unit.

Cat.3 (Rep) C Fly The aircraft can be flown to the contractor's works after temporary repair, if necessary, under restricted flight conditions.

Cat.3 (Rep) C Deferred The aircraft may be flown under limiting conditions specified by the holding unit until a suitable repair date is agreed with the controlling authority. Cat.3 (Rep) C Deferred aircraft will ultimately be repaired by a contractor while a Cat.3 (Rep) S Fly Deferred aircraft will be handled by a suitable Service unit.

Cat.4 (Rep) Not repairable on site because special facilities and/or equipment is required. Aircraft in this category will be repaired at a contractor's works after temporary repair, in necessary, and under restricted flight conditions.

Cat.4 (Rogue) The parent unit and/or controlling authority have conducted technical investigations and air tests and are satisfied that the aircraft has unsatisfactory flying characteristics.

Cat.5(c) Beyond economical repair or surplus, but is recoverable for breakdown to components, spares and scrap.

Cat.5(s) Beyond economical repair or surplus, and fit only for disposal for scrap.

Cat.5(gi) Beyond economical repair or surplus, but suitable for ground instructional use.

Cat.5(m) Missing.

A Housing Estate is built

In the 1950s housing for NCO's and Other Ranks was erected in a grid pattern on the area west of the Coddington Hall driveway on what had been Site No.4 and part of the WAAF Site, and on Site No.1 for houses for Officers to supply married quarters for 150 RAF families connected not only to Winthorpe but to nearby RAF stations (Scampton, Digby, Cranwell, Waddington and Coningsby); it was based around Harvey Avenue and five more roads and became known locally as Coddington Camp.

CHAPTER TWENTY

Central Servicing Development Establishment

CSDE unit badge – Mike Smith/Newark Town Hall Museum

Between 1953 and 1958 the RAF Central Servicing Development Establishment, a part of Maintenance Command, was based at Winthorpe, before moving on to RAF Swanton Morley.

Formed in March 1947 as the Air Ministry Servicing Development Unit it moved to RAF Wittering in April 1950 and became the Central Servicing Development Unit. In February 1953 it moved to Winthorpe and became the Central Servicing Development Establishment (CSDE).

Its commanding officer from 1953 to 1955 was W/Cdr. Victor Charles Otter OBE. He joined the RAF as an apprentice in 1929 and then went on to pilot training. On the 12th December 1936 he was seriously injured whilst piloting Handley-Page Heyford K6900 (pictured is an example). His aircraft crashed into high ground near Hebden Bridge instantly killing two of his crew and injuring his co-pilot, who died on the way to hospital.

He spent two years undergoing plastic surgery by Mr Archie McIndoe for his facial burns. When he returned to No.102 Squadron, he was pronounced unfit for further flying duties. Granted a wartime commission in 1940 and a permanent commission in 1946 he retired from the RAF as an AVM in 1969.

Sir Archibald McIndoe CBE FRCS (1900–1960) was a pioneering New Zealand plastic surgeon. In 1938 he was appointed consultant in plastic surgery to the RAF.

Handley-Page Heyford – Expired Crown Copyright Image by RAF via website

When World War II broke out McIndoe founded a Centre for Plastic and Jaw Surgery.

There, he treated very deep burns and serious facial disfigurement like loss of eyelids. Patients at the hospital formed the 'Guinea Pig Club', initially a drinking club, whose aim was to help rehabilitate its members during their long reconstructive treatments; formed in June 1941 with 39 patients its members were aircrew patients and the surgeons and anaesthetists who treated them. Aircrew members had to be serving airmen who had gone through at least ten surgical procedures. By the end of the war the club had 649 members. McIndoe worked at times at RAF Hospital Rauceby, Sleaford during the war.

On arrival (the main party on the 9th March) the unit strength was 28 Officers, 143 SNCOs and 187 other ranks, the MT section used 20 vehicles which covered 12,596 miles in the month of March 1953. Conditions at Winthorpe were not ideal and a number of reports record the fact; both buildings for work and accommodation were poor.

Kenneth Simmons was posted to RAF Winthorpe in 1953 as a SAC Driver/Mechanic, he describes the camp as '... *rather primitive at the time, lacking many modern facilities...*' As well as vehicle maintenance his duties included ferrying various personnel to and from their quarters at other bases – Cranwell, Digby, Waddington and Scampton using coaches, personnel carriers and staff cars and to and from their places of work all over the country, Standard Vanguard cars were used for these journeys. He says *'We never knew the nature of the tasks carried out by CSDE on camp or on assignments; we were not allowed to know anyway'.*

Thomas Anderson arrived at Winthorpe as an AC2 Recruit U/T Storeman Electrical and Instruments in Trade Group 18, training 'on the job'; he progressed to the rank of SAC before going to the Supply Trade School at RAF Hereford. He lived in a Nissen hut with around 20 other men, mainly Stores personnel with 2 pot-bellied coke stoves for heating.

Five Officers and 98 airmen took part in a Coronation Day Parade and Church service in Newark on the 31st May 1953. Jeff Burland remembers it absolutely pouring with rain during the Station Parade in the morning and watching the ceremony on a TV in the NAAFI, and on 2nd June some 80 volunteers took part in the Coronation Festivities on Sconce Hills with Tug-of-War, Fencing and Judo demonstrations and a mock attack on a fort.

In July 1953 the unit was given responsibility for the servicing aspects of Guided Weapons with a new section established for the purpose, and in the month the station played 5 cricket matches winning 4 and personnel took part in shooting at Bisley and sailing on the Isle of Wight. In July the station cricket team were runners up to Collingham in the Newark Hospital Cup and Sgt. White won a sailing competition in Germany.

In September No.54 MU, which had arrived in March, left for North Coates which allowed the unit to re-organise its accommodation and on the 20th 75 personnel took part in the Battle of Britain parade and Church Service in Newark.

At the end of 1953 the strength was 45 Officers, 173 SNCOs and 245 other ranks. The station took part in matches against local teams and RAF stations in Football, Hockey, Badminton, Table Tennis and Shooting, the shooting teams were noted as being top of their respective Newark league divisions.

In January 1954 the Commanding Officer visited detachments at Messrs. Ferranti (Manchester), Bristols (Filton) and English Electric (Luton). The first service in the recently rehabilitated station Church took place on the 30th January.

In April Messrs. Richmond commenced building 15 Officers and 84 Airmen's Married Quarters. The unit won Maintenance Commands Pistol Championship and the A and B shooting teams won their respective Newark League divisions. In May the MT section won the Command's 'Division A' Group Efficiency Competition and the station came 3rd in the Command Dining Hall Competition, and as it was reported, giving a fillip to those involved and enhanced the esprit de corps of the unit.

Towards the end of 1954 the general standard of accommodation was causing concern with damp the main culprit, extra rations of fuel were authorised to be issued.

On the 17th January 1955 W/Cdr. A. S. Knowles AFC took command and W/Cdr. Otter was posted to No.2 TAF Germany.

Corporals Club card – Jeff Burland   Barrack block photo – Jeff Burland

National Serviceman Jeff Burland had arrived at CSDE in May 1953 as an AC2 U/T Clerk Personnel working in the Orderly Room on personnel records of SNCOs and airmen. He progressed through the ranks and around 3 months before his national service ended he was promoted to substantive (from acting) Corporal rank. As a Corporal he had to carry out Orderly Corporal duties during the week and some weekends and also was the Corporal in charge of his barrack block (in the picture Jeff is standing at the back with his hands on his chest).

Tuesday night was 'bull' night when the accommodation, washrooms and toilets were cleaned ready for inspection on Wednesday morning and on the first Saturday of the month a COs parade was held followed by a full kit inspection.

Jeff in his spare time helped with the Coddington Scouts and in an attempt to improve himself attended Newark Technical College one evening a week on a typing course '... I didn't make much progress; the consolation is there was myself and sixteen to twenty girls studying ...'

Nearing his demob Jeff went on 'rehabilitation visits' to Ransome and Marles, John Players in Nottingham and a Brewery in Newark. One particular memory he recalls was the day the '... COs driver got 28 days confined to barracks after one of the wheels on the COs car came off as he was being driven into camp one morning. Fortunately there were no injuries ...' Jeff was demobbed from what he describes as '... basically very happy...' RAF Winthorpe in February 1955 and returned home to Hartlepool.

A report in March 1955 describes Winthorpe as 'an abandoned wartime station with most of the buildings used and still used by a local farmer. Most of the existing Airmen's' barrack huts are due to be demolished to make way for married quarters. Plans for rehabilitation have been under consideration since RAF Winthorpe was reoccupied. It is only by means of self help that the buildings in use have been made temporarily usable. Fortunately a steady supply of material for self help is available from unoccupied buildings which collapse and become derelict. The standard of accommodation at Winthorpe, both domestic and functional, is poor and far from ideal'.

Proposals for improvements and new buildings were estimated at £91,020 (over £2.2 million in 2013); the functional space (working offices) was reported to be 13,200 sq ft housed in 11 Laing and 10 Nissen huts whereas the total reported requirement was 15,200 sq ft. Just over half of the work was already approved including over £9,200 (£205,000) for a new SHQ and £2,500 (£55,500) for street lighting.

Five Officers Married quarters were occupied during May but delays in providing the electrical supply delayed any occupation of the Airmen's quarters. In June 39 SNCOs were sent to RAF Cranwell for accommodation. In July the first 2 Airmen's Married Quarters were occupied.

In September 18 Airmen's Married Quarters were taken over from the contractor and 12 were occupied and work commenced on a number of station buildings and installation of street lighting. The station soccer team lost all 5 of its matches; the only sports team to record a win was in Table Tennis.

Building 52 a brick building was altered and provided accommodation for 47 SNCOs in November and 67 Airmen's MQs were now occupied, the sale of poppies raised £13/1/4d (£13.5½p - £303.44 in 2013) doubling the amount from 1954. S/Ldr. Pope and P/O Boon led 30 SNCOs in the Remembrance Day Parade in Newark.

During December parties were located at Rolls Royce Derby on the Avon engine, RAE Farnborough, Vickers Weybridge on the Valiant, Saunders Roe Eastleigh on the Skeeter, RAF Wittering, Shorts Belfast on the Seamew, Handley-Page Radlett on the Victor and de Havilland Hatfield on the Comet; a total of 37 home and 6 overseas tasks were completed in 1955. The new SHQ and PBX buildings were occupied. The MT section travelled 13,065 miles using 17 vehicles in the month. The station strength was 29 Officers, 21 WOs and Master Technicians, 227 SNCOs and 214 other ranks.

The role of CSDE as defined in 1956 covered the investigation of 1st and 2nd line servicing requirements and the development of efficient methods and techniques both prior and subsequent to the introduction of equipment into the service; the unit was also responsible for the production of servicing schedules and the scaling of servicing equipment. Its tasks also included appraisal of design for ease of servicing, service trials and spares provisioning. These included not only aircraft but guided and atomic weapons and MT and marine craft. During 1956 personnel was; 32 Officers. 252 SNCOs and 215 other ranks with 6 civilians with single accommodation at Winthorpe for 13 Officers, 107 SNCOs and 227 other ranks (12 Officers and 107 NCOs and airmen were allocated married quarters).

Flight Magazine in June 1957 reported:-

Central Servicing Development Establishment. This establishment is at Winthorpe, and is under the command of G/Cpt. A. Pyke. Its purpose is to secure uniformity in the approach to servicing policy. The scope of the establishment covers investigation of future servicing requirements and the development of efficient methods and techniques before, and subsequent to, the introduction of aircraft and other equipment into the Service. It is responsible for the production of servicing schedules, the scaling of servicing equipment, the detailing of manpower establishment scales and advising on suitable trade structures.

C.S.D.E. officers work inside the aircraft firms on an equal partner basis with Ministry of Supply project teams, with the result that C.S.D.E. recommendations, made with an eye on the practical aspect of servicing in the R.A.F., can often influence design changes. Fundamentally, it is C.S.D.E.'s task to ensure that aircraft designs impracticable from the maintenance point of view do not get beyond the drawing board stage. The range of C.S.D.E. activity includes servicing aspects not only of aircraft and ancillary equipment but also of guided and atomic weapons. The establishment is becoming increasingly involved as the "new look" policy for air armament is developed. C.S.D.E. is under the direct control of Air Ministry.

26245 G/Capt. Alan Pyke OBE FIMechE AFRAeS joined the Electrical and Wireless School, Flowerdown, in 1927 and graduated from Cranwell as a pilot in 1931. He served with Nos.16 and 20 Squadrons (flying Westland Wapitis in India) and joined Maintenance Command HQ in 1941. He then held technical appointments, and took RAF and Joint Services' Staff College courses and became a CBE in 1960. He retired from the RAF in 1961 as an Air Commodore.

CSDE site map – NAM archives/Author

CSDE occupied the area around Coddington Hall which had been parts of the old domestic site as shown by the map and plan guide.

The CSDE left Winthorpe and moved to RAF Swanton Morley in January 1958

Records show that in February 1958 Winthorpe had Technical buildings, drawing office, test bays, etc in Temporary Brick (TB) buildings along with Nissen and Laing hutting. Equipment stores, station workshops and a PBX (telephone exchange) were in TB and Nissen. SHQ was in SECO, Guardroom in TB, leisure rooms and Indoor miniature range in SECO.

There were quarters for 13 single officers, 107 SNCOs and 212 airmen with married quarters for 15 Officers and 128 airmen. There were no WRAF and SSQ had 8 beds. There was a Gymnasium, NAAFI institute, Chapels and a hired sports field (the Holes Brewery Sports Ground – Castle Brewery Sports and Social Club). There was no electrical standby facility.

CSDE site plan guide – NAM archives/Author

Although many of the buildings have been demolished, one, a Nissen hut, still exists and in almost daily use as a garage (pictured right) within Nottinghamshire. It was part of the MT complex at CSDE Winthorpe and was removed and re-erected in 1959.

Garage photo – Howard Heeley

The end of an RAF Station

In 1956 Winthorpe was transferred to Home Command (responsible for maintenance and training of reserve organisations) and was allocated to the USAF for use as a hospital, but was never occupied by them, and control reverted to the MOD on 30th June 1958.

Following the departure of the CSDE in January and closure in July 1959 the airbase was reduced to 'inactive status' and transferred to Maintenance Command care. In 1964 two hundred acres of RAF Station Winthorpe were purchased by the Newark and Nottinghamshire Agricultural Society. With the approval of the Society, Newark Air Museum's first aircraft was flown into the Showground in 1967, a former RAF Cranwell Percival Prentice training aircraft.

The central Winthorpe airbase buildings, the Communal Site and Site No.2, around Coddington Hall were demolished and the site auctioned off in 1969; Coddington Hall itself had become unsafe and by 1968 most of it had been demolished – a local firm Hough Bros. won the contract and some of the materials were recycled in village properties.

The Harvey Avenue housing built in the 1950s was disposed of by the MOD and taken over by Newark and Sherwood District Council in the 1970s which continued to use it. The estate became rundown and was eventually vacated and in 1999 sold to a private developer who demolished it in 2001 with the area re-developed as Thorpe Oaks, with 255 new private houses. These started to be occupied in July 2002, and were completed in July 2006.

What was No.1 Site is today Parklands Close and No.2 Site is Old Hall Gardens.

In 1988 work started on building a relief road for the A17 to bypass Newark town centre; the western end of the road used to begin at the junction in Newark-on-Trent where Queens Road meets Northgate (the former A46). It then followed Sleaford Road and Beacon Hill Road out of the town and through Coddington towards Beckingham.

The new road began at a new A1/A46/A17 junction at Winthorpe, crossing the southern end of the airfield passing over the main runway and to the north of the technical site

and then crossing Drove Lane before meeting the old carriageway a little further on – photograph above.

The Control Tower (pictured below in the 1980s) and its associated buildings were demolished at this time. The attached PABX or telephone exchange is to the right and the Fire Control building is just behind the tower.

The main technical site buildings which had been used as farm buildings were finally demolished to make way in May 2007 for DSGi (Currys/Dixons) to open Europe's largest electrical distribution centre in Newark. The centre occupies a 100 acre site.

There is little left of the airfield today; parts of the runways (09/27 is practically intact) but the main 04/22 runway has been 'cut-off' at either end – Drove Lane crosses the northern end and a go-kart track occupies part of it, and the new A17 and Dixons warehouse crosses and covers the other end. Some taxiways are still there and can be recognised and a couple of frying pans (Hard-standings) where the air museum is located but all the rest has been demolished.

The former RAF Station is today (2014) 'home' to Newark & Nottinghamshire Agricultural Society, Newark Indoor Bowls Centre (where a T2 Hangar once stood by the side of the A46 road), Newark Golf Centre Driving Range, Newark Motor Auctions, Diamond Driver Training and Safe Start Driving Centre, Go Kart Express, DSGi (Currys/Dixons) Warehouse, with some land farmed and Newark Air Museum.

Winthorpe Memorials

Newark Air Museum has two significant memorials connected to the sites former role as a training base and its personnel. They remember those that at some time were stationed at RAF Winthorpe and sadly did not survive to see the end of the War. In addition there is a memorial plaque to Guy Gibson.

The RAF Winthorpe/No.1661 HCU Memorial

This was unveiled on the 24th September 2000 and is in the form of a stone cairn which

features a part of a Shorts Stirling propeller hub from aircraft EF186 GP-V, which was then based at RAF Winthorpe. The memorial is dedicated to all those who served at RAF Winthorpe.

The aircraft was on a night training exercise to practice recovery from unusual flight attitudes and after entering cumulonimbus cloud crashed out of control at Breeders Hill near Grantham, Lincs, on December 4th 1944 carrying a crew of nine, there were no survivors.

The crew were F/O G. R. Campbell RAAF Staff pilot (Instructor), F/Sgt. D. J. Standring Pilot, Sgt. L. G. Diggins Flight Engineer, Sgt. E. W, Heaton Navigator, Sgt. A. L. Terry Air Bomber, Sgt. A. Winn Wireless Operator/Air

Winthorpe memorial – Howard Heeley

Gunner, Sgt. B. Stowe Rear Gunner, Sgt. K.C. Glinz RCAF Mid-upper Gunner and Sgt. W. L. Howarth Flight Engineer.

Nine weeping cherry trees are planted around the memorial to commemorate each of the nine aircrew with each tree marked with the name of an individual aircrew member.

Lancaster ME846

On June 11 2005, a plaque was unveiled at Newark Air Museum in memory of the crew of Avro Lancaster I ME846.

In March 1944 the crew trained on Short Stirlings with No.1661 HCU at RAF Winthorpe and later they were posted to No.619 Squadron at RAF Dunholme Lodge, Lincolnshire.

The crew were Pilot P/O Mark Anthony Hamilton Davis, Wireless Operator Sgt. Thomas A 'Tom' Newberry, Flight Engineer Sgt. Dennis 'Geordie' Belshaw, Navigator F/Sgt. Leslie 'Tag' Taylor, Bomb Aimer F/Sgt. Peter Edmund Knox RAAF, Mid-upper Gunner Sgt. George Harry Moggridge and Rear Gunner P/O John Earnest Ralph 'Porky' Bowering RCAF.

ME846 memorial – Howard Heeley

Entries from John 'Porky' Bowering's logbook showing his time spent training at RAF Winthorpe – NAM archives

The target on their eighth sortie was a synthetic fuel hydrogenation plant at Wesseling near Cologne, Germany and they took off from Dunholme Lodge on the night of June 21st/22nd 1944. At approximately 0120 British Standard Time (BST) the Lancaster was hit by ground fire and flames engulfed the starboard engine. The pilot gave the order to abandon the aircraft and at the same time turned to port, descending onto a reciprocal course, all but the rear gunner responded to the call to bale out; although uninjured the pilot stayed with the aircraft.

Despite the aircraft being badly damaged Pilot Officer Davis remained at the controls of the aircraft, allowing four members of the crew to bale out successfully, but he, with the Rear Gunner Pilot Officer Bowering and the

Mid-Upper Gunner Sergeant Moggridge did not survive the crash. It is thought that Moggridge went to the aid of Bowering. However, before anything could be done, the starboard wing became detached at about 3,000 feet and the falling aircraft exploded close to the ground. The aircraft crashed near Antwerp just northeast of Postel Abbey in Bladel Woods, on the Belgian side of the border with Holland.

Of the four who baled out, Sgt. Knox was found by a farmer and was passed on to the resistance, who helped him escape back to England. The other three survivors, Taylor, Belshaw and Newberry were captured and became prisoners of war.

The two gunners are buried at the Schoonselhof Cemetery in Antwerp, Belgium; to date unfortunately the remains of the pilot and the aircraft have never been found.

W/Cdr. Guy Penrose Gibson VC DSO DFC

Gibson plaque – Howard Heeley

The memorial plaque to Guy Gibson, on loan to Newark Air Museum, by Jan van den Driesschen who tends Guy Gibson and Jim Warwick's graves in Holland.

Much had been written and recorded of 'Dambuster' Guy Gibson and his career that it need not be repeated here, Jim 'Paddy' Warwick who died with him had previously been stationed at Winthorpe.

S/Ldr. Warwick DFC and W/Cdr. Gibson VC DSO DFC rest together in Steenbergen-en-Kruisland Cemetery, Noord-Brabant Holland.

Other Memorials

There are other small memorials and displays at the museum in remembrance to others including one to the Polish Air Force (right) in the form of a commemorative plaque from RAF Faldingworth for the Polish Air Force Squadrons that were stationed there.

A tree has also been planted close to the RAF Winthorpe Memorial in memory of members of the Polish Air Force who served at RAF Winthorpe. Later in the war many of those same personnel would go on to serve at Faldingworth.

Faldingworth plaque – Author

Manchester

The following Manchesters are known to have operated from Winthorpe:

The aircraft are listed showing their service history in the RAF, their resulting fates and with the hours flown where known.

L7281 Delivered to the Aircraft and Armament Experimental Establishment (A&AEE) 7th December 1940. It subsequently served with No.1654 Flight, No.49 Squadron and 1661HCU struck off charge (SOC) on the 14th September 1943 having flown a total of 327hrs.

L7296 No.49 Squadron (Y) Conversion Flight during December 1940, it was transferred to 1661HCU, and SOC at Benson on the 18th April 1943.

L7297 Rolls-Royce Derby, No.83 Squadron and 1661HCU, overshot at Winthorpe on the 19th May 1943.

L7398 No.97 Squadron during April 1941, it served with Nos.106, 49 and 97 Squadrons and 1661 and 1660HCUs until it was finally scrapped on 30th April 1943 having flown a total of 286hrs.

L7401 No.408 Squadron, 1654HCU, No.1485TT Flight, 1654/61HCUs, Wrecked 15th October 1943.

L7402 The first record for this aircraft is with No.420 Conversion Flight based at RAF Waddington, delivery would have been no earlier than 16th May 1942, the transfer to 1661HCU would have involved a simple move across the airfield, SOC 1st March 1943.

L7415 No.50 Squadron during May 1941, Nos.61 and 408 Squadrons, 1654/60/61HCUs, it was finally SOC 1st October 1943, 267hrs flown.

L7420 No.25 Operational Training Unit (OTU), No.49 Squadron and 1660/61HCUs. It was utilised by USAAF for ditching training in 1945 and then by the RAF. It was dumped in a sandpit in Lincolnshire in 1956.

L7425 Nos.97, 207, 50, 408 and 9 Squadrons, 1661HCU and No.8 AGS, became 3741M.

L7430 No.25 OTU July 1941, No.44 Conversion Flight and 1661/54HCU's, SOC 1st September 1943.

L7453 Nos.97 (OF-X), 83, 49 and 44 Squadrons and 1661HCU, belly landed after take off at Swinderby 24th March 1943, SOC 1st May 1943.

L7455 Nos.207 (EM-G), 50 and 9 Squadrons, 1661HCU and No.8 AGS, became 3742M.

L7461 Nos.97 and 106 Squadrons, 1661/54/60HCUs and No.3 SoTT, became 4278M.

L7467 No.25 OTU, No.97 Squadron Conversion Flight and 1661HCU, wrecked 25th September 1943.

L7477 No.61 Squadron October 1941, 1661HCU, No.1485 Flight and 1654HCU, SOC 1943.

L7480 Nos.207, 61, 50 and 44 Squadrons and 1661HCU, scrapped 30th April 1943, 261hrs flown.

L7481 No.25 OTU, No.44 Squadron Conversion Flight and 1661HCU, SOC September 1943, 323hrs flown.

L7493 No.25 OTU, No.49 Squadron August 1943, 1661HCU, SOC October 1943, 392hrs flown.

L7524 No.25 OTU, No.49 Squadron, No.1485 Flight, 1661 and 1668HCU's, SOC October 1943, 276hrs flown.

L7525 Nos.97, 106, 83 and 50 Squadrons, No.1485 Flight and 1661HCU, SOC August 1943, 423hrs flown.

R5769 No.25 OTU March 1942, Nos.106, 50 and 98 Squadrons and 1661HCU, SOC December 1943, 285hrs flown.

R5790 Nos.207, 83, 49 and 44 Squadrons and 1661HCU, became 3774M.

R5835 Nos.207, 83, 49 and 408 Squadrons and 1654/61HCU's, SOC October 1943, 471hrs flown.

R5836 Nos.83 and 49 Squadrons and 1661HCU, wrecked landing at Scampton 1st December 1942
R5838 Nos.83 and 9 Squadrons and 1661HCU, overshot at Wickenby and crashed 12th March 1942, Crew OK.

R5839 Nos.106 March 1942 and 49 Squadrons and 1661HCU (GP-G), SOC October 1943, 299hrs flown.

Lancaster

The following Lancasters are known to have operated from Winthorpe, all Mk.1 or Mk.3 with the exception of DS786 a Mk.2:

The aircraft are listed showing their service history in the RAF, their resulting fates and with the hours flown where known.

L7530 No.44 Squadron 28th December 1941, No.207 Squadron Conversion Flight 25th February 1942, No.467 Squadron, 1661HCU, flew into the ground on overshoot at Winthorpe 1st February 1943 and SOC 12th February 1943.

L7583 No.207 Squadron (EM-A), 1661HCU (GP-X), No.5 LFS, Scrapped November 1946.

R5492 Nos.44 and 106 Squadrons and 1661HCU, dived into ground at Exeter on the 3rd September 1943, over 600hrs flown.

R5540 No.61 Squadron, No.44 Squadron Conversion Flight and 1661HCU, crashed and caught fire 28th January 1943.

R5542 No.44 Squadron, No.106 Squadron Conversion Flight, Nos.24 and 46MU, No.83 Squadron, 1667HCU, No.3 LFS, 54MU, No.3 LFS, 1660 and 1661 HHCU's; SOC October 1945 after five crashes.

R5547 No.44 Squadron and 1661HCU, Crashed at Balderton on the 8th September 1943, 506hrs flown.

R5549 No.207 Squadron, 1661HCU, No.12 Squadron, 1667HCU, No.1 LFS, 1656HCU, SOC November 1944.

R5556 No.44 Squadron (KM-C) April 1942 and 1661HCU, crashed near Cromwell, Notts. 12th March 1943, 304hrs flown.

R5624 No.44 Squadron May 1942 and 1661HCU November 1942; Nos.24, 46 and 5 MU's scrapped May 1947.

R5635 No.207 Squadron 1st June 1942 and 1661HCU February 1943 became 3508M.

R5668 Nos.106 and 207 Squadrons; Bomber Development Unit, 1661HCU, No.5 LFS, Became 4901M at No.4 SoTT St Athan.

R5751 Nos.49 and 57 Squadrons, 1661HCU, No.1 LFS, 1656/62/68HCU's Became 5257M.

R5756 No.207 Squadron, 46MU; 1667/51/60/61HCU's; SOC October 1945.

R5757 Nos.49, 156 and 61 Squadrons, 1661HCU, No.5 LFS, No.46MU, scrapped January 1947.

R5842 Avro 5th January 1942, No.61 Squadron March 1942, Nos.44 and 49 Squadrons Conversion Flights, 1661HCU (GP-S), No.5 LFS, No.46MU, AAEE(ETPS), Crashed 27th March 1946.

R5846 Nos.61 and 44 Squadrons, 1661/68/54HCUs, Nos.15, 622 and, 75 Squadrons, Nos.5 and 3 LFS; Collided mid-air with R5674 near Hockwold, Norfolk on the 18th December 1944.

R5850 Nos.83 and 44 Squadrons and 1661HCU, Burnt out at Winthorpe on the 19th February 1943, 229hrs flown.

R5855 No.49 Squadron Conversion Flight, 1661HCU, Nos.5 and 6 LFS, No.231 Squadron, Scrapped March 1949.

R5865 Nos.207 and 57 Squadrons, 1661HCU, No.46MU, 1668HCU, became 4950M.

R5889 Nos.49 and 97 Squadrons and1661HCU (GP-M), Burnt out in crash 9th July 1943, 519hrs flown.

R5892 No.49 Squadron 13th July 1942 and 1661HCU February 1943, SOC February 1943, 86hrs flown.

R5904 No.9 Squadron and 1661HCU (GP-D) November 1942, No.15 Squadron missing 21st July 1944, 504hrs flown.

R5908 No.207 Squadron August 1942, No.49 Squadron Conversion Flight and 1661HCU, Crashed 28th November 1942.

W4113 Nos.49 and 156 Squadrons, 1661HCU (GP-J), No.5 LFS, Became 4969M.

W4122 No.9 Squadron (WS-U) September 1942, 1661HCU November 1942, No.5 LFS, Scrapped November 1946.

W4132 No.9 Squadron, 1661 (GP-N) and 1667HCUs, No.1 LFS, Crashed 3rd February 1944, 388hrs.

W4164 Nos.207 and 9 Squadrons and 1661HCU. Became 4443M.

W4183 No.49 Squadron and 1661HCU November 1942 crashed 11th January 1943. 71hrs.

W4190 No.57 Squadron September 1942 and 1661HCU (GP-A) February 1943, crashed 23rd August 1943, 579hrs flown.

W4249 No.9 and 97 Squadrons, 1661HCU, No.3 LFS, No.46MU, Scrapped January 1947.

W4258 No.49 Squadron, 1661HCU (GP-U), No.5 LFS, W4383 landed on top 27th May 1944.

W4271 No.1661HCU (GP-O), No.3 LFS, Swung landing at Swannington 13th August 1944.

W4355 No.97 Squadron, 1661HCU, No.15 Squadron, missing 23rd February 1944, 795hrs flown.

W4358 Nos.49 and 57 Squadrons, 1661HCU, No.9 Squadron, No.5 LFS, 1653HCU, became 4968M.

W4381 Nos.67 and 61 Squadrons, 1661HCU March 1943, crashed 24th August 1943, 516hrs flown.

W4775 No.57 Squadron October 1942 and 1661HCU April 1943 Crashed 5th May 1943.

W4902 No.156 Squadron, 1661/54HCUs; hit ground at Hackthorn 19th November 1943.

W4929 Nos.617 and 619 Squadrons, 1661HCU, Crashed with all crew killed 5th September 1943, 471hrs flown.

W4937 No.156 Squadron March 1943, 1661/60HCU's; Crashed 26th September 1943, 456hrs flown.

W4947 No.156 Squadron March 1943, 1661HCU May 1943, missing 17th July 1943, 258hrs flown.

DS786 Mk.II, No.514 Squadron (JI-E), 1668/61HCU's, Became 4976M at 1661HCU Winthorpe.

DV246 No.617 Squadron (AJ-U) August 1943, 1661/1654HCUs, No.5MU, SOC August 1947.

ED308 Nos.9 (WS-R) and 57 Squadrons, 1661HCU, No.50 Squadron, lost 18/19th March 1943, 423hrs flown.

ED323 No.97 Squadron, 1661HCU May 1943, No.15 Squadron December 1943, lost 28th January 1944, 745hrs flown.

ED437 Nos.50 and 617 Squadrons, 1661HCU, No.622 Squadron, Nos.3 and 5 LFS became 5060M.

ED801 No.106 Squadron, 1661HCU, No.207 Squadron, 1653HCU, Crashed March 1945, 46MU, Scrapped November 1947.

ED822 No.156 Squadron, 1661HCU, Lost 30th July 1943.

ED823 No.156 Squadron, 1661HCU crashed at Halam, Notts. 10th April 1943.

ED944 Nos.57 and 630 Squadrons, No.5 LFS November 1943, 1661HCU April 1944, Became 5455M.

EE128 No.156 Squadron June 1943, Navigator Training Unit (PFF), 1661 HCU (KB-H), Became 5295M.

HK566 No.115 Squadron, 1654/65/61HCUs, No.279 Squadron August 1945, No.5MU, Scrapped November 1946.

HK572 Nos.115 (KO-Y), 149 and 115 Squadrons, 1661/54HCUs, scrapped August 1946.

HK737 No.1661HCU, No.58MU, 1661HCU, No.5MU August 1945, Scrapped May 1947.

HK738 No.1661HCU (KB-D) crashed near Langford, Notts. 24th March 1943 following failure of flaps to retract when carrying our 3 engine overshoots.

JA876 No.106 Squadron, 1661HCU, No.622 Squadron, No.46MU, RAE, No.20MU, scrapped at No.2 MPRD November 1947.

LM307 No.1661HCU, Hit the ground near South Muskham 16th December 1943, 443hrs flown.

LM308 No.1661HCU and No.5 LFS crashed near Syerston 29th January 1945.

LM724 No.514 Squadron September 1944, 1661 February 1945 and 1668HCUs, Crashed13th August1945.

ME312 No.630 Squadron, 1661HCU December 1944, No.20MU March 1946, scrapped August 1946.

ME324 No.32MU, No.106 Squadron, 1661HCU, No.20MU, Became 5794M at No.1 Radio School.

ME371 No.1661HCU December 1944, No.279 Squadron August 1945, MU September 1945, SOC May 1947.

ME431 No.1661HCU (KB-Z) January 1945, No.279 Squadron August 1945, No.5MU, Scrapped January 1948.

ME433 No.1661HCU January 1945, No.10MU August 1945, Scrapped January 1947.

ME435 No.1661HCU (KB-M) January 1945, No.5MU August 1945, SOC May 1947.

ME480 No.1661HCU 15th February 1945, No.20MU August 1945, Scrapped May 1946.

ME495 No.1661HCU 15th February 1945, No.5MU August 1945, Scrapped May 1947.

ME759 No.9 Squadron April/May 1944, No.46MU, 1661HCU, No.227 Squadron, Lost 2/3rd February 1945.

ND450 Nos.97 and 635 (F2-Y) Squadrons, Navigator Training Unit (PFF), 1669/61HCUs, No.20MU, Scrapped May 1946.

ND809 No.635 (F2-C) Squadron April 1944, 1661HCU December 1944, No.20MU, SOC May 1946.

ND862 Nos.582 and 207 Squadrons, 1661HCU, No.20MU, SOC in Middle East October 1946.

ND882 32MU, No.1546 Squadron April 1944, No.46MU, 1661HCU February 1945, No.5MU, scrapped September 1947.

ND959 No.460 (AR-T) Squadron (crash 11th January 1945), 1661HCU May 1945, No.1323 AGLT (Automatic Gun Laying Turret) Flight, scrapped February 1947.

NE122 No.7 Squadron May-November 1944, 1669/61HCUs, No.20MU, Became 5895M at No.1 Radio School.

NG396 No.1661HCU December 1944, No.44 Squadron January 1945, Lost Sassnitz, Rugen Island 6/7th March 1945.

NG397 No.1661HCU December 1944, No.44 Squadron June 1945, No.39MU, scrapped January 1947.

NG416 No.1661HCU December 1944, No.189 Squadron January 1945, Missing Harburg 7/8th March 1945.

NG417 No.1661HCU December 1944, No.189 Squadron January 1945, Missing Harburg 7/8th March 1945.

PA194 No.1661HCU December 1944, Nos.106 and 7 Squadrons, SOC as target 1949.

PA966 Nos.35 and 156 Squadrons, 1661 and 1660 HCUs, accident 2nd September 1946 and SOC.

PB116 No.1661HCU, No.1323 Flight July 1945, No.39MU October 1945, SOC November 1946.

PB205 Nos.44 and 619 Squadrons, 1661HCU January 1945, No.20MU August 1945, scrapped May 1947.

PB213 No.460 Squadron, 1661HCU, crashed at Hall Farm, Oxton, Notts. 15/16th April 1945.

PB227 No.460 Squadron, 1661HCU, swung landing at Winthorpe 25th May 1945.

PB283 No.44 (KM-K) Squadron July 1944, 1661HCU January 1945, scrapped December 1946.

PB285 No.460 Squadron, 1661HCU April 1945, No.1323 Flight June 1945, crashed 11th September 1945.

PB352 Nos.460, 218 and 149 Squadrons, 1661HCU, 1323 Flight, No.39MU, scrapped January 1947.

PB575 No.582 Squadron September 1944, 1661HCU (KB-G) December 1944, No.20MU, scrapped May 1947.

PB582 No.7 (MG-T) Squadron, 1661/60/53HCUs, No.10MU, scrapped October 1947.

PB733 No.32MU, No.44 Squadron, 1661HCU (KB-Q) December 1944 crashed 2nd May 1945 on night circuit practice at Winthorpe.

PB758 No.619 Squadron, 1661HCU, BTU, SOC after second crash 1st February 1946.

PB865 No.1661HCU January 1945, No.10MU 3rd August 1945, scrapped October 1946.

PB869 No.1661HCU (KB-L) January 1945, No.5MU September 1945, scrapped January1947.

PB901 No.1661HCU January 1945, No.5MU September 1945, scrapped November 1946.

PD381 No.44 Squadron. 1661HCU, Radio Warfare Establishment, damaged 16th March 1947, scrapped at No.2 MPRD November 1947.

SW256 No.1661HCU, Nos.49 and 57 Squadrons, Lindholme January 1946, SOC February 1946.

Additionally the following although never actually based at Winthorpe are linked to it:

JA909 Nos.156 (GT-B) 405 and 467 Squadrons crashed near Winthorpe 4th June 1945.

W4964 No.9 Squadron (WS-J) April 1943 and completed 106 operational sorties with the Squadron before being reduced to a maintenance airframe as 4922M in December 1944. It was struck off charge in November 1949.

Part of the second production batch of 200 aircraft from Metropolitan-Vickers Ltd., Trafford Park, Manchester, under Contract No.B69275/40 built at the Mosley Rd. Works, Manchester; 170 were Mk.Is; the remaining 30 aircraft Mk.IIIs (Packard-Merlin engines). Deliveries commenced in September 1942 and were completed in May 1943 (an average rate of production of 6 aircraft per week).

The first operation by the aircraft was to Stettin, Germany (now Poland) on the 21/22nd April and it completed the 100th by dropping a 12,000 lb Tallboy on the Tirpitz moored in KaFjord. The operation, by Nos.9 and 617 Squadron aircraft, was flown from Yagodnik in USSR and the Tirpitz was hit by a single Tallboy bomb - it is believed that it was dropped by W4964. The crew were F/O J. Melrose DFC (pilot), Sgt. E. C. Selfe (Flight Engineer), F/O J. W. Moore RAAF (Navigator), F/O S. A. Morris DFC (Bomb Aimer), F/O R. G. Woolf RAAF (Wireless Operator), Sgt. E. Hoyle (Mid-upper Gunner) and Sgt. E. E. Staley (Rear Gunner).

Johnny Walker advertisement – NAM archives

The aircraft had some distinctive nose art as pictured in this 1944 advertisement; it featured the Johnny Walker whisky symbol with the firm's equally famous motto, *'Still Going Strong'*.

The artwork included the ribbons from four DFM's and two DFCs that were awarded to her aircrew, a chevron indicating a year's service on active duty and below were three wound stripes including one for a container of fifty, 4lb incendiary bombs that were dropped from above the aircraft and passed through the aircraft's wing.

Below these was the medal ribbon for the 1939-1945 star, followed by a swastika indicating an enemy fighter shot down and a marking for a searchlight that was shot out at low level also a red Soviet star recalling the aircraft's visit to Russia en-route to bombing the Tirpitz. The bomb tally indicated 104 regular night operations, one day operation, and a larger bomb indicating the 12,000lb Tallboy bomb that it is said struck the Battleship Tirpitz.

Part of the Mid-fuselage section survives and is on public display at Newark Air Museum.

Stirling

The following Stirlings are known to have operated from Winthorpe:

The aircraft are listed showing their service history, the number of operations in the RAF and their resulting fates where known.

BF562 Nos.214 and 622 Squadrons and 1661HCU, SOC 19th July 1945.

BK654 No.15 Squadron and 1661HCU, unable to maintain height when 2 engines failed the crew abandoned the aircraft which crashed at Gosberton near Spalding, Lincs. 28th June 1944.

BK719 No.15 Squadron and 1661HCU, SOC 24th April 1945.

BK761 Nos.7 and 218 Squadrons (38 operations) and 1661HCU (GP-S), SOC 19th July 1945.

BK766 Nos.15 and 622 Squadrons (25 operations) and 1661HCU (GP-M), SOC 25th April 1946.

BK818 No.15 Squadron (25 operations) and 1661HCU, SOC 18th May 1945.

EE907 No.15 Squadron (20 operations) and 1661HCU (GP-K), control lost when the flaps were lowered on a three engined approach, crashed and burst into flames at Housham Wood, Morton near Swinderby 28th October 1944.

EE956 No.214 Squadron (13 operations) and 1661HCU, control lost due to icing and the aircraft broke up in the air and crashed in an ironstone quarry at Rothwell, Northants. 17th May 1944.

EE965 No.214 Squadron, 1660 and 1661HCUs (GP-P), SOC 28th March 1946.

EE967 No.214 Squadron (5 operations), 1660 and 1661HCUs (KB-Q), corrected swing on a hurried takeoff then deliberately swung to avoid another aircraft, the undercarriage collapsed and the aircraft broke in two and scrapped 3rd August 1944.

EF115 No.214 Squadron (3 operations), 1660, 1661 and 1654HCUs, on a three engined landing at Wigsley the aircraft swung and the undercarriage was sheared off by a tree trunk 20th September 1944.

EF122 No.622 Squadron (8 operations) and 1661HCU (GP-Q), three engined landing at Carnaby, Bridlington, Yorks. The aircraft overshot the runway and collided with a lorry, deemed BER and SOC 10th November 1944.

EF125 No.214 Squadron (3 operations), 1660, 1661 and 1654HCUs (GP-B), SOC 25th April 1946.

EF127 No.622 Squadron (9 operations) and 1661HCU, crashed at Edwinstowe, Notts. After suspected fuel shortage, heard to call 'Mayday' by Syerston but unable to contact the aircraft 26th February 1944.

EF151 No.622 Squadron (3 operations) and 1661HCU, port outer engine failed, with the undercarriage only partly down became tail heavy and hit trees on landing and crashed at Glebe Farm, Brough, Notts. 21st January 1944.

EF177 Nos.622 and 15 Squadrons (3 operations) and 1661HCU (GP-S), unable to feather the port outer engine the propeller flew off hitting the port inner engine and fuselage the aircraft was abandoned which crashed at Alverston, Gloucs. 30th October 1944.

EF186 Nos.622 and 15 Squadrons (3 operations) and 1661HCU GP-V), crashed out of control at Breeders Hill, Grantham, Lincs. after entering cumulonimbus cloud whilst practising recovery from unusual attitudes 4th December 1944.

EF194 No.623 Squadron (2 operations) and 1654 and 1661HCUs (GP-W), SOC 25th April 1946.

EF208 No.622 Squadron and 1661HCU, unable to maintain height on 2 engines the aircraft force landed at Wiggenhall St. Peter, Norfolk 9th December 1944.

EF266 No.1661HCU (GP-M), undershooting the runway on 3 engines the aircraft swung hard to starboard when full power was applied and crashed near Collingham, Notts. 4th November 1944.

EF289 No.1661HCU (GP-D), SOC 27th December 1945.

EF290 No.1661HCU (GP-Y), SOC 31st January 1946.

EF444 No.214 Squadron (22 operations), 1660 and 1661HCUs (GP-F), port outer engine feathered due to oil leak, starboard outer 'shaky' and starboard inner developed an oil leak and feathered, the artificial horizon became u/s the crew baled out and the aircraft came down at Dawsons Corner, Farsley, Yorks. 20th July 1944.

EF447 No.214 Squadron (14 operations), 1660 and 1661HCUs (GP-G and -A), SOC 5th June 1947.

EF461 Nos.15 and 622 Squadrons (19 operations) and 1661HCU, SOC 28th March 1946.

EF512 No.75 Squadron (20 operations) and 1661HCU, SOC 28th March 1946.

EF518 No.15 Squadron (5 operations) and 1661HCU (GP-E), hit a snow bank on takeoff and swung to port and the undercarriage broke off 1st March 1944 deemed BER and SOC.

EH879 Nos.15 and 149 Squadrons (1 operation), 1651 and 1661HCUs, SOC 28th February 1946.

EH921 Nos.214 and 622 Squadrons (19 operations), 1661 (GP-E and -L) and 1654HCUs, SOC 24th April 1945.

EH929 Nos.75 and 15 Squadrons (17 operations) and 1661HCU (GP-F), SOC 19th July 1945.

EH940 Nos.15 and 218 Squadrons (10 operations) and 1661HCU, engine fire at 1,800ft and control lost and following a diving turn to starboard the aircraft crashed at Park Farm, Kettlethorpe, Lincs. 21st June 1944.

EH988 No.218 Squadron (1 operation) and 1661HCU crashed out of control at Home Farm, Annesley Park, Hucknall, Notts. following starboard engine fire 14th January 1945.

EH992 No.622 Squadron (14 operations), 1661 and 1657HCUs, SOC 27th December 1945.

EJ118 No.1661HCU, SOC 31st January 1946.

LJ468 No.1661HCU, SOC 28th February 1946.

LJ469 No.1661HCU, SOC 27th December 1945.

LJ515 No.1661HCU, SOC 25th April 1946.

LJ523 No.1661HCU (GP-E), unable to contact either base or diversion airfields given green to land at Harlaxton, Lincs., overshot in bad weather and hit a gun pit 17th September 1944 deemed BER and SOC.

LJ527 No.1661HCU (GP-A), SOC 25th April 1946.

LJ529 No.1661HCU, after 3 attempts to land with engine problems at Port Ellen, Islay, Scotland the aircraft crashed behind the watch office 25th February 1944.

LJ532 No.1661HCU, SOC 5th June 1947.

LJ533 No.1661HCU, port outer engine failed and would not feather the aircraft landed in a field near Syerston and hit some trees 21st March 1944.

LJ535 Nos.1654, 1661, 1654 and 1660HCUs, SOC 31st May 1945.

LJ540 No.1661HCU, SOC 28th February 1946.

LJ558 Nos.1654 and 1661HCUs, swung on landing and hit BK766 and a workshop building 5th May 1944 deemed BER and SOC.

LJ575 Nos.1654 and 1661HCUs (GP-E), port tyre burst on takeoff from Waddington and undercarriage collapsed 15th May 1944, the aircraft was recovered and given the serial TS266 with No.570 Squadron, SOC 5th June 1947.

LJ584 No.1661HCU (GP-O), SOC 25th April 1946.

LJ586 No.1661HCU (GP-Y and -X), unable to maintain height due to icing at 17,500ft, broke through cloud at 3,000ft and crashed at Iwerne Minster, Blandford, Dorset 28th October 1944.

LJ592 No.1661HCU (GP-X), SOC 21st June 1947.

LJ593 No.1661HCU (GP-W), SOC 28th February 1946.

LJ623 No.149 Squadron (19 operations) and 1661HCU, SOC 24th April 1945.

LK389 No.75 Squadron (2 operations), 1661HCU and No.196 Squadron (1 operation), SOC 5th June 1947.

LK393 No.15 Squadron (1 operation) and 1661HCU (GP-B), SOC 31st January 1946.

LK404 No.1661HCU (GP-P), SOC 24th January 1945.

LK407 No.1661HCU, SOC 28th March 1946.

LK409 Nos.1661 and 1654HCUs, SOC 25th April 1946.

LK429 No.1661HCU, SOC 28th February 1946.

LK438 No1661HCU (GP-U), SOC 19th July 1945.

LK447 Nos.1661 and 1651HCUs, SOC 28th March 1946.

LK456 No1661HCU (GP-T), crashed out of control after engine fire shortly after takeoff 11th April 1944.

LK460 No1661HCU (GP-O) and Signals Flying Unit, belly landed at Wittering after starboard undercarriage stuck up 31st December 1944.

LK462 No.1661HCU (GP-P), SOC 28th March 1946.

LK485 Nos.1661HCU (GP-K) and 1332HTCU, SOC 22nd May 1945.

LK491 Nos.1660 and 1661HCUs and 1332HTCU, SOC 24th April 1945.

LK494 Nos.1654 and 1661HCUs, tyre burst on takeoff and undercarriage collapsed 1st August 1944 and deemed BER and SOC.

LK497 Nos.1661HCU and 1332HTCU, overshot the runway at Nutts Corner, Antrim, N. Ireland and undercarriage collapsed when hitting a ditch 4th January 1945.

LK535 No.1661HCU (GP-D), SOC 28th February 1946.

LK537 Nos.1661HCU (GP-N) and 1332HTCU, SOC 22nd May 1945.

LK538 No.1661HCU (GP-J), SOC 28th February 1946.

LK546 No.1661HCU (GP-N), overshot with 3 engines defective at Culmhead, Taunton, Devon and hit trees 19th May 1944 deemed BER and SOC.

LK547 No.1661HCU (GP-H), SOC 28th February 1945.

LK561 No.1661HCU (GP-A), starboard outer propeller flew off, port inner feathered for no reason and then would not give power, the aircraft was abandoned and it crashed at Point Clear, Bradwell Bay, Essex 25th September 1944.

LK562 Syerston, No.1661HCU (GP-V), hit by EE907 at Winthorpe on the 7th June 1944, recovered and renumbered TS265 with No.190 Squadron, the aircraft failed to return from SOE Operation Blinkers 2 on the 15th April 1945 on its third operation.

LK572 No.1661HCU (GP-T), SOC 28th February 1946.

LK573 No.1661HCU (GP-F), SOC 5th June 1947.

LK574 No.1661HCU, SOC 5th June 1947.

LK590 Syerston, Central Navigation School, Nos.295 and 570 Squadrons, Syerston, Nos.1660, 1654 and 1661HCUs (GP-L), SOC 28th March 1946.

LK591 Syerston, No.1661HCU, on a 'Bullseye' operation the oxygen failed at 15,500ft, port outer engine failed followed by fire in the port inner, low approach to Gaydon but could not gain height and crashed short of the runway 25th July 1944.

LK595 No.1661HCU (GP-L), SOC 30th August 1945.

LK599 No.1661HCU, SOC 24th April 1945.

LK605 No.1661HCU, SOC 28th March 1946.

LK606 No.1661HCU, SOC 5th June 1947.

LK616 No.1661HCU (GP-G) overflew Syerston on return from a night cross-country and crashed near the AA camp at Hawton, Newark, Notts. 27th August 1944.

LK617 No.1661HCU (GP-V), unable to retract the undercarriage the dinghy blew out and the under carriage collapsed on landing at Woodbridge, Suffolk 10th October 1944 deemed BER and SOC.

The two following aircraft although not from 1661HCU suffered damage at Winthorpe:

EE899 from 1654HCU at Wigsley stalled after 3 engined landing and the undercarriage collapsed at Winthorpe 2nd July 1944, the aircraft had 23 recorded operations.

EH978 from 1660HCU Swinderby, lost port tailplane and elevator hitting an oak tree on takeoff from Winthorpe 24th July 1944, the aircraft had 28 recorded operations.

Halifax

The following Halifax aircraft are known to have operated from Winthorpe:

The aircraft show their type and service history in the RAF, their resulting fates and with the hours flown where known.

L9613 B.1, No.138 Squadron and 1661 (GP-A) and 1662HCUs, belly landed at Blyton 20th April 1944.

R9428 B.2, Nos.35 and 10 Squadrons, No.10 Squadron Conversion Flight, 1661 and 1662HCUs, became 4867M.

W7711 B.2, Telecommunications Flying Unit, Bomber Development Unit, No.35 Squadron, 1661 and 1662HCUs, tyre burst on landing at Wittering and undercarriage collapsed 14th March 1944. SOC 21st June 1947.

W7781 B.2, Nos.460 and 76 Squadrons, 1658, 1661 and 1662HCUs, swung on takeoff from Blyton, ground looped and undercarriage collapsed 5th February 1944.

BB213 B.2, No.158 Squadron, 1658, 1661 and 1662HCUs, bounced on landing at Blyton and undercarriage collapsed 22nd February 1944.

BB243 B.2, No.102 Squadron, No.102 Squadron Conversion Flight, No.10 Squadron, 1661 and 1656HCUs, SOC 25th January 1945.

BB260 B.2, Nos. 1658, 1661 and 1656HCUs, crashed and burnt out at Hatfield Woodhouse 30th July 1944.

BB383 B.2, No.102 Squadron, 1654, 1661 and 1662HCUs hit a tree 1 mile from Blyton during a forced landing after engine failure 25th April 1944.

DG305 B.5, Nos.1661 and 1667HCUs, swung on takeoff at Sandtoft and undercarriage collapsed 27th March 1944.

DJ997 B.5, Nos.1661 and 1667HCUs, SOC 1st November 1945.

DJ998 B.5, Nos.1661 and 1667HCUs, spun into the ground at Belton, Lincs. and burnt out 8th March 1944.

DJ999 B.5, Nos.1661, 1654, 1656 and 1667HCUs, SOC 1st November 1945.

DK114 B.5, Nos.1661, 1662 and 1667HCUs, No.1 Ferry Unit, SOC 30th April 1946.

DT643 GR.2, No.77 Squadron, 1654, 1661 and 1662HCUs, crash landed and burnt out near Caenby Corner, Lincs. after Starboard outer engine caught fire 2nd September 1944.

DT671 GR.2, Nos.77, 158 and 51 Squadrons, 1652 and 1661HCUs, SOC 6th March 1945.

DT693 GR.2, No.51 Squadron, 1661and 1662HCUs, rudder stall on takeoff and crashed at Wharton, Gainsborough, Lincs. 22nd January 1944.

DT703 GR.2, Nos.158 and 102 Squadrons, 1654, 1661 and 1656HCUs, SOC 17th July 1944.

JP191 GR.2, No.428 Squadron, 1664 and 1661HCUs, SOC 1st November 1945.

58MU

Work carried out by Sgt. C. R. Machin and his team from their No.58 MU base in Newark

JOB:	AIRCRAFT TYPE:	LOCATION:	CATEGORY:
1	Stirling	Wigsley	B
2	Spitfire	Kirton	B
3	Stirling	Wigsley	B
4	Lancaster	Skellingthorpe	B
5	Stirling	Winthorpe	E2
6	Beaufighter	North Ormsby	B
7	Lancaster	Waddington	E1
8	Spitfire	Kirton	E1
9	Master	Kirton	E1
10	Master	Hibaldstow	E1
11	Mosquito	Rippendale	E2
12	Tiger Moth	Orom Grange (??)	B1
13	Wellington	Normanton-on-Soar	E2
14	Spitfire	Kirton	B
15	Stirling	Wigsley	E2
16	Lancaster	Waddington	
17	Proctor	Cranwell	B
18	Proctor	Cranwell	B
19	Proctor	Cranwell	B
20	Proctor	Cranwell	B
21	Lancaster	Syerston	B
22	Halifax	Blyton	E1
23	Wellington	Newton	C
24	Anson	Newton	E1
25	Lancaster	Dunholme	B
26	Halifax	Blyton	E1
27	Mosquito	Bawtry	E2
28	Spitfire	Crowle	E2
29	Halifax	Blyton	E1
30	Spitfire	Market Rasen	A
31	Blenheim	Grantham	E1
32	Lancaster	Skellingthorpe	B
33	Spitfire	Hibaldstow	E1
34	Anson	Grantham	E2
35	Lancaster	Bottesford	E1
35a	Lancaster	obstruction at Hemswell	
36	Oxford	Sutton Bridge	E2
37	Master	Sutton Bridge	E1
38	Lancaster	Bardney	E2

39	Lancaster	lifted to remove bombs	
40	Lancaster	Bardney	E2
41	Stirling	Bardney	E2
42	Anson	Newton	E2
43	Anson	Newton	E2
44	Lancaster	Elsham Wolds	B
45	Harvard	Leverton, nr. Boston	Ac
46	Lancaster	Woolfox Lodge	E1
47	Oxford	Market Deeping	E2
48	Hurricane	Gamston	E1
49	Liberator	Wickenby	E1
50	Lancaster	Woolfox Lodge	E2
51	Wellington	Haughton	E2
52	Wellington	Worksop	E2
53	Martinet	Skellingthorpe	E1
54	Spitfire	Hucknall	B
55	Tiger Moth	Castle Bromwich	E2
56	Lancaster	Metheringham	B
57	Hotspur	Wellesborne, nr. Warwick	B
58	Lancaster	Bottesford	C
59	Lancaster	Swinderby	E2
60	Lancaster	Kemble (to Bardney on exhibition)	E2
61	Lancaster	Bardney	C
62	Lancaster PD368	Bardney	Crash on takeoff 1st January 1945
63	Lancaster NG252	Bardney	Burnt after takeoff crash 1st Jan 1945
64	Stirling	Bardney	

The following damage/repair categories were used by the RAF between 1941 and 1952:-

Cat. U   Undamaged

Cat. A   Aircraft can be repaired on site

Cat. Ac   Repair is beyond the unit capacity, but can be repaired on site by another unit or a contractor

Cat. B   Beyond repair on site, but repairable at a Maintenance Unit or at a contractor's works

Cat. C   Allocated to Instructional Airframe duties (for ground training)

Cat. E   Write-off

Cat. E1   Write-off, but considered suitable for component recovery

Cat. E2   Write-off and suitable only for scrap

Cat. E3   Burnt out

Cat. Em   Missing from an operational sortie (Missing aircraft were categorised 'Em' after 28 days).

In addition to the above the cause of damage was occasionally indicated by a prefix or suffix:-

FA	Flying Accident	FB	Operational Loss
GA	Ground Accident	T	Technical Cause
EA	Enemy Action		

Stan Bray – his qualifications and flying hours

1232381 Aircraftman Stanley Bray joined the RAF in 1941

06/08/42 - Qualified as Target
Tug Operator with No.1 AACU
(Anti Aircraft Co-operation Unit)
Aberporth

06/10/42 – Qualified as Wireless
Operator with No.2 Signals School
Madley

Hawker Henley TTIII of No.1 AACU – HU92999 of the Imperial War Museum

12/12/42 – Qualified as Air Gunner with No.1 Air Gunnery School Pembury

Flying Units

06/08/42 to 23/08/42
with Q Flight, No.1 AACU at Aberporth [18 hours 55 minutes] on Henleys

02/09/42 to 06/10/42
with Air Operations Section No.2 Signals School Madley [14 hours 10 minutes] on
Dominies

21/11/42 to 02/12/42
with No.1 Air Gunnery School Pembury [9 hours for the course] on Blenheims

Course notes
– Sighting instruction was given in accordance with 25 Group standards
– Course included ground firing, Air to Ground, Beam, Beam R.S., Under Tail,
  Quarter and Air Tracer
– Exam marks 83%, final average number of hits to rounds fired 6.33%
– Remarks 'Finished 2nd on the Course. Has been an excellent pupil'

27/01/43 to 09/04/43
with No.29 OTU flying from Bruntingthorpe [and satellite stations Woolfox Lodge and
North Luffenham] on Wellington IIIs

Flying Hours
January   3 hours [day]
February   15 hours 25 minutes [day]; 6 hours 25 minutes [night]
March   23 hours 55 minutes [day]; 21 hours 45 minutes [night]
April   8 hours [day]; 16 hours 45 minutes [night]
Course Total 50 hours 20 minutes [day]; 44 hours 55 minutes [night]

Date	Hour	Aircraft Type and No.	Pilot	Duty	Remarks (including results of bombing, gunnery, exercises, etc.)	Flying Times Day	Flying Times Night
					1661 CONVERSION UNIT — WINTHORPE NOTTS. Time carried forward :—	9225	44·55
		MANCHESTER					
11·5·43	1145	L7401	F/LT GREEN	WIRELESS O/P	CIRCUITS LANDINGS OVERSHOOTS	2·35	
11·5·43	1603	"	SGT McCLELLAND	" "	" " "	·40	
17·5·43	10·00	"	" "	" "	X COUNTRY Ex 3	2·30	
19·5·43	11·45	R5769	" "	" "	BOMBING · LANDINGS · OVERSHOOTS	2·20	
		LANCASTER.					
22·5·43	17·20	W4253	P/O WEST	" "	Ex 1 & 2.	1·55	
26·5·43	15·25	5547	F/L GREEN.	" "	Ex 1 · 2 & 3.	2·55	
26·5·43	18·20	"	SGT McCLELLAND	" "	CIRCUITS & LANDINGS	·40	
28·5·43	11·45	ED826	" "	" "	X COUNTRY 2D.	1·40	
28·5·43	14·25	5547	F/LT GREEN	" "	EVASIVE ACTION	1·05	
30·5·43	19·00	L7296	SGT McCLELLAND	" "	X COUNTRY & BOMBING	3·15	
4·6·43	13·10	W4253	" "	" "	X COUNTRY & BOMBING	5·05	
5·6·43	13·40	"	" "	" "	FIGHTER AFFILIATION	1·00	
5·6·43	14·40	"	" "	" "	" "	1·15	
					TOTAL TIME ...	119·20	44·55

Stan's logbook entries for his training at Winthorpe – NAM archives/Howard Heeley

11/05/43 to 12/06/43

on Course 8 1943 with No.1661 HCU RAF Winthorpe on Manchesters and Lancasters

Flying Hours

Manchester times	8 hours 5 minutes [day]
Lancaster times	18 hours 50 minutes [day]; 18 hours 40 minutes [night]
Course Total	26 hours 55 minutes [day]; 18 hours 40 minutes [night]

17/06/43 to 16/12/43

on No.467 [RAAF] Squadron 'B' Flight at Bottesford and Waddington on Lancasters

Flying Hours

June	5 hours 45 minutes [day]; 29 hours 10 minutes [night] – 4 Operations
July	5 hours 15 minutes [day]; 20 hours 35 minutes [night] – 4 Ops
August	6 hours 20 minutes [day]; 35 hours 30 minutes [night] – 5 Ops
September	5 hours 20 minutes [day]; 34 hours 45 minutes [night] – 5 Ops
October	30 minutes [day]; 13 hours 20 minutes [night] – 2 Ops
November	3 hours 55 minutes [day]; 25 hours [night] – 4 Ops
December	1 hour [day]; 7 hours 20 minutes [night] – 1 Op

End of first tour

01/02/44 to 24/07/45
with No.1661 HCU RAF Winthorpe as Instructor

Flying Hours

February 1944	Stirlings 1 hour 50 minutes [day]; 1 hour [night]
April 1944	Stirlings 2 hours 35 minutes [day]
May 1944	Stirlings 4 hours 50 minutes [day] Forced landing at Little Staughton - EF125
June 1944	Stirlings 4 hours 55 minutes [day]
July 1944	Stirlings 4 hours 35 minutes [day] Leeds crash - EF444
August 1944	Stirlings 2 hours 55 minutes [day]
September 1944	Stirlings 10 hours 30 minutes [day]
October 1944	Stirlings 2 hours 40 minutes [day]; 5 hours 45 minutes [night]
November 1944	Stirlings / Oxfords 3 hours [day]
December 1944	Stirlings / Lancasters 10 hours 20 minutes [day]
January 1945	Lancasters 1 hour 15 minutes [night]
February 1945	Lancasters 9 hours 35 minutes [day]
March 1945	Lancasters 8 hours 25 minutes [day]
April 1945	Lancasters 5 hours 20 minutes [day]
May 1945	Lancasters 5 hours [day]
June 1945	Lancasters 6 hours 20 minutes [day]
July 1945	Lancasters 12 hours 15 minutes [day] Two sorties to view bomb damage [Cap Griz-Nez; Aachen; Cologne; Ruhr Valley; Hamm; Munster; Wesel; Antwerp; Ostend; Calais]

Total Hours as Instructor 95 hours 40 minutes in a 16 month period

07/09/45 – 28/09/45
No.72 W/Op Air Course at No.14 Radio School RAF St. Athan on Ansons 12 hours 15 minutes [day]

25/10/45 – 08/11/45
with No.1660 HCU RAF Swinderby

October	Lancasters 9 hours 45 minutes [day]
November	Lancasters 7 hours 40 minutes [day]

Total Flying Time from his Observer's & Air Gunner's Flying Log Book
263 hours 55 minutes [day]
212 hours 30 minutes [night]

Air Ministry (1956) *The Royal Airforce Builds for War; A History of Design and Construction in the RAF 1935-1945*. London: the Stationery Office.

Betts, A. (1995) *Royal Air Force Airfield Construction Service 1939-46*. Ware: Airfield Research Publishing

Blake, R., Hodgson, M., Taylor, B. (1984) *Airfields of Lincolnshire Since 1912*. Leicester: Midland Counties Publications

Chorley, W. R, (2003) *Royal Air Force Bomber Command Losses Vol. 8, Heavy Conversion Units & Miscellaneous Units 1939-1947*. Midland Publishing: Hinckley

Fairhead, R. (1982) *An Airman's Diary*. New Horizon: Bognor Regis

Falconer, J. (1992) *RAF Bomber Airfields of World War 2*. Shepperton: Ian Allan Ltd.

Francis, P. (1996) *British Military Airfield Architecture*. Yeovil: Patrick Stevens Ltd.

Finn, S. (1973) *Lincolnshire Air War 1939-1945*. Lincoln: Brayford Press Ltd.

Finn, S. (1983) *Lincolnshire Air War 1939-1945 Book Two*. Lincoln: Brayford Press Ltd.

Gomersall, B. B. (1987) *The Stirling File*. Tonbridge: Air Britain (Historians Ltd.).

Glover, A. P. and R. M. (2010) *Nottinghamshire Aviation Diary; Aviation Incidents 1930-1945*. Horsburgh Publishing

Higham, R. (1998) *Bases of Air Strategy, Building Airfields for the RAF 1914-1945*. Shrewsbury: Air Life Publishing Ltd.

Hill, R E. (2000) *Survivor a true story of one mans war*. Privately published

Hope, B. (2010) *Royal Air Force Station Winthorpe 1940-1945*. Sutton in Ashfield: Self Published.

Keltie, C. (2013) *Riding in the Shadow of Death*. London: Chris Keltie Publishing

Lyall, G. (1968) *Freedom's Battle, Volume two: the War in the Air 1939-1945*. London: Hutchinson.

Mallory, R. (1987) *Newark in World War Two*. Newark: Millgate Folk Museum

Mallory, R. (1995) *Newark in the Second World War*. Newark: Newark and Sherwood District Council.

McKinstry, L. (2009) *Lancaster, the Second World Wars Greatest Bomber*. London: John Murray

Needham, D. (2008) *Nottinghamshire Air Crashes*. Ashbourne: Landmark Publishing.

Nesbit, R. C. (1995) *An Illustrated History of the RAF, (6th edition)*. Colour Library Books Ltd.: Godalming

O'Brien, T. (2012) *Royal Air Force Syerston*. Bingham: Tobbit Publishing.

Overy, R. (1997) *Bomber Command 1939-1945*. London: Harper-Collins Publishers

Penrose, H. (1980) *British Aviation. The Ominous Skies 1935-1939*. Her Majesty's Stationery Office: London

Read, S. (2006) *The Killing Skies, RAF Bomber Command at War*. Stroud: The History Press.

Roberts, R.N. (compiler) (1982) *The Halifax File*. Tonbridge: Air Britain (Historians Ltd.).

Robertson, B. (1964) *Lancaster – the Story of a Famous Bomber*. Letchworth: Harleyford Publications Ltd.

Robertson, B. (1960) *Spitfire – the Story of a Famous Fighter*. Letchworth: Harleyford Publications Ltd.

Sands, J. (2011) *Airborne Radar*. Ontario: Privately published

Sands, J. (no date) *Footprints in the Sands of Time*. Ontario: Privately published

Smith, D. J. (1981) *Wartime Wreck Recovery*. Article in Aviation News 13-26 March 1981

Sturtivant, R., Hamlin J. and Halley J. J. (1997) *Royal Air Force Flying Training and Support Units*. Tonbridge: Air Britain (Historians Ltd.

Taylor, W. (1984) *RAF Winthorpe, a History 1940-1945*. Lincoln: Brayford Press.

Taylor, W. (1994) *RAF Winthorpe, Photographic Memories and Anecdotes 1940-1945 Volume Two.* Retford: Burgess Photoprint.

Wilson, K. (2005) *Bomber Boys - the Ruhr, the Dambusters and Bloody Berlin.* London: Weidenfield and Nicholson.

Online sources:

http://adb.anu.edu.au/biography/martin-sir-harold-brownlow-mick-14937
Australian Dictionary of Biography Martin, Sir Harold Brownlow (Mick) (1918–1988) by John McCarthy

http://history.coddington-pc.x10.mx/index.php?option=com_content&view=article&id=170:winthorpe-airbase-and-
Coddington, Notts. History Group, Winthorpe Airbase and the RAF Estate

http://orb.polishaf.pl/unit/300sqn
ORB for No.300 Squadron

http://ses.library.usyd.edu.au/bitstream/2123/664/2/adt-NU20050104.11440202whole.pdf
Britain 1939 – 1945: The Economic Cost of Strategic Bombing by John Fahey University of Sydney, Australia

http://www.bomberhistory.co.uk/49squadron/Aircrew/Aircrew_Index.html
Index to all aircrew who served with No.49 Squadron during WW2 (information on S/Ldr. Warwick).

http://www.bomberhistory.co.uk/49squadron/Files/Tom%20Page%20Service%20Career.pdf
My Service Career in the Royal Air Force 1940/1968 Including Bomber Operations With No.49 Squadron in 1943/44 by Squadron Leader T J Page DFM

http://www.dambusters.biz/after-the-dams/raids/antheor/
Dambusters Raids, Antheor Viaduct

http://www.dambusters.biz/operation-records/
ORB for No.617 Squadron

http://www.dambusters.biz/after-the-dams/raids/saumur/
Dambusters Raids, Saumur Tunnel

http://www.dambusters.biz/after-the-dams/raids/tirpitz/
Dambusters Raids, Tirpitz

http://www.elsham.pwp.blueyonder.co.uk/raf_bc/
Royal Air Force (RAF) Bomber Command 1939-1945 Rob Davis

http://www.flightglobal.com/pdfarchive/view/1940/1940%20-%201268.html
Flight Magazine May 2 1940 Pages 17/18 Keeping the RAF in the Air

http://www.flightglobal.com/pdfarchive/view/1957/1957%20-%200895.html
Flight Magazine June 28 1957 page 901 Central Servicing Development Establishment

http://www.pegasusarchive.org/pow/cSL_3_Fifty.htm
Stalag Luft III and the Great Escape Mark Hickman

http://www.polishsquadronsremembered.com/300/300Squadron.html
History of No. 300 Polish Bomber Squadron Wilhelm Ratuszynski

http://www.polishsquadronsremembered.com/301/301_story.html
History of No. 301 Polish Bomber Squadron Wilhelm Ratuszynski

http://www.rafbombercommand.com/
RAF Bomber Command

http://www.raf.mod.uk/history/bombercommandno617squadron.cfm
No. 617 Squadron

http://www.raf.mod.uk/history/worldwarii.cfm
Royal Air Force Bomber Command

http://www.raf.mod.uk/history/bombercommandno5group.cfm
Bomber Command No.5 Group

http://www.raf.mod.uk/history/raftimelinehomepage.cfm
RAF History Timeline

http://www.raf.mod.uk/rafcms/mediafiles/F21D57C4_9913_5321_BB9830F0BB762B4E.pdf
A Short History of the Royal Air Force Chapter 3, the Second World War 1939-45

http://www.raf-lincolnshire.info/
Royal Air Force and Airfield History in Lincolnshire

http://www.rafweb.org/Biographies/Butler_ES.htm
Air of Authority - A History of RAF Organisation, Air Vice-Marshal E S Butler (05235)

http://www.rafweb.org/Biographies/Otter_VC.htm
Air of Authority - A History of RAF Organisation, Air Vice-Marshal V C Otter (44999)

http://www.rafweb.org/Biographies/Pyke_A.htm
Air of Authority - A History of RAF Organisation, Air Commodore A. Pyke (26245)

http://www.rafweb.org/Biographies/Ward_ELS.htm
Air of Authority - A History of RAF Organisation, Air Commodore E L S Ward (16211)

http://www.rafweb.org/Sqn450-467.htm
Air of Authority - A History of RAF Organisation, No.450 - 467 Squadron Histories

http://www.rafweb.org/Stations/Stations-W.htm
Air of Authority - A History of RAF Organisation, RAF Stations - W

http://www.rquirk.com/cdnradar/cdnradar.htm
The Canadian Radar History Project

http://www.rquirk.com/cdnradar/Sands/Radar%20book%202.pdf
James Sands ex F/O RCAF Airborne Radar Personal Recollections

Personal recollections:

Alan Geeson

Alan Roberts (his Fathers Winthorpe log book entry and flying career)

David Hallam

G. H. Davis

Geoff Lewis

Gerald Baggaley

James Daubney (his Father's photograph album)

James Sands

Mrs. Jane Cooper (information on her Father F/O W. Eager DFC)

Jeff Burland

Mrs. Joyce Golland

John Dove

John Knowles

John W. Dean

Maurice Price

Sidney Coles

Tony Driver (his Fathers photographs and log book entries)

Personal recollections from the Museum Archives:

Colin Ewen

E. G. 'Nobby' Clark

Harry Le Marchant

John F. Grime

John Hyman

Keith Slade

Kenneth Simmons

P. P. Cockerton

Ray Darney

Ronald W. Bridgland

Roy Hill

S. E. Liddicoat

Stan Jolly

Stan Matthews

Stan R. Liversedge

Thomas Anderson

Email correspondence with:

D.W. Gardner, Director, RAAF Museum, RAAF Williams, Point Cook, VIC 3027.

Carol Morgan, Archivist, Institution of Civil Engineers, One Great George Street, Westminster, London SW1P 3AA.

James Sands, Smith Falls, Ontario, Canada (ex RCAF)

de Havilland Aircraft Heritage Centre (Phil Catton, Martin Bronkhorst, and Ian Thirsk)

Public records office KEW:

AIR 14/1101
Organisation of No.7 Group and aircrew schools July 1944 – Feb 1946

AIR 14/1877
Bomber Command. Intake and output of crews in OTUs and Heavy Conversion Units 01 Mar 1943 - 30 Apr 1945

AIR 14/2525
RAF Swinderby: operations log book Aug 1940 - Aug 1941

AIR 14/3894
R.A.F. Swinderby: operations room log book (also Air 14/2442 - 67 & Air 14/2525) 01 Mar 1942 - 30 Jun 1942

AIR 2/10536
ROYAL AIR FORCE: Stations (Code B, 67/36): Winthorpe: deployment policy 01 Feb 1944 - 31 Jan 1964

AIR 2/11537
ROYAL AIR FORCE: Maintenance Command (Code B, 67/17): Central Servicing Development Establishment, RAF Station, Winthorpe: terms of reference

AIR 2/11538
RESEARCH & DEVELOPMENT ESTABLISHMENTS (Code B, 65): Central Servicing Development Establishment, RAF Station, Winthorpe: terms of reference

AIR 2/11760
RESEARCH & DEVELOPMENT ESTABLISHMENTS (Code B, 65): Charter for Central Servicing Development Establishment (CSDE): re-deployment, policy and plans July 1957 Jan 1959

AIR 25/109A
No.5 Group Operations record book Sept 1937 – Dec 1943

AIR 25/110
No.5 Group Operations record book Jan 44 – Dec 45

AIR 27/2128*
No 617 Squadron: Operations Record Book Apr 1943 – May 1945

AIR 28/41
BALDERTON Operations Record Books, Royal Air Force Stations. BALDERTON. with appendices 01 Sept 1944 - 30 Apr 1945

AIR 28/796
Operations Record Books SWINDERBY Aug 1940 – Dec 1943.

AIR 28/797
Operations Record Books SWINDERBY Jan 1944 – Dec 1945.

AIR 28/799
Operations Record Books, Royal Air Force Stations. SYERSTON 1 January 1944 - 31 October 1945

AIR 28/800
Operations Record Books, Royal Air Force Stations. SYERSTON loose Appendices. 1 March 1943 - 31 October 1945

AIR 28/952*
Operations Record Books, Royal Air Force Stations. WINTHORPE. With appendices 01 May 1943 - 30 Sept 1945

AIR 29/1015
4 Salvage Centre, formed Newark August 1938; became 58 Maintenance Unit, October 1939; moved to Skellingthorpe November 1945

AIR 29/1017
61 Maintenance Unit, formed at Handforth July 1941; includes Sub-Unit at Hooton Park October - December 1944 (MU UK) with appendices 1941 July – 1945 Dec.

AIR 29/1058
Maintenance Unit, formed at Newark January 1942; disbanded December 1945.

AIR 29/1071
203 Equipment Disposal Depot, formed at Balderton June 1945; became 254 Maintenance Unit, June 1945; disbanded July 1946

AIR 29/1518
No. 61 MU Handforth, B'ham with appendices Jan. 1946 – Dec.1950

AIR 29/1974
No. 1333 Transport Support Training Unit, Syerston, Notts Aug 1946 – Dec 1947.

AIR 29/1975
No. 1333 Transport Support Training Unit, Syerston, Notts, appendices only Aug 1946 – Dec 1947.

AIR 29/2037
No. 54MU Rufforth (and other locations) with appendices July1952 – Oct. 1957

AIR 29/2405*
Operations Record Books Central Servicing Development Establishment Jan 1951 Dec 1955

AIR 29/2406
Central Servicing Development Establishment. Includes 9 photographs depicting: RAF Winthorpe, inspection parades and march past (no information given). Dated 1953.

AIR 29/2407
Central Servicing Development Establishment appendices only Jan-Dec 1954

AIR 29/2408
Central Servicing Development Establishment. Includes 10 photographs depicting: (1) RAF Winthorpe, inspection parades and march pasts (2) RAF Winthorpe, site including married quarters. Dated 1955.

AIR 29/2733
MISCELLANEOUS UNITS. Central Servicing Development Establishment, Winthorpe. Appendices only 01 Dec 1956 - 31 Jul 1957

AIR 29/2734
Central Servicing Development Establishment, Winthorpe. Includes 19 photographs depicting: Central Servicing Development Establishment, RAF Winthorpe: AOC's inspection - personnel not identified; missile, complete with launcher frame, on loading trolley, loading trolley connected to launcher, launcher frame mated to launcher. Dated 1957.

AIR 29/2735
Operations Record Books. Central Servicing Development Establishment, Winthorpe 01 Feb 1956 - 30 Nov 1960

AIR 29/2969
Operations Record Books, EXPERIMENTAL/DEVELOPMENT UNITS. CSDE, Winthorpe. appendices only. 01 Jan 1956 – 31 Dec 1956

AIR 29/611 1333

(Transport Support) Conversion Unit. Based at Leicester East (UK) from February 1945. Contains numerous group photographs of training course participants (all individuals named). with appendices Date: Feb1945 – July1946

AIR 29/613*

Operations Record Books, 1661 Conversion Unit. Formed at Waddington in Nov 1942. Operated from Waddington and Scampton. Moved to Winthorpe in January 1943. 01 Nov 1942 – 31 Jan1944

AIR 29/614 1668

Conversion Unit (became 5 Lancaster Finishing School in Nov 1943). Formed at Balderton in Aug 1943. Moved to Syerston in November 1943. Unit disbanded at Syerston March 1945

AIR 29/854

RAF 56 Base, Syerston, UK; includes news booklets and a group photograph of personnel Oct. 1944- Apr. 1945.

AIR 29/871

5 Group Training Flight, Scampton, later became 1485 Target Towing and Gunnery Flight, then 1485 (Bomber) Gunnery Flight at Dunholme, Fulbeck, Skellingthorpe and Syerston (UK) with appendices Aug1941 – Feb 1944.

AIR 29/882

1690 Bomber Defence Training Flight; based at various locations including Syerston, Swinderby, Scampton and Metheringham (BDT UK) with appendices Mar 1944 – Oct 1945.

*NB Items marked with an * are record copies held by Newark Air Museum*